SHOT ON
THIS SITE

Books by William A. Gordon

"How Many Books Do You Sell in Ohio?":
A Quote Book for Writers

The Ultimate Hollywood Tour Book

Four Dead in Ohio:
Was There a Conspiracy at Kent State?

SHOT ON THIS SITE

A Traveler's Guide to the Places and Locations Used to Film Famous Movies and TV Shows

William A. Gordon

A Citadel Press Book
Published by Carol Publishing Group

A Citadel Press Book
Published by Carol Publishing Group
Citadel Press is a registered trademark of Carol Communications, Inc.
Editorial Offices: 600 Madison Avenue, New York, N.Y. 10022
Sales and Distribution Offices: 120 Enterprise Avenue, Secaucus, N.J. 07094

In Canada: Canadian Manda Group, One Atlantic Avenue, Suite 105, Toronto, Ontario M6K 3E7

Queries regarding rights and permissions should be addressed to Carol Publishing Group, 600 Madison Avenue, New York, N.Y. 10022

Carol Publishing Group books are available at special discounts for bulk purchases, sales promotion, fund-raising, or educational purposes. Special editions can be created to specifications. For details, contact: Special Sales Department, Carol Publishing Group, 120 Enterprise Avenue, Secaucus, N.J. 07094

Manufactured in the United States of America

10 9 8 7 6 5 4 3 2 1

Library of Congress Cataloging-in-Publication Data

Gordon, William A., 1950–
   Shot on this site : a traveler's guide to the places and locations used to film famous movies and television shows / by William A. Gordon.
        p.   cm.
   ISBN 0-8065-1647-X (pbk.)
   1. Motion picture locations—United States—Guidebooks.
2. Television program locations—United States—Guidebooks.
3. United States—Description and travel.   I. Title.
PN1995.67.U6G47   1995
791.43 ′025 73—dc20
                                                    94-46370
                                                       CIP

Contents

Preface

This book is designed to help tourists find where their favorite movies and television series were filmed and covers all but two of the fifty states in the Union. The only states not covered are Idaho and North Dakota, and that is because even though both states have hosted a few movies, officials from the Idaho and North Dakota film commissions could not recommend any sites still in existence that they would consider to be of interest to tourists.

Idaho and North Dakota, of course, hope to attract major productions in the future and undoubtedly will, once directors and location scouts—who are always on the lookout for new locations—discover that there are still two states whose resources have been largely untapped.

In the other forty-eight states this book reveals where just under nine hundred movies and over ninety weekly television series were filmed.

Although this is the first comprehensive guidebook to movie and television sites, *Shot on This Site* is neither all-inclusive nor definitive. The reason for that should be fairly obvious to readers. Since the advent of the talkies in 1929, more than twenty thousand feature films have been released theatrically by the major studios in this country alone. No single book—or even a multivolume encyclopedia—could begin to cover more than a fraction of these movies. In fact, it is doubtful that anyone would want or could use an all-encompassing volume, since a significant percentage of movies released theatrically are deservedly forgotten. The same could be said about most television series, many of which are filmed on soundstages in Los Angeles.

I figured readers would want to know only about the most popular movies, so I concentrated my efforts on box-office favorites released over the past fifteen years and on the few pre-1980 classics that were not filmed on soundstages.

To find out what was shot where, I contacted each of the 189 film commissions currently in existence. Some kept very good records or at least had locations specialists on staff who could tell me where the most important productions in the state were filmed. Oftentimes, though, only sketchy records were kept, or the commissions were so new that they were unable to help. (Most of the commissions were formed in the 1970s and 1980s, when Hollywood started making a concerted effort to find new locales and when many states and cities began to fully appreciate how much revenue filmmaking could bring into their communities.)

Whenever the film commissions were unable to help, I tracked down local film buffs or location managers who worked on the movies I knew were filmed in their cities or geographic regions. In all, I interviewed a few dozen location managers, who were most helpful in enabling me to fill in the blanks.

In selecting the locations used in this book, I had two criteria. The first was: Were the locations easily accessible? This book includes a number of hotels, restaurants, airports, college campuses, and national parks, all of which are open to the public.

If the locations were not directly accessible, I asked: Can a tourist at least drive past them or see them from a distance? In this category I've included many office buildings and factories.

I have also included a few private residences, but only when the home either played an integral part in the story or has since become a tourist attraction in its own right. The homes in *E.T. The Extraterrestrial* (1982), *Mrs. Doubtfire* (1993), *Pacific Heights* (1990), and *The Hand That Rocks the Cradle* (1992), all fit into that category.

Readers are cautioned *not* to disturb the occupants of these homes. There is nothing wrong with driving by and gawking, but the privacy of the occupants should be respected at all times.

Outside of the larger cities, I also incorporated geographic reference points found on most maps to help readers locate the more important entries. The reader will probably want to use this book in conjunction with existing tour books and maps.

It is hoped that *Shot on This Site* will make your next vacation destination more enjoyable and give you plenty of ideas as to where you might want to travel in the future.

Happy sightseeing.

SHOT ON
THIS SITE

Chapter 1

California

Southern California

Hotel del Coronado
1500 Orange Avenue, Coronado

Hollywood first discovered the Hotel del Coronado in 1927, when the hotel (or the Del, as locals affectionately call it) was featured in the MGM silent production of *The Flying Fleet*, which starred Ramón Novarro and Anita Page. Since then, the Del, considered one of the finest resort hotels on the West Coast, has appeared in a dozen or so features. Most memorably, it was the Florida resort hotel in Billy Wilder's *Some Like It Hot* (1959). Many believe that Marilyn Monroe gave her best performance in the picture. Jack Lemmon and Tony Curtis costarred as two musicians who witness a gangland murder and pose as women in Monroe's all-girls band to escape a mob hit.

The Stunt Man (1980), starring Peter O'Toole, was also filmed at the Del.

Hotel del Coronado, Some Like It Hot (courtesy Hotel del Coronado)

Simon & Simon Offices
802 Fifth Avenue (at F Street), San Diego

Mismatched brothers A.J. and Rick Simon, the TV detectives played by Jameson Parker and Gerald McRaney in *Simon & Simon*, operated out of an office on the third floor of the Keating building in San Diego's Gaslamp Quarter. The series ran on CBS from 1981 to 1988.

Other Locations in San Diego

San Diego's beaches, harbors, and naval facilities have appeared in a number of other films, among them: *Here Comes the Navy* (1934), *Hellcats of the Navy* (1957), *Little Nikita* (1988), and *Splash* (1984), but as local film officials point out, the locations have been so well disguised that tourists would never recognize them. The most popular movie based in San Diego, *Top Gun* (1986), was filmed primarily at the Miramar Naval Air Station and on North Island, which is off-limits to civilians, and aboard the USS *Ranger*, an aircraft carrier that was decommissioned in 1993.

Fans of *Top Gun* (particularly naval personnel and their families) still sometimes go to the Kansas City Barbeque at 610 West Market Street, across from Seaport Village. At the end of the movie, Tom Cruise comes back to see Kelly McGillis here. The restaurant has a *Top Gun* Room with photographs from the movie, and sells *Top Gun* T-shirts and fighter-pilot hats.

Hoag Memorial Hospital
301 Newport Boulevard, Newport Beach

This hospital, which is visible from the Pacific Coast Highway, served as the exterior of the hospital seen in the NBC sitcoms *Empty Nest* and *Nurses*.

Hyatt Regency Beach
200 South Pine Avenue, Long Beach

Last Action Hero (1993) was Arnold Schwarzenegger's first box-office bomb, but Arnold's fans (and there are still plenty of them) might be interested in seeing where some of the film's best action stunts were staged. The stunts start out on the hotel's roof, where Schwarzenegger crashes a gangster's funeral, steals the corpse, and while dodging the gangsters' gunfire, jumps onto an outdoor glass elevator (added especially for the movie), only to have to dodge artillery fire from a helicopter. Schwarzenegger shoots out the helicopter, but the elevator collapses, forcing him to make a midair grab onto the corpse, which is dangling from a conveniently placed crane. Schwarzenegger falls again, this time into a specially created Hollywood version of the La Brea Tar Pits (located in real life about thirty miles north of Long Beach). Fortunately, Schwarzenegger's movie daughter arrives just in time with a change of clothes.

Other Locations in Long Beach

• The Queen Mary, docked on Pier J at the end of the Long Beach Freeway, has appeared in over two hundred productions, most notably the disaster film *The Poseidon Adventure* (1972). In *Someone to Watch Over Me* (1987), Mimi Rogers witnesses a murder in the passenger liner's swimming pool, which the set designers had transformed into a New York art museum.

• Former vice president Dan Quayle's favorite movie, *Ferris Bueller's Day Off* (1986), was also filmed in part in Long Beach. Although the movie was set in Chicago, a house at 4160 Country Club Drive was used as Matthew Broderick's home.

• Meg Ryan's famous faked orgasm scene in *When Harry Met Sally* (1989) was filmed in the area as well, at the Port Cafe, located at 955 South Neptune Avenue, in neighboring Wilmington. The cafe, however, has since been razed.

Torrance High School
2200 West Carson Street, Torrance

Tourists frequently drive past Beverly Hills High School, thinking they will see the fictional West Beverly High of the hit television series *Beverly Hills 90210*. Beverly Hills High is famous for other reasons: mostly its prestigious alumni—the producers of *90210*, which was filmed at Torrance High School, located about forty minutes south of Los Angeles.

The reason Torrance stood in for Beverly Hills had to do with economics. The city of Beverly Hills charges more than $850 a day for film permits. Torrance charges $346 for the first day and half that ($178) for filming on additional days.

The cheaper permit costs are why, one movie-location scout told me, many films and television shows supposedly set in Beverly Hills, such as *Beverly Hills Cop* (1984), are primarily filmed elsewhere.

Los Angeles and Environs

Even though Los Angeles suffers from what industry insiders call "runaway production" (the loss of filming to other states and municipalities), the city still is the entertainment capital of the world. On any given day there are dozens of feature films and television programs shooting somewhere in Los Angeles, either on studio soundstages or on the streets of Los Angeles County.

In fact, there are so many movie and television locations that Los Angeles deserves its own book, which I have already written. It is *The Ultimate Hollywood Tour Book*, which is updated at least once a year.

Readers planning trips to Los Angeles may want to consult the book, since it includes information of interest to entertainment buffs (celebrity homes and haunts, the studios, sites of Hollywood scandals, murders, and suicides, and other sites where entertainment history was made).

There are so many L.A. filming locations to choose from that in this book I decided (somewhat arbitrarily) to limit the choices to approximately fifty of the top sites. This section includes movie and television locations in neighboring Beverly Hills, Malibu, Santa Monica, and Pasadena, all of which are separate cities in Los Angeles County.

Greystone Park and Mansion
905 Loma Vista Drive, Beverly Hills

The grounds include a magnificent fifty-five-room mansion that was once the largest and most expensive home in Beverly Hills. It was built by oilman Edward L. Doheny, whom scholars of presidential scandals will remember from the Teapot Dome scandal. Doheny, who was not content with his personal fortune of $100 million (in 1920s dollars), was accused of giving President Warren G. Harding's secretary of the interior, Albert B. Fall, a $100,000 interest-free "loan" in return for secretly leasing naval oil reserves at Teapot Dome, Wyoming, and Elk Hills, California. Doheny was acquitted and in 1928 built the mansion as a gift for his only son, Edward Jr., who moved in with his wife and children. A few weeks later, however, Edward Jr. and his male secretary were both found dead in Doheny's bedroom, giving rise to unconfirmed rumors that they died in a lovers' quarrel.

The property was later sold to Henry Crown, the owner of the Empire State Building, who subdivided it. It is now a public park owned and operated by the city of Beverly Hills.

The mansion has frequently been used as a filming location. It has been featured on such television programs as *Dynasty*, *Falcon Crest*, and *Knots Landing*. *Ghostbusters* (1984), *All of Me* (1984), *The Witches of Eastwick* (1987), *The Fabulous Baker Boys* (1989), *Guilty by Suspicion* (1990), *The Marrying Man* (1991), *The Bodyguard* (1992), *Memoirs of an Invisible Man* (1992), *Death Becomes Her* (1992), and *Indecent Proposal* (1993) have all made use of the mansion.

The Beverly Hillbillies Mansion
750 Bel Air Road, Bel Air

The house that Jed Clampett and his family called home in *The Beverly Hillbillies*, the enormously popular television show that aired from 1962 to 1970, was once known as the Kirkeby estate and was considered one of the great homes of Beverly Hills. It was bought in 1986 by Hollywood producer and agent Jerrold Perrenchio. Perrenchio, whose net worth was estimated by *Forbes* magazine at about $665 million, paid $13.6 million for the mansion, dismantled it, bought the three neighboring properties for an additional $9 million, and built what one writer called what "looks to be a modern monument to himself."

Although the gates are almost always closed, blocking all views of the new house, the property itself is still one of Los Angeles's hottest tourist attractions.

(*Note:* Ronald Reagan's retirement home is next door, at 668 St. Cloud Road.)

Regent Beverly Wilshire Hotel
9500 Wilshire Boulevard, Beverly Hills

In *Pretty Woman* (1990), Richard Gere is a wealthy businessman who stays in the penthouse suite of the Regent Beverly Wilshire with Julia Roberts, playing a hooker he picks up on Hollywood Boulevard and eventually courts. The fantasy struck a responsive chord, and the hotel still gets inquiries from prospective guests who want to stay in the $3,000-a-night "*Pretty Woman* Suite" (which actually was re-created on a soundstage). Only the lobby and the exterior of the hotel were featured in the movie. One Texas businessman even asked the hotel's concierge to locate the dressmaker who made Julia Roberts's dress so that it could be duplicated for his girlfriend when they stayed at the hotel.

Regent Beverly Wilshire Hotel, Pretty Woman *(courtesy Bob Dennison Photography/Regent Beverly Wilshire)*

Paradise Cove
28100 block of Pacific Coast Highway, Malibu

Located about a half hour's drive from Santa Monica, Paradise Cove is where all of Frankie Avalon and Annette Funicello's beach movies—*Beach Party* (1963), *Muscle Beach Party* (1964), *Beach Blanket Bingo* (1965), and *Back to the Beach* (1987)—were filmed and where, in *Indecent Proposal* (1993), Woody Harrelson proposes to Demi Moore. The couple, seemingly destroyed by Robert Redford's offer, later reunite on the pier next to the beach.

In the NBC series *The Rockford Files*, James Garner parked his trailer in the parking lot adjacent to the Sand Castle Restaurant on the beach. William Conrad lived in the first beach house south of the restaurant in the CBS crime show *Jake and the Fatman*.

Venice Fishing Pier
at the end of Washington Boulevard, Venice

Falling Down (1993) starred Michael Douglas as a recently displaced and divorced defense worker who one day descends into madness. A police lieutenant, played by Robert Duvall, finally catches up with Douglas at the pier, where Douglas meets his fate.

Fox Plaza
2121 Avenue of the Stars, Century City

This was the Nakatomi Corporation building in *Die Hard* (1988), which starred Bruce Willis as New York policeman John McClane, who single-handedly rescues his wife (played by Bonnie Bedelia) and other hostages from terrorists.

Ironically, the building, which was owned by Twentieth Century-Fox (which is situated next door), was later sold to a Japanese concern.

After retiring from public office, former president Ronald Reagan set up his offices in the building.

Fox Plaza and Century Plaza Towers, Die Hard *(Julian Wasser)*

J. W. Marriott Hotel
2151 Avenue of the Stars, Century City

I have included the Marriott not because it is particularly memorable in movie history but because it is next door to the Fox Plaza and tourists cannot miss it. The hotel has been featured in *Point of No Return* (1993; Bridget Fonda blows up some floors here); *Lethal Weapon 2* (1989; Mel Gibson and Danny Glover guard Joe Pesci in a suite and then jump out of a window into the hotel's swimming pool); and in *Pacific Heights* (1990), in which Melanie Griffith tracks Michael Keaton, her tenant from hell, to a room in the hotel.

Century Plaza Towers
2029 and 2049 Century Park East, Century City

These twin office towers served as the exteriors of Cybill Shepherd and Bruce Willis's Blue Moon Detective Agency in *Moonlighting* and Stephanie Zimbalist and Pierce Brosnan's Steele Investigations in *Remington Steele*.

It is probably not a coincidence that both series were created by producer Glenn Gordon Caron.

The Source
8301 Sunset Boulevard (at Sweetzer)

This natural-foods restaurant, located on the Sunset Strip, is where Diane Keaton dumps Woody Allen in *Annie Hall* (1977).

77 Sunset Strip
8532 Sunset Boulevard

Although fans of the popular 1950s television series would never recognize it today, the front door of the Tiffany Theater is where Efrem Zimbalist Jr. and Roger Smith played private eyes at the fictitious address 77 Sunset Strip.

The restaurant next to their offices, Dino's Lodge (which was once owned by Dean Martin), is also long gone. It has been replaced by an office building housing Casablanca Records.

Hollywood Studio Museum
2100 North Highland Avenue, Hollywood

The museum, which is dedicated to early Hollywood moviemaking, is located in the barn where Cecil B. DeMille directed *The Squaw Man* (1914), the first feature-length film shot entirely in Hollywood. Some books give the erroneous impression that the barn is where the first Hollywood movie was made, but as museum director Kari Johnson points out, several filmmakers set up shop in Santa Monica and in downtown Los Angeles as early as 1906, eight years before *The Squaw Man*'s release. The movie's "real claim to fame," says Johnson, "is that it was the first nationally successful feature-length western." Its success inspired other filmmakers to follow the lead of DeMille and producer Jesse Lasky and set up shop in Hollywood.

The barn, which originally was located a few miles east of its present site (at the intersection of Selma and Vine streets), was subsequently moved to Paramount's back lot, where it was later used as the railroad station in *Bonanza*. Eventually, the barn was donated by Paramount Pictures and the Hollywood Chamber of Commerce to Hollywood Heritage, Inc., which operates the museum.

High Tower
at the north end of Hightower Drive, Hollywood

Fans of the 1991 suspense thriller *Dead Again* will immediately recognize this unusual-looking Italian tower. It was here—and in the studio apartment immediately to the right of the tower—that the climactic scene played out. The location was chosen deliberately (and even included in the original script) because the producers wanted to show that the character played by costar Emma Thompson, who lived in the apartment, was literally cut off from outside help.

The five-story tower houses an elevator that services the homes and apartments built into the hillside. The elevator is inaccessible to the public, but the area offers some interesting photo opportunities.

Incidentally, Elliott Gould, playing detective Philip Marlowe, lived in the same apartment in Robert Altman's *The Long Good-bye* (1973).

High Tower, Dead Again
(William A. Gordon)

First United Methodist Church of Hollywood
6817 Franklin Avenue, Hollywood

This is the church where Earthlings prayed when it appeared that invading Martians would destroy them in the 1953 classic *The War of the Worlds*. The gym inside was also used for the filming of the "Enchantment Under the Sea" dance in the first two *Back to the Future* (1985 and 1989) movies. Several scenes in *Sister Act* (1992) were also filmed in the church.

Ozzie And Harriet House
1822 Camino Palmero, Hollywood

The Nelson family—Ozzie, Harriet, David, and Ricky—lived here for over twenty-five years, and the outside of the house was seen in their ABC-TV show *The Adventures of Ozzie and Harriet*, which aired from 1952 to 1966.

Mann's Chinese Theater
6925 Hollywood Boulevard, Hollywood

This theater, which is undoubtedly the most famous in the world, has been on the screen too many times to count. Originally known as Graumann's Chinese Theater, it still holds ceremonies in which celebrities immortalize their handprints in concrete. The ceremonies are always held a few days before the star's movie opens at the theater.

Paramount Studios
5555 Melrose Avenue, Hollywood

Paramount is the only major studio still located in Hollywood (the others have all fled to the suburbs), and it offers a little-publicized walking tour of its back lot.

One of its main attractions is the famous wrought-iron side gate at the corner of Bronson Avenue and Marathon Street (not to be confused with the main gate on Melrose Avenue). The side gate was immortalized in *Sunset Blvd.* (1950) and has appeared in countless other films.

*Paramount Studios
(William A. Gordon)*

Happy Days Home
565 North Cahuenga Avenue, Hancock Park

The façade of this house served as the Cunningham home in the long-running hit television series *Happy Days*.

Ambassador Hotel
3400 Wilshire Boulevard, Los Angeles

The Ambassador, once a Hollywood hot spot, perhaps is best known as the site where Robert F. Kennedy was assassinated while running for the presidency in 1968. The hotel closed in 1990 and today is used exclusively for location filming. Public records indicate that the Ambassador was L'Idiot Restaurant in *L.A. Story* (1991), where maître d' Patrick Stewart cross-examines Steve Martin; a Wrigley Field bathroom in *Opportunity Knocks* (1990), in which Dana Carvey pretends to be George Bush; the setting for a downtown meeting between Robert De Niro, playing a blacklisted writer, and his attorney, played by Sam Wanamaker in *Guilty by Suspicion* (1991); Meryl Streep's hotel in *Defending Your Life* (1991); and both a Catskill resort and a glitzy Las Vegas showroom in Billy Crystal's *Mr. Saturday Night* (1992).

The Academy Awards were presented in the hotel's famous Cocoanut Grove six times between 1930 and 1943. In 1947, Marilyn Monroe started as a model at Emmaline Snively's Blue Book Modeling Agency, located in the hotel.

Chemosphere
7776 Torreyson Drive, Hollywood Hills (one block north of Mulholland Drive)

Even if you were not a fan of Brian DePalma's 1984 film *Body Double* (in which Craig Wasson, playing a struggling actor, house-sits here and is set up as a pawn in a convoluted murder scheme), you will enjoy looking at this house. Shaped like an eight-sided flying saucer (and sometimes mistaken for one, particularly at night), the Chemosphere sits atop a single concrete post several hundred feet above Torreyson Drive. To get to the house, the occupants have to either climb more than a hundred steps or take a cable car which runs from the street level to the house's front door.

The house was designed by the famed architect John Lautner, who also designed Bambi and Thumper's house in the James Bond film *Diamonds Are Forever* (1971), as well as a house down the street at 7436 Mulholland. In *Lethal Weapon 2* (1989), that house is the residence of South Africa's evil ambassador, and Mel Gibson brings the house down from its pedestal by tying it to a pickup truck.

Hollywood Sign
atop Mount Lee, Hollywood Hills

The Hollywood sign, which is probably more recognizable worldwide than the Statue of Liberty or the White House, is actually a giant billboard with letters over fifty feet high and thirty feet wide. It was originally constructed in 1923 as "Hollywoodland" to advertise homes sold by the Hollywoodland Realty company (still in existence in Beachwood Canyon). When the last four letters fell off, the sign became a symbol of the entertainment industry.

Until recently, it was possible to hike to the sign from Mulholland Highway. However, a gate was erected a few years ago to discourage vandalism and suicide.

Invasion of the Body Snatchers Stairs
corner of Belden and Beachwood drives, Hollywood Hills

While some of the most memorable scenes in the original *Invasion of the Body Snatchers* (1956) were filmed in the town square of Sierra Madre, a small community just northeast of Pasadena (it was there that Kevin McCarthy and Dana Wynter hide from the pod people), the scenes of their escape were filmed at the corner of Beachwood and Belden drives. The couple run eastward up the hill on Belden Drive and then up a flight of 148 steps located one block north of that intersection, at the corner of Beachwood and Woodshire drives.

Griffith Park Observatory
2800 East Observatory Road, Hollywood Hills

Griffith Park is the largest urban park in the United States. Sometimes it is referred to as an unofficial Hollywood back lot, since so many productions—over a thousand a year—are filmed there. According to the park's film coordinator: "When companies need green space or a road that doesn't have buildings on it, they come up here."

The park's famous observatory was the site of the final fight scenes in *Rebel Without a Cause* (1955). A bust of James Dean stands on the planetarium's west lawn.

Arnold Schwarzenegger beams down to earth at the observatory in the beginning of *The Terminator* (1984), and in one of the sillier

Griffith Park (courtesy Los Angeles Convention and Visitors Bureau/ copyright 1991 Michele and Tom Grimm)

scenes in *The Rocketeer* (1991), hero Bill Campbell and the Mafia combine forces to fight off invading Nazis.

Dorothy Chandler Pavilion
135 North Grand Avenue, downtown Los Angeles

Site of most of the Academy Awards presentations in recent years. Los Angeles's Shrine Auditorium, located at 649 West Jefferson Boulevard, is also sometimes used.

Westin Bonaventure Hotel
404 South Figueroa Street, downtown Los Angeles

The futuristic-looking Bonaventure has appeared in more than a dozen movies, including *Rain Man* (1988), where Tom Cruise, having met Jerry Molen, the recipient of his brother's trust, is offered, but turns down, $250,000 to walk away from his brother. In *True Lies* (1994) the Bonaventure appeared as the Washington, D.C. hotel in which Arnold Schwarzenegger, riding a horse in pursuit of a nuclear terrorist, gallops through the lobby and takes the elevator to the top floor. The terrorist manages to evade him by driving a motor scooter off the roof and into a neighboring hotel's swimming pool.

The Bonaventure is probably most famous, though, as the hotel where Clint Eastwood foils John Malkovich's presidential assassination attempt in *In the Line of Fire* (1993).

Bonaventure Hotel, Rain Man, In the Line of Fire, True Lies (courtesy Westin Bonaventure Hotel and Suites)

L.A. Law Building
444 South Flower, downtown Los Angeles

The building was seen in television's *L.A. Law*. It has also been filmed in *Baby Boom* (1987) and served as CIA headquarters in *Gotcha!* (1985). In *Beverly Hills Cop II* (1987), Gilbert Gottfried had an office there.

Biltmore Hotel
506 South Grand Avenue, downtown Los Angeles

Since it opened back in 1923, the Biltmore has hosted kings, presidents, Hollywood celebrities, and virtually every major league baseball team. In 1960, John F. Kennedy set up the official head-quarters for the Democratic National Convention in suite 8315. It was here that he—and his brother Bobby—decided on Lyndon Baines Johnson as a running mate.

Over the past twenty years at least three hundred feature films, television programs, and commercials have been filmed at the hotel. The Crystal Ballroom served as the setting for the bookie joint in *The Sting* (1973), the fight arena in *Rocky III* (1982), the prom scene in *Pretty in Pink* (1986), the banquet scene in *Alien Nation* (1988), the singing scenes in *The Fabulous Baker Boys* (1989), and the guests-getting-slimed scenes in the original *Ghostbusters* (1984).

Vertigo (1958) used the eleven flights of ornate, wrought-iron back stairs to create its dizzying scenes, and scenes from *Bugsy* (1991) were filmed at the Biltmore Health Club.

In *Beverly Hills Cop* (1984), the Biltmore was called the Beverly Palm. Eddie Murphy, playing wisecracking Detroit detective Axel Foley, cons his way into the hotel, stuffs bananas in the tailpipe of detectives following him, and later keeps some of the bathrobes as souvenirs.

The Biltmore was also the setting of eight early Academy Award ceremonies: in 1931, 1935–1939, 1941, and 1942.

Biltmore Hotel (courtesy The Biltmore, Los Angeles)

Southern California Gas Company Tower
555 West Fifth Street, downtown Los Angeles

This fifty-two-story high-rise, which is directly across the street from the Biltmore, is where Keanu Reeves rescues hostages trapped in an elevator in the 1994 action film *Speed*.

Bradbury Building
304 South Broadway, downtown Los Angeles

The Bradbury was Harrison Ford's home in *Blade Runner* (1982), the publishing offices where Jack Nicholson works in *Wolf* (1994), Christian Slater's law office in *Murder in the First* (1995), and the setting of several television and movie private-eye melodramas, including *Chinatown* (1974). Sam Hall Kaplan, Los Angeles's premier architectural critic, writes: "With its magical interior court bathed in light filtered through a glass roof and ornate ironwork and reflected off glazed yellow brick walls, the 1893 structure is one of the city's architectural treasures."

Los Angeles City Hall
200 North Spring Street

"City Hall," writes *Los Angeles Times* researcher Cecilia Rasmussen, "has starred in more movies and television series than most Hollywood actors." Perhaps best known as the *Daily Planet* in the popular 1950s television series *Superman*, City Hall, inside and out,

Los Angeles City Hall (courtesy Los Angeles Convention and Visitors Center/copyright 1991 Michele and Tom Grimm)

has been seen in *Seems Like Old Times* (1980), *48 Hrs.* (1982), *Another 48 Hrs.* (1990), *Die Hard II* (1990), *Dragnet* (1987), and *Ricochet* (1991). "Although it was destroyed by Martians in *The War of the Worlds* (1953)," Rasmussen notes, "it somewhere survived to portray the U.S. Capitol in *The Jimmy Hoffa Story* and the Vatican in *The Thorn Birds*. ... You might have caught a glimpse of City Hall in the series *Kojak*, *Cagney and Lacey*, *The Rockford Files*, *Matlock*, *Hill Street Blues*, *L.A. Law*, *Equal Justice*, *The Trials of Rosie O'Neill*, and *The Big One: The Great Los Angeles Earth-quake*."

Puente Hills Mall
Colima Road, City of Industry

In *Back to the Future* (1985), Christopher Lloyd is seemingly gunned down by terrorists in the parking lot near the mall's J. C. Penney department store. Michael J. Fox avoids them by taking Lloyd's DeLorean back in time.

The Bat Mansion
380 South San Rafael Avenue, Pasadena

Although tourists sometimes drive by the property, the mansion, used as the Wayne Manor in the popular 1960s television series *Batman*, and later as Kenneth Branagh's home in *Dead Again* (1991), is not visible from the street.

Gamble House
4 Westmoreland Place, Pasadena

In the *Back to the Future* series, Christopher Lloyd ("Doc") lived in this house. It is an internationally recognized architectural landmark, a product of the turn-of-the-century arts and crafts movement, and is open to tourists.

Pasadena City Hall
100 North Garfield Avenue, Pasadena

The producers of the *Beverly Hills Cop* movies filmed the exteriors of Pasadena's historic City Hall and pretended it was the Beverly Hills City Hall. The reason: filming permits cost four times as much in Beverly Hills as they do in Pasadena.

Castle Green Apartments
99 South Raymond Avenue, Pasadena

One of Pasadena's premier resort hotels before the turn of the century, the Castle Green is a popular location site because of its unusual Middle Eastern architecture. The outside of the building was used as the Hotel de Nacional in *Bugsy* (1991), as a Russian consular office in San Francisco in *Sneakers*, and as a restaurant in *The Marrying Man* (1991). It was featured in *Wild at Heart* (1990) and was where "the sting" took place in *The Sting* (1973).

The Carrington Mansion
1145 Arden Road, Pasadena

This is not the house seen in the opening credits of *Dynasty*. That one, located in the San Francisco suburb of Woodside, is featured on pages 31–32. This one, known formally as Arden Villa, is, however, the mansion used for close-up outdoor scenes with the actors and for the garden and pool shots, including the famous catfights between Linda Evans and Joan Collins.

The twenty-thousand-square-foot mansion has been a frequent filming site, dating back to the 1933 Marx Brothers' classic *Duck Soup*. According to owner Charles Morton, who handles film and corporate-affairs rentals, Arden Villa has appeared in at least two hundred productions since 1980, including four television movies about the Kennedys, *Nixon's Last Days*, several episodes of *Hart to Hart*, *Flamingo Road*, and Charles Bronson's *Death Wish* (1974).

Carrington Mansion from Dynasty *(William A. Gordon)*

The house also served as the Knight Rider Foundation in the NBC series *Knight Rider*, and was where Eddie Murphy ran his scam in the opening scenes of *The Distinguished Gentleman* (1992).

Father of the Bride House
843 South El Molino Avenue, Pasadena

Although Steve Martin's narrative in the 1991 remake of *Father of the Bride* identifies Martin and Diane Keaton's residence as being in San Marino, the house was actually located in Pasadena, a few blocks north of San Marino (another city which discourages film-making by charging one of the highest permit fees in Los Angeles County).

The producers considered the house almost a character in the story. They looked for a home in an old-fashioned, idealized community and considered this white clapboard residence perfect.

thirtysomething House
1710 Bushnell Avenue, South Pasadena

The façade of this house was used for the Philadelphia residence of Ken Olin and Mel Harris on TV's *thirtysomething*. It was also Jeff Daniels's home in *Welcome Home, Roxy Carmichael* (1990) and is across the street from a group of houses used in the first two *Back to the Future* movies. According to Scott Carter, a film buff who lives on the street, 1809 Bushnell was the house in which the bully Biff lived; 1803 was the house where Biff takes away a ball from kids; and 1727 was where Lea Thompson and her family take in Michael J. Fox after Thompson's father hits him with an automobile. (In 1985, Fox returned to 1727 Bushnell, which was used as his family home in *Teen Wolf*.) Also, 1705 was used as Elisabeth Shue's house, and both 1621 and 1615 were used for Bill Cosby's *Ghost Dad* (1990). One block west of this house, at 1623 Fletcher, is Patricia Wettig and Timothy Busfield's *thirtysomething* home.

The Beverly Hillbillies Movie Home
1284 Oakland Avenue, South Pasadena

The exterior of this mansion, once owned by a mistress of deposed dictator Ferdinand Marcos, was used for the exterior shots, including the wedding scenes, in *The Beverly Hillbillies* (1993).

The mansion is directly across the street from another at 1365 South Oakland, which was the governor's mansion in the ABC television series *Benson*, which aired from 1979 to 1986.

Rialto Theater
1023 South Fair Oaks, South Pasadena

The Rialto played itself in *The Player* (1992), in which Tim Robbins, as amoral studio executive Griffin Mill, meets an aspiring writer who Robbins thinks is sending him threatening postcards. Robbins tries to win over the writer, played by Vincent D'Onofrio, with promises of meetings but ends up killing him in the alley behind the theater. Robbins proceeds to seduce D'Onofrio's girlfriend and not only gets away with murder but also climbs the studio ladder of success.

Beverly Hills 90210 House
1675 East Altadena Drive, Altadena

The Walsh family home in the Fox series *Beverly Hills 90210* is actually located in Altadena, about four miles northeast of downtown Pasadena and a good forty minutes' drive from Beverly Hills.

Los Angeles State and County Arboretum
301 North Baldwin Avenue, Arcadia

The Queen Anne cottage seen in the ABC series *Fantasy Island* is located at the Arboretum, which is about a ten-minute drive southeast of downtown Pasadena. The Arboretum is a 127-acre botanical

Los Angeles State and County Arboretum, Fantasy Island

park that features exotic trees and shrubs arranged by their continent of origin. The opening sequence of *Fantasy Island* included stock footage of an airplane landing on the lake and Herve Villechaize's character, Tatoo, ringing the bell in the cottage tower, yelling, "De plane, de plane." The producers filmed only a few episodes at the Arboretum and then constructed a replica on the studio lot.

The Arboretum also has appeared in well over two hundred television episodes and films, including eight Tarzan movies, *The African Queen*, *Road to Singapore*, and others with jungle settings.

Occidental College
1600 Campus Road, Eagle Rock

This private liberal arts college, located in the tiny community of Eagle Rock (nestled between Glendale and Pasadena), became the fictitious California University in the Fox series *Beverly Hills 90210*. Most of the filming took place in the campus's quadrangle—while students were walking to classes. The university's Faculty Club (not open to the public) became the Keg House fraternity, and Thorne Hall was where Shannen Doherty took theater classes.

NBC Studios
3000 West Alameda Avenue, Burbank

NBC is today the only television network that offers a tour of its studios. Moreover, it is possible to see a taping of the *Tonight* show and other shows filmed at its studio. The studio's ticket counter opens at 8:00 A.M. and distributes tickets for shows taping that evening. Ticket requests are also honored by mail if you write to the studio giving the name of the show and enclose a self-addressed stamped envelope.

NBC Studios, Burbank
(William A. Gordon)

Warner Bros. Studios
4000 Warner Boulevard, Burbank

Warner Bros. offers a two-hour tour of its back lot and studio facilities. The tour, Warner spokespersons point out, "is not a charade created for mass audiences" (an obvious jab at Universal's tour) "but is, in fact, designed for small groups—no more than twelve persons—so that they may learn about the various components that go into the making of a film." The tour includes a walk through the busy back lot of Warner Bros. and oftentimes (although there is no guarantee) onto stages where Warner television programs are being filmed.

Universal Studios Hollywood
100 Universal City Plaza, Universal City

Universal Studios Hollywood is so popular that the theme park actually makes more money every year than do the company's movies. The park offers stunt shows, technical attractions, and a tram tour through Universal's back lot, where hundreds of movies and television shows have been filmed. The Bates Motel, seen in *Psycho* (1960), is there, as are the sets used in *Back to the Future* (1985; the Hill Valley courthouse), *The Sting* (1973), and such television series as *Murder, She Wrote*, *Matlock*, *McHale's Navy*, *Leave It to Beaver*, *The Munsters*, and *Nancy Drew*.

Universal Studios/Psycho House (courtesy Universal Studios Hollywood)

Brady Bunch House
11222 Dilling Street, North Hollywood

The exterior of this house, which is located only a short drive from Universal Studios, was used as the Brady household in the popular ABC-TV show, which aired from 1969 to 1974.

E.T. House
7121 Lonzo Street, Tujunga

When Steven Spielberg's location scouts searched for a house to use as Elliot's in *E.T. The Extraterrestrial* (1982), they looked for a typical suburban home that looked as if it had a magical mountain and a redwood forest behind it. They found it in the northwest section of the San Fernando Valley, situated in front of one of the highest peaks of the San Gabriel Mountains. In the movie, E.T. takes up residence here after being stranded by his fellow travelers, and Elliott hides him until both were discovered by government agents.

The Halloween street scenes and the chase scenes, though, were filmed on several different streets of Porter Ranch, another community in the northwestern portion of the San Fernando Valley. The famous scene in which Elliott and his friends, seemingly cornered by police cars, fly away into the air on their bicycles was filmed on White Oak Boulevard in Northridge, between Tribune and San Fernando Mission roads.

Vasquez Rocks County Park
10700 Escondido Canyon Road, Agua Dulce (northeast of Newhall on Route 14)

Dozens of westerns and science-fiction movies have been filmed here. They include the first and fourth *Star Trek* features (1979 and 1986), *Star Wars* (1977), and the original *Star Trek* television series.

The Flintstones *set at Vasquez Rocks (Sam Renzi)*

The rocks, which were once the hideout for a notorious nineteenth-century bandit named Tiburcio Vasquez, also served as the backdrop for Bedrock in *The Flintstones* (1994). They are located about seventy miles northeast of downtown Los Angeles.

Two Bunch Palms
67-425 Two Bunch Palms Trail, Desert Hot Springs (thirteen miles north of Palm Springs)

Manager Jerry Greenbach reports that the inn's mud-bath business significantly increased after *The Player* showed stars Tim Robbins and Greta Scacchi (a regular customer in real life) "immersed up to their necks in relaxing goo." Greenbach adds that 76 percent of the resort's clientele are celebrities from the movie and recording industries. "Most come to the spa because it is secure, secluded, and here they can walk around in their bathrobes or cover-ups and nobody would say boo."

California's Central Coast

Santa Barbara

Although a number of features have been shot in Santa Barbara, most, including Brian DePalma's *Scarface* (1985) and the 1992 version of John Steinbeck's *Of Mice and Men*, were filmed on private estates, where sightseers are not permitted.

One site that can be seen, though, is the Santa Barbara County Courthouse at 1100 Anacapa Street. It appeared in the opening credits of ABC-TV's *Owen Marshall, Counselor at Law*. The series, which ran from 1971 to 1974, starred Arthur Hill as a warm-hearted, *Marcus Welby, M.D.*–type attorney who practiced in Santa Barbara.

The only recognizable scenes from the long-running soap opera *Santa Barbara*, are those in the opening credits of the elegant Four Seasons Biltmore Hotel, located at 1260 Channel Drive, and some mansions nearby. *Santa Barbara* aired on NBC from 1984 to 1992.

Fans of the 1981 remake of *The Postman Always Rings Twice*, starring Jessica Lange and Jack Nicholson, sometimes trek to the gas station just south of the Sandpiper Golf Course at the Holister Avenue–Winchester Canyon exit of the 101 Freeway, where much of the action in the movie takes place.

In addition, the Santa Barbara Airport masqueraded as the site of an international arms show in the 1984 Chevy Chase feature *Deal of the Century*. North of Santa Barbara, *The Rocketeer* (1990) was filmed extensively at the Santa Maria Airport, which stood in as the 1938

Santa Monica Airport. It was here that star Bill Campbell tested his rocket. The airport was also featured in *The Spirit of St. Louis* (1956), and one of the buildings has been turned into an aviation museum.

Monterey Bay Aquarium
886 Cannery Row, Monterey

In *Star Trek IV: The Voyage Home* (1986), the aquarium was transformed into the Sausalito Cetacean Institute, where William Shatner (Capt. James T. Kirk) and Leonard Nimoy (Mr. Spock) find the two humpback whales they need to bring back to the twenty-third century to save Earth from an alien probe. Many of the key scenes were filmed in the observation-deck area outside, where, in the movie, the two whales, George and Gracie, are released from captivity, and in the Kelp Forest Exhibit, where Spock shocks the other tourists by jumping into the water to do a Vulcan mind meld with the humpback

Monterey Bay Aquarium/Kelp Forest, Star Trek IV *(copyright Monterey Bay Aquarium).*

Gracie. Here Spock tells Gracie what the mission of the crew of the *Enterprise* is and discovers that Gracie is pregnant.

Although Nimoy, who directed the film, originally considered diving into the exhibit himself, that scene was actually filmed on the Paramount studio lot. Nimoy discovered that the water in the Kelp Forest Exhibit was pretty cold and thought Spock would look funny with goose bumps. So they just filmed the tank from the outside—before the dive—as the tour group walks up to the window.

There are, by the way, no whales in the aquarium. Whales are kept in captivity only in oceanariums like Sea World. George and Gracie were actually three-foot-long radio-controlled models.

Through the magic of movies, the filmmakers also added a fake San Francisco skyline behind the aquarium to make it appear as though the institute was close to San Francisco.

Other Locations in Monterey, Carmel, and Pebble Beach

Joe Graziano, a columnist for the *Monterey Herald*, discovered that segments of more than 170 films were filmed in Monterey, Carmel, and Pebble Beach, some dating back to the silent era. Many of those films, Graziano says, could have been filmed anywhere, "but I think filmmakers came here as an excuse, because it's so beautiful."

Among the more memorable: *National Velvet* (1944), Elizabeth Taylor's first starring film, which was shot in part at the polo field in Pebble Beach; Disney's *Escape to Witch Mountain* (1975), starring Eddie Albert, at the old Crocker mansion on the famous 17-Mile Drive; and *Turner and Hooch* (1989), starring Tom Hanks, also on the 17-Mile Drive, and in various locations in nearby Pacific Grove.

Scenes from Clint Eastwood's *Play Misty For Me* (1971) were filmed at the Sardine Factory Restaurant at 701 Wave Street on Fisherman's Wharf in Monterey. Disney's *The Parent Trap* (1961), starring Hayley Mills, as twin daughters who try to reunite their separated parents, was filmed at the Monterey Peninsula Airport, at the Lodge of Pebble Beach overlooking the eighteenth hole of the golf course, and at Cypress Point in Pebble Beach. And *Cannery Row* (1982), starring Nick Nolte and Debra Winger, was filmed at the Cannery Row waterfront made famous in John Steinbeck's novel of the same name, although the street scenes were re-created on a soundstage in Culver City.

Four miles south of Carmel, off Highway 1, is the Point Lobos State Reserve, a state park that visitors have called "an area of astounding beauty." Point Lobos, reportedly the park that Robert

Louis Stevenson used as his model for Spyglass Hill in *Treasure Island*, has also been the setting of at least thirty-four features, including the *Rebecca* (1940), *Lassie Come Home* (1943), *The Sandpiper* (1964), *The Graduate* (1967), *Blind Date* (1986), and *Turner and Hooch*. Whaler's Cabin, the small museum in the park, has a photo exhibit of the different films.

Also south of Carmel and Monterey—in an area known as the Carmel Highlands—is a house on Spindrift Road that served as Sharon Stone's home in the controversial thriller *Basic Instinct* (1991). The house, which in the movie is supposed to be north of San Francisco in Marin County, was selected because of the tall oceanside cliffs directly behind it. The house is behind a six-foot-high fence and is not visible from the street.

The beach scenes in *Basic Instinct*—including the scene where Michael Douglas tells Stone he will nail her for murder and she laughs him off, saying, "You'll just fall in love with me"—were filmed on Garrapatta State Beach, just south of the highlands.

Santa Cruz Boardwalk
400 Beach Street, Santa Cruz

Santa Cruz's famous oceanside boardwalk has been featured in a number of films, including the campy 1987 teenage vampire flick *The Lost Boys*, which starred Kiefer Sutherland, Jason Patric, two Coreys (Feldman and Haim), Jami Gertz, Dianne Wiest, and Edward Herrmann. The "Boys" are teenage vampire-punks who hang out at the amusement park at night. Director Joel Schumacher selected the boardwalk because it "has a jazzy carnival atmosphere, which is always slightly sinister at night, and it was perfect for our purpose."

Clint Eastwood also filmed the denouement of *Sudden Impact* (1983) on the boardwalk. This was the fourth of the five movies about "Dirty Harry" Callahan, the neofascist "screw-the-rules, screw-their-rights" San Francisco police inspector.

In the film, which Eastwood directed as well as starred in, he harasses a Mafia figure during his daughter's wedding, provoking a heart attack. That scene was filmed at the boardwalk's Cocoanut Grove Ballroom. The movie's climactic scenes, including the ultimate shoot-out with the thugs who have raped costar Sondra Locke, were filmed on and near the park's carousel ride.

The boardwalk also featured in some less popular movies, including *The Sting II* (1982), which features a chase through the park, ending with a stuntman jumping off a moving car of the Giant Dipper ride, and *Creator* (1984), starring Peter O'Toole and Mariel Hemingway. In *Creator*, the boardwalk doubled as Atlantic City.

Mission San Juan Bautista
19 Franklin Street, San Juan Bautista

Located a few miles north of Salinas and ninety-one miles south of San Francisco, this is the mission where Kim Novak jumps to her death in Hitchcock's *Vertigo* (1958).

The famous bell tower, however, was taken down before the filming. The tower seen in the film was built by the studio and optically superimposed onto the mission.

"Cyberdyne Systems" Building
47131 Bayside Park, Fremont

The greatest police shoot-out in cinematic history took place at this forbidding-looking blue-glass office building, located five miles north of San Jose, at the corner of Gateway Boulevard and Bayside Park. Set designer Joseph Nemec III selected the building for *Terminator 2: Judgment Day* (1991) because its exterior struck him as being very cold. In the movie the building is the headquarters of Cyberdyne Systems, which manufactures the weapons responsible for a nuclear holocaust (Judgment Day) on August 29, 1997. Arnold Schwarzenegger, Linda Hamilton, and Joe Morton go to the building in an attempt to neutralize the machines of destruction.

Since the building had just been erected and was not occupied at the time, a real explosion was staged, and a few floors were blown out. One of the more spectacular stunts involved the evil Termina-

Terminator 2 *building,*
Fremont (William A.
Gordon)

tor (Robert Patrick) riding a motorcycle out of a second-story office window and onto a helicopter. A stuntman actually flew through the air for about forty-five feet before a safety harness broke the launch. He then landed safely on a stack of cardboard boxes.

Great America Amusement Park
Great America Parkway, Santa Clara

This family entertainment center was transformed into Wonder World in *Beverly Hills Cop 3* (1994). While investigating the murder of his Detroit police captain and a counterfeiting ring here, Eddie Murphy saves children trapped on the Triple Wheel, a birdcage-shaped Ferris wheel.

The park was also one of the amusement parks to which Ted Danson takes his son (Macauley Culkin) in *Getting Even With Dad* (1994).

Other San Jose–Area Locations

• *Birdy* (1984), a psychodrama starring Matthew Modine as a traumatized Vietnam veteran who thinks he is a bird, was filmed on the west campus of the Agnews Developmental Center, a state mental institution at the corner of Montague Expressway and De la Cruz, in San Jose.

• The Tech Mart building, at the corner of Great America Parkway in Santa Clara, was used as the setting of Argo Motors, the auto manufacturer implicated in a class-action suit in *Class Action* (1990).

• *The Rookie* (1990), starring and directed by Clint Eastwood, was filmed in various locations around San Jose, including Highways 680 and 87, where a spectacular opening chase sequence was shot; Villa Montalvo, 15400 Montalvo Road, Saratoga, an arboretum that was once the private estate of Sen. James Duval Phelan; and at the San Jose International Airport, where the climax took place.

• Scenes from *The Candidate* (1972), starring Robert Redford, were filmed in Eastridge Mall. Brian DePalma's *Raising Cain* (1992), starring John Lithgow and Lolita Davidovich, was also shot in various locations around Palo Alto (including the Stanford Shopping Center), Los Altos, Menlo Park, and Mountain View, whose city hall was used.

Filoli
Canada Road, Woodside

Filoli is the Georgian mansion seen from the air in the opening credits of the long-running (1981–1989) ABC-TV series *Dynasty*. According to director Anne Taylor, the series pilot was shot there, and the producers then re-created the mansion's living room (actually Filoli's library), hallway, and staircase on a sound stage.

The house also served as Warren Beatty's home in *Heaven Can Wait* (1978) and as a Shanghai mansion in *The Joy Luck Club* (1993).

The estate and gardens which are open to tourists, are located in Woodside, about twenty-five miles south of San Francisco.

Filoli (courtesy Filoli)

San Francisco and the Bay Area

Pacific Heights House
corner of Texas and 19th streets

The town house where Michael Keaton torments Melanie Griffith and Matthew Modine in the 1990 thriller of the same name is not in Pacific Heights. It is at the top of San Francisco's Potrero Hill section, a location chosen because it provided spectacular panoramic views of the city.

The Queen Anne Victorian looks much smaller and in better shape than it does on the screen. When the production company discovered it, the house had been recently repainted. To create a "distressed" look, they masked the entire house with sound-blasting frisket, a substance with light adhesive on one side and paper on the other. The painted side was treated with chemicals to make the exterior look cracked and aged.

After two days' filming, the crew removed the frisket.

The interior scenes were filmed on soundstages at Culver Studios in Los Angeles.

Burger Island
901 Third Street (corner of Townsend)

In *Sudden Impact* (1983), his fourth appearance as San Francisco inspector "Dirty Harry" Callahan, Clint Eastwood breaks up a

Burger Island, Sudden Impact (*William A. Gordon*)

robbery in progress here and kills two villains. Then, when one robber takes a waitress hostage, putting a gun to her head, Eastwood makes his memorable threat: "Go ahead. Make my day."

Although the restaurant is unpretentious, French and German tourists flock here.

(*Note:* Burger Island is a short drive from Moscone Center North, where, before the center was built, Leilani Sarelle, Sharon Stone's girlfriend in *Basic Instinct*, tries to run down Michael Douglas and crashes into a construction pit.)

North Beach

The San Francisco Film and Video Office does not have any record of movies being filmed inside the Transamerica Pyramid, the city's tallest and most identifiable office building. (The forty-eight-story-tall structure is capped by a 212-foot spire.) However, the building, located at 600 Montgomery Street, has been featured in the background of virtually every recent San Francisco film. In *Shattered* (1991), Tom Berenger plays Merrick, a San Francisco developer who works in the building.

Four blocks north of the Pyramid, at 261 Columbus Street, is City· Lights, one of the most famous bookstores in the country. Founded by poet Lawrence Ferlinghetti and known as a haven for bohemians, City Lights was last seen in *Flashback* (1990), in which a triumphant ex-1960s radical, Dennis Hopper, autographs his autobiography and meets up with FBI agent Kiefer Sutherland. The bookstore was also featured in *Heart Beat* (1980), starring Nick Nolte, Sissy Spacek and John Hurt.

Directly across from the bookstore, at 242 Columbus Avenue, is the Tosca Cafe. The restaurant was not one of the more important locations in *Basic Instinct* (in one scene, Michael Douglas has drinks with his fellow cops there), but the protests outside the restaurant—by gay activists, who attempted to disrupt filming of the movie—made national headlines.

One block north of the Transamerica building, at 847 Montgomery Street (between Pacific and Jackson), is Ernie's. The restaurant was featured prominently in Alfred Hitchcock's classic *Vertigo* (1958), which many film historians consider the most famous movie set in San Francisco. Jimmy Stewart spies on, and later dines with, Kim Novak at the restaurant (although the interior of the restaurant was actually re-created in a Los Angeles soundstage.)

Also within short walking distance is the intersection of Columbus, Kearny, and Pacific avenues, where the crew of the *Enterprise* divided into teams in *Star Trek IV* (1986), and William Shatner and Leonard Nimoy board a bus to Sausalito. Nearby, the Bank of America Building, at 555 California Street, is where Irwin Allen's famous disaster movie *The Towering Inferno* (1974) was set. The bank building was used as the base of a skyscraper, and the film-makers "added" eighty-six fictional stories above it to make it appear as the world's tallest skyscraper.

Also in North Beach—in Washington Square—is the renowned Saints Peter and Paul Church, on 666 Filbert Street. It appears in a scene from *Dirty Harry* (1971) in which a rooftop sniper aims a high-powered rifle across Washington Square at a Saints Peter and Paul priest, among others.

Telegraph Hill

A few blocks north of North Beach, on Telegraph Hill, is the art deco apartment at 1360 Montgomery Street where Lauren Bacall lived in *Dark Passage* (1947). The movie is about an innocent man, played by Humphrey Bogart, whom Bacall helps escape from San Quentin.

According to an August 9, 1988, article in the *San Francisco Chronicle* ("Starring San Francisco" by Ruthe Stein), San Francis-co's famous "Coit Tower was transformed into Rita Hayworth's Tele-graph Hill mansion in [the 1957] musical *Pal Joey*, starring Frank Sinatra. On the lawn behind the tower a vast terrace was built of wood painted gray to simulate stone, and the entrance to the tower was changed to make it look more like a house."

In another article, "The Movies Go to San Francisco," by Howard Baldwin (*Voyager*, January 1986) reports: "Above Broadway, Tele-graph Hill holds a treasure trove of filmgoer and tourist delights. At the corner of Vallejo and Kearny, Susan Anspach left Woody Allen in *Play It Again Sam*. It was near here that Dudley Moore . . . took Goldie Hawn in *Foul Play*; her apartment was at 430 Vallejo, just a few blocks away. . . . Further up the hill, Donald Sutherland lived on Union Street near the corner of Castle in *Invasion of the Body Snatchers* (1978). When it became obvious that the apartment was being surrounded by aliens, the stars—Sutherland, [Brooke] Adams, [Veronica] Cartwright and [Jeff] Goldblum—took off down Mont-gomery Street to the wooden Filbert Street steps. An elegant, secluded spot, the Filbert Street steps would be worth a stroll even if they didn't have cinematic significance.

Above the intersection of Montgomery and Filbert is the house where Julie Christie lived in *Petulia*."

Hyatt Regency
5 Embarcadero Center

In *High Anxiety* (1978), Mel Brooks plays a psychiatrist who is deathly afraid of heights but is forced to take a room on the hotel's top floor while attending a convention.

Brooks survives that experience (and his assistant's jokes), but he barely escapes when he is framed for murder in the hotel's lobby. A hit man wearing a Mel Brooks face mask (Rudy DeLuca) shoots a fellow conventiongoer and then hands the gun to an unsuspecting Brooks.

The Regency was also featured in *The Towering Inferno* (1974; the bar scenes were filmed there) and in *Time After Time* (1979), a time-travel movie in which H. G. Wells (Malcolm McDowell) pursues Jack the Ripper (David Warner) into twentieth-century San Francisco. It is at the Regency that Warner discovers that San Francisco is his kind of town. In one memorable scene he tells McDowell: "This world has caught up and surpassed me. Ninety years ago I was a freak. Today I'm an amateur."

Union Square

Wiretapper Gene Hackman surreptitiously tapes the conversations of Cindy Williams and Frederic Forrest as they wander through Union Square in *The Conversation* (1974).

In *Vertigo* (1958), Kim Novak's character rents an apartment, under the name of Carlotta Valdez, at the Empire, which is now the York Hotel, at 940 Sutter Street.

In *Heart and Souls* (1993), the horrendous bus accident which claims the lives of four San Franciscans at the exact moment Robert Downey Jr. is born, was staged at the Stockton Street Tunnel on the Chinatown side.

And the Sir Francis Drake Hotel, located at 450 Powell, at the corner of Sutter, played a role in cinematic history. It was at the Sir Francis, in 1921, that actress Virginia Rappe died after a sexual encounter with screen comedian Fatty Arbuckle. Although three juries later acquitted him of rape, his career was destroyed by the scandal.

Fairmont Hotel
California Street at Mason (atop Nob Hill)

The Fairmont, one of the classiest luxury hotels in San Francisco, became the St. Gregory Hotel in the ABC series *Hotel*.

Across the street, at 1000 Mason Street, are the Brocklebank Apartments, made famous as Kim Novak's house in *Vertigo*. The elegant high-rise is also featured in *The Woman in Red* (1984), in which Gene Wilder totters on its ninth-story window ledge, hiding from Kelly LeBrock's husband.

San Francisco City Hall

In *A View to a Kill* (1985), the last James Bond movie starring Roger Moore, City Hall is set on fire by a psychopath, Max Zorin (played by Christopher Walken), who tries to cover up the murder of a city official and get rid of Moore at the same time.

Moore, of course, escapes, rescuing Tanya Roberts as well. But when the San Francisco police mistake Moore for the killer, Moore hijacks a hook-and-ladder fire truck and leads San Francisco police on a chase down Market Street to a drawbridge (the Third Street Bridge), where the police end up crashing their cars into each other.

The courtroom scenes in *Class Action* (1990) were also filmed at City Hall. Gene Hackman's wife, Mary Elizabeth Mastrantonio's mother, dies of a heart attack as she descends the stately City Hall stairs.

City Hall also doubled as a San Francisco courthouse in *Murder in the First* (1995), a Chicago courthouse in *Tucker* (1988), and the fourth floor became a corridor of power in Washington, D.C., in *The Right Stuff* (1983).

City Hall was also the site of the November 27, 1978, murder of former San Francisco mayor George Moscone and supervisor Harvey Milk by former supervisor Dan White as well as the January 14, 1953, marriage of San Francisco resident Joe DiMaggio and Marilyn Monroe.

(*Note:* Around the corner from City Hall, at 101 Grove Street, is San Francisco's Department of Public Health, where Donald Sutherland works as a deputy health inspector in the 1978 remake of *Invasion of the Body Snatchers*, and Ted Danson and his friends pull off a coin heist in the 1994 feature *Getting Even With Dad.*)

Alamo Square
Steiner Street

On Steiner Street, between Hayes and Fulton streets, is a row of Victorian houses that may be the most photographed houses in America. Sometimes called "postcard row," the houses have been seen in the opening credits of several TV series set in San Francisco, including *Too Close for Comfort* (which ran from 1980 to 1986) and *Full House* (1987–1995). Ted Knight's and Bob Saget's families supposedly lived in these houses.

Brooke Adams lives at 720 Steiner Street in Philip Kaufman's 1978 remake of *Invasion of the Body Snatchers*—next door to 722 Steiner Street, the house occupied by Glenn Close in *Maxie* (1985). During the filming of that movie the producers reportedly borrowed the owners' phone and ran up a $200 bill.

Gene Wilder and his movie wife, Judith Ivey, also lived in one of the Painted Ladies in *The Woman in Red* (1984). In *So I Married an Axe Murderer* (1993), Mike Myers breaks up with his girlfriend Nancy Travis, whom he suspects is an ax murderer, in the park across the street from the house.

Although the houses on Steiner Street are virtually indistinguishable from hundreds of other Victorians throughout San Francisco, the backdrop of the downtown skyscrapers makes the street irresistible to filmmakers.

Alamo Square (courtesy San Francisco Convention and Visitors Bureau)

Mrs. Doubtfire House
2640 Steiner Street

The house at the corner of Steiner Street and Broadway in Pacific Heights, featured in *Mrs. Doubtfire* (1993), has become a major San Francisco tourist attraction. In the movie, Robin Williams, divorced from Sally Field, impersonates an English nanny so he can be close to his own children.

Golden Gate Bridge

In *A View to a Kill* (1985), the climactic scenes—in which Christopher Walken's getaway blimp becomes entangled in the cables and Walken fights to the death with Roger Moore—were filmed atop the bridge's east tower.

Parts of the stunt fight were staged on the cables seven hundred feet above the water. Originally, bridge officials refused to allow the filmmakers to stage the stunt, fearing it might cause unsuspecting motorists below to have accidents. However, Eon Productions worked out a compromise with the Golden Gate Bridge, Highway and Transportation District, which included an agreement to refrain from throwing a dummy off the bridge. (The bridge is already San Francisco's favorite suicide spot, and the city did not want to encourage any more attempts.)

In the original *Superman* (1978), Christopher Reeve saves a school bus and the bridge from earthquake destruction, and in *Star Trek IV* (1986) the bridge withstands severe storm lashings. Tom Cruise sucks the life out of Christian Slater as the latter drives across the bridge in *Interview With the Vampire* (1994).

Golden Gate Bridge (courtesy San Francisco Convention and Visitors Bureau)

Fort Point

Historic Fort Point, situated in the shadow of the Golden Gate Bridge, has long been a favorite movie location. Humphrey Bogart's climactic fight scene in *Dark Passage* (1947) was staged here. In *Vertigo* (1958), James Stewart rescues a suicidal Kim Novak by jumping into the San Francisco Bay after her.

In 1978, Mel Brooks paid tribute to *Vertigo* director Alfred Hitchcock by deliberately shooting *High Anxiety* scenes at the same spot. One of the film's funnier moments occurs when a hit man tries to strangle Brooks while he is on the phone with Madeline Kahn, who thinks she has just received an obscene phone call.

In *Star Trek IV*, William Shatner (Captain Kirk) walks with Leonard Nimoy (Mr. Spock) and convinces him to tone down his "colorful metaphors" (swear words).

Golden Gate Park

In *Star Trek IV*, the crew of the *Enterprise* supposedly parked its Klingon "Bird of Prey" here. But the scenes were actually filmed at Will Rogers State Park in the Pacific Palisades (14253 Sunset Boulevard).

The park served as Sherwood Forest in *The Adventures of Robin Hood* (1938), starring Errol Flynn. The Conservatory of Flowers in the park is where Robert Downey Jr. finally commits to Elisabeth Shue in the teary ending of *Heart and Souls* (1993).

Sister Act Church
221 Valley Street (at Church)

In *Sister Act* (1992), St. Paul's Catholic Church was transformed into St. Katherine's Convent, the church where Whoopi Goldberg hides while waiting to testify against ex-boyfriend Harvey Keitel. Goldberg, playing Dolores von Cartier, accidentally witnesses Keitel (Vince) murder his limo driver, who has turned into an informant against Vince. To escape a contract on her life, Goldberg poses as unorthodox Sister Mary Clarence, who organizes the choir, bringing San Franciscans back to the church.

To make the neighborhood look like a ghetto, the filmmakers put blackmesh in front of the doors, brought trash and abandoned cars to the street, hired extras as bag ladies and street people, and turned a real estate company, Hall Realty, across the street, into a porn shop.

In real life the neighborhood is as safe as any in San Francisco.

Sister Act *church*
(William A. Gordon)

Mission Dolores
16th and Dolores streets

Another key location in *Vertigo*. It's here that Kim Novak visits the grave of her great-grandmother, Carlotta Valdes, whose identity she assumes. Monsignor Patrick O'Shea told the *San Francisco Chronicle:* "The tombstone was there for a number of years afterwards. It was one of the highlights of the Greyhound tour. People passed by the real tombstones to see Carlotta Valdes. But the bishop thought he better get rid of it because everything else [in the graveyard] was real."

In *Class Action* (1990), Mary Elizabeth Mastrantonio's mother is also buried at the mission.

Alcatraz Island

The U.S. National Parks Service conducts tours of the island's former maximum-security federal penitentiary, which once housed such notorious criminals as Al Capone, "Doc" Barker, and "Machine Gun" Kelly. On the tour you can visit the cell occupied by real-life convicted killer Robert Stroud, immortalized by Burt Lancaster in the 1962 film *Birdman of Alcatraz.*

Escape from Alcatraz (1979) was based on the story of the only still unresolved escape attempt from the supposedly impenetrable prison. On June 11, 1962, Frank Norris (played in the movie by Clint Eastwood) and John and Clarence Anglin (Jack Thibeau and Fred Ward) escape from their cells by using makeshift tools that allow them to get into a ventilation grille. From there they enter a shaft running the length of the cell block and onto the roof of the prison.

Although they were presumed drowned in the freezing waters outside the island, law enforcement agencies never found their bodies. Of the thirty-nine other men who tried to escape from the prison, twenty-six were captured, seven were shot, and three others drowned.

The Enforcer (1976), the third in Clint Eastwood's "Dirty Harry" series, was also filmed at Alcatraz, as was *Murder in the First* (1995), starring Christian Slater and Kevin Bacon. *Murder* was a dramatized account of a true story; the real-life events had prompted a federal investigation into punishment practices and treatment of prisoners at Alcatraz.

Alcatraz (courtesy San Francisco Convention and Visitors Bureau)

Other San Francisco Locations

• *The Doctor* (1991), starring William Hurt as a surgeon who develops cancer and finds out what it is like to be a patient, was filmed at the Rincon Towers apartment building on Stewart and Howard. The building was dressed up to appear as a hospital.

• The Rawhide 2 Country and Western Bar at 280 Seventh Street, a gay bar, was turned into the Stetson in *Basic Instinct*, a bar where Sharon Stone dances with Michael Douglas and her jealous girlfriend, Leilani Sarelle.

• The three-story brick mansion lived in by Joan Crawford and Jack Palance in *Sudden Fear* (1952) is located at 2800 Scott Street. Nearby, the stairs in Alta Plaza Park are where Barbra Streisand and Ryan O'Neal appear in a manic chase scene in *What's Up, Doc?* (1972). The chips in the stairs are still visible.

• *Vertigo* also filmed at the California Palace of the Legion of Honor in Lincoln Park, where a portrait of Carlotta Valdes hung in Gallery 6 alongside medieval tapestries and paintings, and at the Palace of Fine Arts, on 3601 Lyons Street. *So I Married an Axe Murderer* (1993) was also filmed at the Palace of Fine Arts, which served as the backdrop to a scene in *Forrest Gump* (1994) in which Tom Hanks gives Robin Wright his Congressional Medal of Honor.

• *So I Married an Axe Murderer* was filmed at the Rococo Showplace, on 165 Tenth Street, which served as the Cafe Roads, and at a North Beach butcher shop, R. Iacopi Meats, on 1462 Grant Avenue at Union, where Nancy Travis worked.

Oakland and the East Bay

Dunsmuir House and Gardens
2960 Peralta Oaks Court, Oakland

Located in the Oakland foothills, about a half hour's drive from downtown San Francisco, the city-owned thirty-seven-room Colonial Revival mansion is the most frequently filmed home in Oakland. In *A View to a Kill*, the 1985 James Bond thriller, Roger Moore fights off thugs who are harassing Tanya Roberts, who supposedly owns the house. Later, Moore romances Roberts while Q sends in a mobile robot to try to find him.

In *So I Married an Axe Murderer*, the Dunsmuir was transformed into the bed-and-breakfast Poet's Corner, where Mike Myers and Nancy Travis honeymoon.

The house is rented frequently for private events, including corporate parties and weddings. It also has appeared as the mausoleum in *Phantasm* (1979), as Bill Cosby's home in his embarrassing *Leonard Part VI* (1987), and in the 1976 horror movie *Burnt Offerings*, starring Karen Black, Bette Davis, and Oliver Reed.

Tour hours vary during the year.

Dunsmuir House and Gardens (William A. Gordon)

Bridges Restaurant
44 Church Street, Danville

In *Mrs. Doubtfire* (1993), Robin Williams has to shuttle back and forth between his family and Robert Prosky, the owner of the television station where Williams works as a shipping clerk. Danville is located approximately fourteen miles east of downtown Oakland.

Oakland/Alameda County Coliseum
7000 Coliseum Way, Oakland

Because of scheduling conflicts, the 1994 remake of *Angels in the Outfield* was filmed at the Coliseum, the home of the Oakland Athletics, instead of Anaheim Stadium, the home of the California Angels and the setting of the story. The foster home where Joseph Gordon-Levitt (Roger) and Milton Davis Jr. (J.P.) live is at the corner of Douglas and Hale.

H. Tulanian & Sons Rug Company
2998 College Avenue, Berkeley

The rug company was transformed into Whoopi Goldberg's African Queen Bookstore in *Made in America* (1993).

Other Movies Filmed in Oakland

• *The Principal* (1987), which starred James Belushi as a principal who tries to teach a gang-ridden high school some lessons about human compassion and self-respect, was filmed on the former Merritt College campus on Martin Luther King Jr. Way.

• Oakland Technical High School, at 4351 Broadway, was where Nia Long graduated in the 1993 comedy *Made in America*. The movie ends with an inspirational singing sequence at her high school graduation ceremonies, led by costars Whoopi Goldberg and Ted Danson.

• *Made in America* was also filmed at a parking lot at the corner of 14th and Madison streets in downtown Oakland, where the moviemakers constructed Jackson Motors, the new-car lot owned by Hal Jackson, played by Ted Danson. The site was chosen because of its proximity to Lake Merritt, where, in the movie, Danson rides one of the animals he uses in his commercials, a four-ton pachyderm, into the waters of Lake Merritt.

• *Sneakers* (1992) made use of the Fox Theater at 1815 Telegraph Avenue in downtown Oakland, which served as the office of Robert Redford and his fellow computer hackers. Telegraph Avenue was also one of several locations used to create scenes of Chicago at the end of World War II in Francis Ford Coppola's *Tucker* (1988), which starred Jeff Bridges as innovative car designer Preston Tucker, who, in the 1940s, builds his own automobile and is crushed by the giants in the industry. Other *Tucker* locations included Oakland City Hall, at One City Hall Plaza and 14th Street, and the old Hotel

Oakland, now a senior housing facility on the corner of Alice and 13th streets. The latter was transformed into a Chicago courthouse.

• Oakland's city council has been so willing to accommodate film-makers that in 1988 it actually vacated its offices at 901 39th Street so that courtroom scenes for *True Believer* could be filmed in council chambers. The film starred James Woods as a burned-out 1960s civil liberties lawyer who defends an Asian immigrant accused of murder.

• Oakland also appeared in *Basic Instinct* (1991). Michael Douglas and his partner, played by George Dzundza, go into an office building, where Dzundza is murdered. That scene was filmed at the old John Breuner Company building at 2201 Broadway. Douglas also shoots Jeanne Tripplehorn there.

• Janet Jackson's first movie, *Poetic Justice* (1993), was also filmed in the neighborhood of 18th and Market streets. Some scenes were shot at the Saeed Dobahi Market at 1000 18th Street and at the Lakeside Motel, on 122 East 14th Street.

Northern California

University of the Pacific
Stockton

The university's Conservatory of Music was used as Harrison Ford's archaeology classroom in *Raiders of the Lost Ark* (1981). Because the campus has an Ivy League look, director Rob Reiner turned it into a winter wonderland in *The Sure Thing* (1985). Reiner used a classroom in Sears Hall, dormitory rooms in Grace Hovell Hall and South/West Hall, the Anderson Quad, and Khoury Hall, which served as the exterior for a swimming pool. The movie was about a college student (John Cusack), obsessed with scoring, who is lured to Los Angeles with the promise of a "sure thing" (Nicollette Sheridan), only to find true love (Daphne Zuniga) on the trip there.

Petaluma and Santa Rosa

Peggy Sue Got Married (1985) is the story of a mother of two (Kathleen Turner) facing a divorce, who faints at her twenty-fifth high school reunion. She wakes up back in the 1960s, giving her an opportunity to change the course of her life.

The story was filmed at a number of locations in Petaluma, including a Queen Anne–style house at 226 Liberty Street that served as Peggy Sue's girlhood home; 1006 D Street, which served as the home of Peggy Sue's boyfriend (played by Nicolas Cage); and

Millie's Chili Bar, at 600 Petaluma Boulevard, which was turned into the Donut Hole Cafe.

The high school reunion was held at Santa Rosa High School, on 1235 Mendocino Avenue, in the city of Santa Rosa, approximately seventeen miles north of Petaluma, on Highway 1. Santa Rosa has also appeared in *Stop or My Mom Will Shoot!* (1992). The movie, best forgotten as one of Sylvester Stallone's comedic bombs, includes an elaborate action sequence that was filmed at the Santa Rosa Air Center.

According to Dick and Pat Alexander, travel writers who chronicled northern California filming in the magazine *Northern Exposure* (March 1993), Santa Rosa was also "the location for the original *Shadow of a Doubt*, a movie Hitchcock described as his favorite. . . . A two-story residence at 904 McDonald Avenue is featured as the house where the sinister uncle comes to visit his niece. *Pollyanna*, a 1959 Disney production with Jane Wyman and Hayley Mills, was filmed at the Mableton mansion at 1015 McDonald Avenue. *Storm Center*, a 1955 movie that included Santa Rosa's old Carnegie Library, is the story of a small-town librarian (Bette Davis) who gets fired when she refuses to remove a Communist book from the shelves."

The Birds Schoolhouse
17110 Bodega Lane, Bodega

Each year, some fifteen thousand visitors flock to the tiny village of Bodega, some sixty miles north of San Francisco, to see where Hitchcock filmed *The Birds* (1963). The schoolhouse is still there. It is now a bed-and-breakfast named the School House Inn.

Point Arena Lighthouse
at the end of Lighthouse Road (off Highway 1), Point Arena

Hopeless romantics loved—and many critics hated—*Forever Young* (1993), a romantic drama starring Mel Gibson as a test pilot who is cryogenically frozen in 1939 after the woman he finally summons the nerve to ask to marry him is struck by a car and becomes comatose. In the film, Gibson is awakened more than fifty years later by a fatherless young boy (Elijah Wood). Eventually Gibson discovers his girlfriend is still alive, and goes searching for her.

The lighthouse at Point Arena played a pivotal role in the movie. It is where Gibson and his girlfriend (Isabel Glasser) had played as children and are reunited in the movie's weepy end.

The lighthouse, located on the Mendocino coast about 128 miles north of San Francisco, is open daily for tours. Do not expect to see the Berkeley shingle cottage and gazebo featured in the movie. They were constructed by the film's production designer, Gregg Fonseca, and later destroyed by the local fire and rescue squad during a fire-suppression exercise.

Heritage House
5200 North Highway 1, Little River

In *Same Time, Next Year* (1978), once-a-year lovers Alan Alda and Ellen Burstyn, each married to someone else, rendezvous at this inn.

Murder, She Wrote House
45110 Little Lake Street, Mendocino

The Victorian home depicted as Angela Lansbury's on the CBS mystery series *Murder, She Wrote* is actually a bed-and-breakfast, Blair House Inn. The inn is located west of Highway 1 and is reach-

Murder, She Wrote *house (courtesy Fort Bragg–Mendocino Coast Chamber of Commerce)*

able by Little Lake Road. For information write to P.O. Box 1601, Mendocino, California, 95460.

Jedediah Smith Redwoods State Park
4241 Kings Valley Road, Crescent City

One of the most memorable battles in *Return of the Jedi* (1983) was staged among the giant redwood trees in this state park, located a few miles north of the small fishing and lumber town of Crescent City, at the northernmost edge of the state. According to the movie's production notes: "For two weeks, the woods were alive with laser gunfire and the voices of Mark Hamill, Harrison Ford and Carrie Fisher as the Rebel Alliance took on the Imperial Forces of the Empire in one of the film's climactic battles. Working among trees as tall as 400 feet and as old as a thousand years . . . the shooting roamed over four different forest locations within several square miles of redwood country."

Lone Pine
east of Sequoia Park

The rocky hills just a few miles west of this tiny town (population: 1,800)—framed by the snow-capped Sierra Nevada mountains—made Lone Pine a popular movie location from the 1930s through the early 1960s, when Westerns were at their peak. Dave Holland, author of *On Location in Lone Pine*, estimates that as many as four hundred movies have been filmed in the area, including *Gunga Dun* (1939), *Rawhide* (1951), and several dozen Hopalong Cassidy pictures. Episodes from *The Lone Ranger, Have Gun Will Travel, Wagon Train, Gunsmoke,* and *Bonanza* were also filmed here.

In 1994, *Maverick* became the first big-budget western shot in Lone Pine in more than twenty years.

Nearby, on the edge of the Owens Dry Lake, just south of Lone Pine, the desert was turned into the otherworldly set of Nimbus III, where Laurence Luckinbill takes hostages in *Star Trek V* (1989).

Most of the movie sets were dismantled after filming, and the only time markers that are erected noting movie locations is during the annual Lone Pine Film Festival (P.O. Box 111, Lone Pine, California, 93545), held every Columbus Day weekend. However, Holland's book does show where many of the movies were filmed. The book is available from Holland House, Box 1120, Lone Pine, California, 93545, and costs $22.70, postpaid.

Other California Locations

• In *Return of the Jedi*, George Lucas filmed the desert planet of Tatooine in Buttercup Valley, near the California border and just west of Yuma, Arizona. Lucas wanted dunes stretching as far as the eye can see and chose this desert area, known as the dune-buggy capital of the world.

• The plane wreck in *Fearless* (1993), which Jeff Bridges walks away from feeling he is immortal, was filmed on Bear Mountain Boulevard, near the intersection of South Union Avenue in Arvin.

• Mammoth Lakes doubled as the Himalayas in *Indiana Jones and the Temple of Doom* (1982) and in *The Golden Child* (1986). In the former movie, Harrison Ford, Kate Capshaw, and Ke Huy Kwan raft down the side of the mountain.

• *Star Trek* V (1989) was also filmed at Yosemite National Park, with William Shatner's rock-climbing fall filmed at Inspiration Point (not El Capitán, as it was identified in the movie). The scenes in which the crew of the *Enterprise* meet God were filmed at the

Trona Pinnacles, Star Trek V *(courtesy Ridgecrest Film Commission)*

Trona Pinnacles, an unusual rock formation located ten miles south of the desert town of Trona and twenty miles east of Ridgecrest.

• *Maverick* (1994) was also filmed at Yosemite. The Shoshone Indian village was set up by Leidig Meadow, and the scene in which the archduke tries to shoot Mel Gibson, who is dressed as an Indian, was filmed at Washburn Point.

• Fresno's new city hall, at 2600 Fresno Street, was dressed up to appear as the city hall in Des Moines, where Eric Thal rescues Julie Warner in *Robert A. Heinlein's The Puppet Masters* (1994).

• The University of California at Berkeley campus served as the fictional Leland University, where Arnold Schwarzenegger and Emma Thompson work as scientists in *Junior* (1994).

• The summer camp in *Addams Family Values* (1993) was on Sequoia Lake in Fresno County.

• The Ehrman mansion, on the south shore of Lake Tahoe, served as Tommy Lee Jones's home in the 1994 biopic *Cobb* and as Robert Prosky's in *Things Change* (1989; see Nevada for north shore locations).

• In *My Blue Heaven* (1990), Joan Cusack works as an assistant district attorney; Melanie Mayron, as a policewoman, at the city hall of Atascadero.

• *Outbreak* (1995) was filmed extensively in Ferndale. The façade of the hospital lab was built around a bank on Main Street.

• A house in Columbia State Park, a train in Railtown, and St. Joseph's Catholic Church in Tuolumne City (where Grace Kelly and Gary Cooper were married) are the major locations shown in the recently instituted annual *High Noon* (1952) tour. For information write to "The Black Hats," Box 162, Sonora, California, 95370.

• Chico's main attraction is Bidwell Park, at Fourth and Pine streets, which served as Sherwood Forest in the original *Adventures of Robin Hood* (1938). For a complete listing of film locations in Chico and Butte County, contact the Chico Visitor and Information Bureau, 500 Main Street, Chico, California, 95928.

Chapter 2

The Pacific Northwest

Oregon

University of Oregon
Eugene

In *Personal Best* (1982), Mariel Hemingway and Patrice Donnelly play athletes who are friends, lovers, and ultimately competitors at the Olympic trials in 1980. Hayward Field, the university's track field, provided the setting for the trials.

The University of Oregon was also the site of *National Lampoon's Animal House* (1978). At the time of the filming, the house was located at 751 East 11th Street, across the street from the campus, and was, appropriately enough, a halfway house for convicts. Delta House, as it was called in the movie, was subsequently converted into apartments for architecture students but fell into disrepair and was torn down in 1986. At that time, bricks were sold as souvenirs for five dollars each.

Still existing on campus—next to where Delta House stood—are the Kappa Sigma fraternity, where the infamous "Toga Party" took place; the Phi Kappa Psi house, which stood in as the snooty fraternity; and the Sigma Nu fraternity that in the movie is the sorority where John Belushi is a peeping Tom.

The university's student union, Erb Memorial Union (EMU), was where the famous Jell-o–eating scene took place; and 110 Fenton Hall was the site of the film's courtroom scene.

Oregon State Mental Hospital
on Center Street between 24th and 25th streets, Salem

Visitors to Salem can drive by the J Building, where Jack Nicholson played a free-spirited rogue who takes over the ward of a mental hospital in the Academy Award-winning *One Flew Over the*

Cuckoo's Nest (1975). Nicholson and Louise Fletcher won Oscars for best actor and actress, Milos Forman won for best director, and Laurence Hauben and Bo Goldman won for best screenplay adapted from other material (in this case, the novel by Ken Kesey).

Timberline Lodge
off the Timberline Road exit of Highway 26 in Government Camp, Oregon, on Mount Hood, sixty miles east of Portland

This is the luxurious hotel at which Jack Nicholson is the off-season caretaker in *The Shining* (1980), director Stanley Kubrick's adaptation of a Stephen King horror story.

There are no mazes or elevators spewing blood in the lodge, and only its exterior was filmed. The lodge's interior was filmed for the first time in *Hear No Evil* (1993), a suspense thriller starring Marlee Matlin, Martin Sheen, and D. B. Sweeney. *New York Times* critic Stephen Holden, who strained to find something nice to say about that film, wrote: "With its gobs of pretty scenery, it is, if nothing else, an effective travel brochure for the Pacific Northwest."

Timberline Lodge, The Shining *(courtesy Timberline Lodge)*

Portland

• Parts of what was once called "J" Town—or Japantown—in downtown Portland were used to re-create Los Angeles's 1936 Little Tokyo in *Come See the Paradise* (1989). The film, directed by Alan Parker, is a love story about a man (Dennis Quaid) whose Japanese wife (Tamlyn Tomita) is sent to a detention camp during World War II. Parker also filmed scenes at the Portland Meadows Race Track, on 1001 North Schmeer Road; Portland International Raceway, at 1940 North Victory Boulevard; and the Moreland Movie Theater, at 6712 Southeast Milwaukee, which became the Brooklyn Movie Theater, destroyed by a fire.

• The outside of the amusement park in *Free Willy* (1993), called Northwest Adventure Park in the picture, was actually Oaks Amusement Park, at the Foot of Southeast Spokane Street. (Yes, that is the address.) The park was also featured in *Breaking In* (1989). Burt Reynolds hides his money there after a bank robbery. Other scenes from *Free Willy*, depicting Jesse's hand-to-mouth life on the streets, were filmed in Portland's Pioneer Courthouse Square and in the warehouse district at the city's skateboard park.

• The house where Madonna kills her aging lover with too much sex in *Body of Evidence* (1993) was the Pittock mansion at 3229 N.W. Pittock Drive, a French Renaissance home built by Henry Pittock, the original owner of the *Oregonian* newspaper. Situated with a view of five snow-capped mountains, the mansion is now a city park open for tourists.

Pittock Mansion, Body of Evidence *(courtesy Pittock Mansion)*

• Matt Dillon and Kelly Lynch lived at the Irving Apartments, 2127 N.W. Irving, in *Drugstore Cowboy* (1989). The pharmacy they rob was the Nob Hill Pharmacy at Northwest 21st and Glisan.

• *The Temp* (1993) was filmed extensively at Portland's historic Princeton Club at S.W. 11th and Alder (now part of the Governor Hotel) in downtown Portland, which served as Mrs. Appleby's Baked Good Companies, where Timothy Hutton, Lara Flynn Boyle, and Faye Dunaway worked. The company picnic, where Boyle tries to seduce Hutton, was filmed at Battle Ground Lake, fifty miles north of Portland in the state of Washington.

Milepost 41 Along Highway 101

In *Shattered* (1991), the accident in which Tom Berenger and Greta Scacchi's car leaps over a seaside cliff was staged at Milepost 41, just north of Neakhanie Mountain. This was, by the way, the film's second car wreck, not the initial one that seriously injures Berenger and sets the stage for his attempts to find out what has happened. That accident was staged on a mountain road near Mount Wilson in Los Angeles.

The same stretch of 101, by Cannon Beach, was also the site of one of the most harrowing scenes in *The Temp*. Timothy Hutton is driving Lara Flynn Boyle down the narrow, winding coastal highway when the brakes of his car suddenly give way. Hutton has to veer off the road onto a precipice to escape death.

About thirteen miles north of Milepost 41 on Highway 101 is Ecola State Park, site of the climactic scene in *Point Break* (1991), starring Patrick Swayze and Keanu Reeves. This is the same beach where the Japanese warriors rode on horseback in *Teenage Mutant Ninja Turtles III* (1993). The grassy park area on a cliff above the beach was the location for the school carnival in *Kindergarten Cop* (1990).

Astoria

The *Hollywood Reporter* recently called Astoria "the hottest small-town filming location in the country," and with good reason. Since 1984, this quaint fishing village (population: just over 10,000) has been the setting of seven major motion pictures: *The Goonies* (1984), *Short Circuit* (1985), *Benji, the Hunted* (1986), *Come See the Paradise* (1989), *Kindergarten Cop* (1990), *Teenage Mutant Ninja Turtles III* (1992), and *Free Willy* (1993).

Astoria's picturesque location, on the Columbia River, is just one of the reasons filmmakers have been drawn to the town. The town also has a number of charming Victorian homes, a dramatic four-mile-long bridge to Washington state, and a fishing port.

That the town does not charge permit fees for filming has not hurt Astoria, either.

Probably the best-known movie filmed in Astoria is *Kindergarten Cop*, which starred Arnold Schwarzenegger as a Los Angeles police detective pressed into service as a kindergarten teacher. In the movie, Schwarzenegger teaches at Astor Elementary School, located at 3550 Franklin Avenue. All the exterior shots of the school were filmed there, while the classrooms, hallways, and stairs were re-created on an enormous set constructed at Universal Studios. With the help of Astor faculty and students, who shipped school posters, bulletins, and artwork to Los Angeles, production designer Bruno Rubeo replicated the entire first floor of the school on Universal's back lot.

Within a short walking distance of the school is a house at 368 38th Street, used in *The Goonies*.

A few blocks away, at 3392 Harrison, is the house where child actor Jason James Richter lived with his foster family in *Free Willy*. In the movie, Richter plays a homeless, abandoned boy named Jesse who befriends a homeless, abandoned whale named Willy. Jesse ultimately sets Willy free when the owners of an amusement park try to kill him for the insurance money.

Nearby, on the Columbia River, at the end of 14th Street, is the 14th Street Dock where Richter hangs out with his delinquent teenage friends and later gets fish scraps to feed Willy.

The dock is a short drive from 197 Hume Street, the home of Ally Sheedy in *Short Circuit*. She plays Stephanie, an animal lover and an operator of a catering truck who rescues "Number Five"—the robot that is alive—from the clutches of military men who want to turn Number Five into a foot soldier.

Other locations include the Astoria-Megler Bridge, which connects Oregon and Washington (seen in the background of each of the Astoria movies), the Red Lion Inn, at 400 Industry Street, where Schwarzenegger takes Penelope Ann Miller and her son to dinner, and the Bayview Hotel at 783 West Marine Drive, where Schwarzengger and his partner, Pamela Reed, stay in rooms 5 and 6 while conducting the investigation.

In addition, in the town of Hammond, a few miles northwest of Astoria, is the Hammond Mooring Basin, the basin referred to as Dawson's Marina in *Free Willy*. It was at Dawson's where Willy is finally freed. The basin is located off the Iredale Street exit of the Fort Stevens Highway.

The Clatsop County Historical Society publishes a brochure, *Shot in Astoria*, which anyone considering a trip to Astoria should send away for. The booklet costs one dollar and is available from the Society at 1618 Exchange Street, Astoria, Oregon, 97103.

Other Movies Filmed in Oregon

- *Stand by Me* (1986), directed by Rob Reiner, which told the story of four teenage boys who stumble across a dead body in the woods, was filmed primarily in Brownsville. The pie-eating contest was held in Pioneer Park, at the end of Park Street (although one of the film's more memorable scenes, in which the boys tempt fate by taking a shortcut over a high-river bridge, with a locomotive in pursuit, was actually filmed near Mount Shasta, California, on a trestle over the McCloud River).
- The riverboat scenes in *Maverick* (1994) were filmed aboard the *Portland*, a historic riverboat docked on the Willamette River near Beacon Rock (along the border with Washington State).
- *The River Wild* (1994), an action adventure starring Meryl Streep and Kevin Bacon, who kidnaps Streep's family, was filmed along the Upper Rogue River between Hog Creek and Argo Riffle.

Washington

State Capitol Building
corner of 14th Street and Cherry Lane, Olympia

The courtroom scenes in *Body of Evidence* (1993) were filmed in the senate chamber of the State Capitol Building, over the objections of Washington's conservative secretary of state Ralph Munro. Munro disapproved of the story line, which has Madonna on trial for murdering an aging lover by having too much sex with him. Willem Dafoe costarred as Madonna's attorney and her next lover. Joe Mantegna plays the prosecutor in this film, which did not turn on very many critics.

The Washington Department of General Administration approved the filming because, in the words of a spokeswoman, "we are not a censoring agency. We've checked over the script, and we feel that since Madonna's got all her clothes on in the courtroom scenes, the use of the facility is totally appropriate for us."

Tacoma

In *Three Fugitives* (1988), the bank a bumbling Martin Short tries to hold up is actually an office building located at the Old Tacoma City Hall, at 625 Commerce Street in downtown Tacoma. When the robbery goes awry, Short takes just-paroled-and-finally-gone-straight bank robber Nick Nolte as a hostage, and the Tacoma police, thinking Nolte is in on the caper, follows them in pursuit.

The Elks Club across the street, at 565 Broadway, was used as the Tacoma Police Station. The club was later used as the site of Dennis Quaid and Tamlyn Tomita's wedding in *Come See the Paradise* and as the police station where the perpetrators of Kevin Kline's attempted murder are questioned in *I Love You to Death* (1990).

Down the street is Colonial Square, formerly the Colonial Hotel, on 7th Street and Commerce, where Shirley MacLaine had an apartment in *Waiting for the Light* (1990). And two blocks away, at 764 Broadway in Tacoma's Antique Row, is the triangular Bostwick Building. The building was transformed into Kevin Kline's restaurant, Joey Boca's Pizzeria, in *I Love You to Death*. The second floor of the building served as the Villa Rosalie apartments, where Kline spent his spare time fixing the "pipes" of his female tenants.

Other Tacoma locations include:

• A house on the 800 block of North Yakima, where nanny-from-hell Rebecca DeMornay seeks revenge in *The Hand That Rocks the Cradle* (1992).

• The Simpson Tacoma Kraft Mill, at 801 Portland Avenue. Debra Winger worked here in *An Officer and a Gentleman* (1981). In the fairy-tale ending, Richard Gere sweeps her off her feet in front of moon-eyed millworkers.

• The McNeil Island Prison. Nick Nolte was paroled from this Washington State prison in *Three Fugitives*.

• The coffeepot-shaped Bob's Java Jive, at 2102 South Tacoma Way, Stadium Bowl High School (111 North "E" Street), and Holy Rosary Church, on 512 South 30th Street, seen in *I Love You to Death*.

• The Rialto Theater, on South Ninth and Court C, where Teri Garr worked in *Waiting for the Light*.

• The Seattle-Tacoma (Sea Tac) International Airport, located midway between Tacoma and Seattle on State Route 99. In *Sleepless in Seattle* (1993), Meg Ryan, looking for Tom Hanks, walks right past him, and Hanks seems smitten when he sees her for the first time.

Seattle

Quite a few recent movies have been set in Seattle, including *Sleepless in Seattle* (1993), a classic romantic comedy that united Tom

Hanks, who plays a recently widowed architect who moves there in an attempt to forget his painful memories, and Meg Ryan, who plays a Baltimore features writer who pursues him cross-country.

Sleepless was filmed aboard a houseboat on Westlake Avenue on private Lake Union, where Hanks and his movie son Ross Malinger live; Alki Beach in West Seattle, where Meg Ryan watches Hanks and Malinger play football; the Arctic Building, on Third Street and James, the site of the New Year's Eve party; the Dalia Lounge, at 1904 Fourth Avenue, where Hanks has a dinner date with a woman who cannot stop laughing; and at the Athenian Inn Restaurant in Pike Place Market, at Pike Street and First Avenue. The inn is where Hanks's friend, played by Rob Reiner, encourages Hanks to start dating again, and where Hanks refers to *tiramisu*, fearing that "some woman is going to want me to do it to her and I won't know what it is." Hanks's character lets his imagination get away from him: Tiramisu is an Italian dessert.

The Pike Place Market has also been featured in three other movies: *Three Fugitives*, as well as *The Vanishing* (1993), and *Black Widow* (1987). It was at the market where Debra Winger, in pursuit of "black widow" Theresa Russell, is approached by the shady private investigator she hires, and almost has her cover blown.

Black Widow was also filmed at the former headquarters of the *Seattle Post-Intelligencer* newspaper, on 521 Wall Street, which served as the Department of Justice offices where Winger worked as an investigator, and at the Burke Museum on the University of Washington campus. In the film, Winger follows Russell to Seattle, where Russell has moved to pursue one of her victims: the wealthy chairman of the Burke Museum Board. The museum displays primitive Northwest Indian and Eskimo artifacts.

Near the campus, adjacent to the Seattle Yacht Club, is West Montlake Park, where Jeff Bridges spies on Kiefer Sutherland and Nancy Travis in *The Vanishing*.

In the Seattle Center, near downtown, is Seattle's famous Space Needle, built for the 1962 World's Fair. In *The Parallax View* (1974), the assassination of a president takes place on the observation deck of the 605-foot-high Space Needle.

The Needle was also featured as a backdrop in *Harry and the Hendersons* (1986), when John Lithgow goes searching for his missing Big Foot, and in *Power* (1985), a thriller about the manipulation of the political processes via market research and advertising.

The historic Smith Tower building, at Second and Yesler, was used for the exterior scenes of DigiCom, the high-tech firm where Demi Moore sexually harasses Michael Douglas in *Disclosure* (1994).

Other Seattle locations include Gas Works Park on Lake Union, which provides what many consider to be the most beautiful view of the city. In *Three Fugitives*, Gas Works Park was called Boswell Park, where Nick Nolte, Martin Short, and Sarah Rowland Doroff, who played Short's daughter, hide from police under bushes.

The Hand That Rocks The Cradle was also shot at several locations in Seattle, including the McGilvra Elementary Schoolyard, 38th Avenue East and East Garfield, where nanny Rebecca DeMornay tells a five-year-old boy bullying Madeline Zima, "I'll rip your fucking head off," if he continues to bother her; and at Auditorium Cleaners, on 3501 Fremont Avenue, where Annabella Sciorra discovers a cigarette lighter in her husband's pocket and is convinced he is having an affair with his former girlfriend, Julianne Moore.

WarGames (1983), which starred Matthew Broderick as a high school hacker who accidentally ties into the NORAD computer system and almost sets off a thermonuclear war, was also set in Seattle. Unfortunately, records no longer exist as to which Seattle locations were used. Location manager Robert Decker does report, though, that Broderick and Ally Sheedy took the Steilacoom Ferry to find the creator of the program, called "Joshua." The creator's (Falken) house and the 7-Eleven store where Broderick is picked up by the FBI were actually filmed in Big Bear, California, and Broderick's house was near Hancock Park in Los Angeles.

The Fabulous Baker Boys (1989) was also set in Seattle. A few scenes were filmed around Pioneer Square, but most were filmed in Los Angeles.

Seattle has also been used as a location for *Singles* (1992), *Cinderella Liberty* (1974), *Harry in Your Pocket* (1973), *Come See the Paradise* (1990), and *An Officer and a Gentleman* (1981).

Although set in Seattle, the NBC series *Frasier* is filmed onstage in Los Angeles. The movie *Stakeout* (1987), starring Richard Dreyfuss and Emilio Estevez, was also set in Seattle but was filmed in Vancouver, British Columbia.

Tides Inn
1807 Water Street, Port Townsend

In *An Officer and a Gentleman*, Richard Gere and Debra Winger and their pals David Keith and Lisa Blount rendezvoused weekends at the Tides Inn. Since the movie's release, so many couples have asked to stay in the same room that Gere and Winger stayed in (room 10) that the hotel rents it out as the *Officer and a Gentleman* room.

Port Townsend, which is northwest of Seattle, is reachable from Seattle by ferry across the Puget Sound. The trip takes about two hours.

Mar-T Cafe
137 West North Bend Way, North Bend

In the ABC series *Twin Peaks*, this was the Double R Diner where Kyle MacLachlan, playing Agent Dale Cooper, ate cherry pie and drank coffee.

One patron told a reporter: "They've had to limit the number of slices of pie you can eat at one time. They keep running out because everybody wants that famous cherry pie and a cup of coffee."

The cafe is located about one mile from the gas station seen in *The Vanishing* (1993) and three miles southwest of Snoqualmie, a logging town twenty-five miles east of Seattle (see the next two entries).

Texaco Gas Station
742 S.W. Mount Si Boulevard, North Bend

Kiefer Sutherland's girlfriend Sandra Bullock mysteriously disappears at this gas station in *The Vanishing*, a psychological thriller centering around his three-year-long compulsion to learn of her fate. Jeff Bridges plays a psychopath who abducts Bullock at the gas station-minimart, identified in the movie as the Titan. The gas station is located off exit 31 of I-90.

Salish Lodge
37807 Southeast Snoqualmie–Falls City Road, Snoqualmie Falls

The exterior of the Great Northern Hotel in *Twin Peaks* was filmed at this resort, which overlooks a 268-foot waterfall.

Roslyn

The CBS series *Northern Exposure*, supposedly set in the remote town of Cicely, Alaska, is actually filmed in this tiny hamlet located about eighty miles east of Seattle. The main locations—the Brick Tavern, Ruth-Anne's General Store, the totem pole, and the storefront offices of Dr. Joel Fleishman (played by Rob Morrow)—are on four-block-long Pennsylvania Avenue, just off Highway 903.

Not all of the citizens of Roslyn appreciated the filming. One woman struck up a petition, signed by 135 of the town's 900 residents, objecting to the crew's presence. The petition read: "We feel that when they are filming, Roslyn is under siege. . . . [Roslyn's] residents . . . have the right to travel unobstructed city streets, perform banking and post office business at their will, and do business along Pennsylvania Avenue unmolested. Roslyn is not a movie set!"

The petition was unsuccessful. Since the show began airing in 1990, tourism in Roslyn has quadrupled, from an estimated five thousand per year to twenty thousand.

Roslyn Cafe, Northern Exposure *(S. Breyfogle Photo)*

Mount St. Michael's Church
Market Street, Spokane

In *Benny and Joon* (1993), a love story about cute eccentrics who find each other, the church became the mental hospital where Mary Stuart Masterson (Joon) is hospitalized. One of the film's more memorable scenes has Johnny Depp, playing a character who is a cross between Buster Keaton and Charlie Chaplin, swinging back and forth on a clock in front of her window, trying to snap her out of her depression.

Other *Benny and Joon* locations include Hilliard Tire at 5404 North Market Street, which was transformed into Benny's Auto Clinic; Riverfront and Manito Parks; and Ferguson's Cafe, at West 804 Garland, where Aidan Quinn's girlfriend, Julianne Moore, waitressed.

(*Note:* Ferguson's was also used as a location in *Vision Quest,* a 1984 high school wrestling movie, which was also filmed in Spokane. It utilized four high schools: Ferris, North Central, Rogers High School, and Shadle Park. Other scenes were filmed at the West Coast Ridpath Hotel, at 515 West Sprague, where star Matthew Modine works as a room-service waiter, Big Foot Tavern, North 9115 Division, and the Armory, an abandoned military armory on Second Street in downtown Spokane.)

Other Movies Filmed in Washington

• *This Boy's Life* (1993), the story of a boy whose mother (Ellen Barkin) marries a tyrannical man (Robert De Niro), was filmed throughout the town of Concrete, about a hundred miles northwest of Seattle. The set decorators converted the entire main street, including the storefronts and signage, to make it look like Washington in the 1950s. The town liked it so much that they maintained the look after the filming.

• A small airport in the town of Ephrata, once used as a World War II training base, was the site of *Always* (1989), a love story set against the background of men and women who fight forest fires.

• The deer-hunting scenes in *The Deer Hunter* (1978) were filmed atop Mount Baker.

• *Come See the Paradise* (1990) was also filmed in Cathlamet, a fishing town on the Washington coast.

• The famous wheatfield scenes in *Toys* (1992) were filmed off Highway 195, near Rosalia, but according to Leslie Lytel, film-location coordinator of the Washington State Film and Video Office: "The road through the wheat field was created strictly for the movie. It was torn up and recycled, and the field was allowed to return to normal."

• *Harry and the Hendersons* (1986) was shot in three mountain locations: in Index, near the Skyomish River, where Don Ameche's North American Museum of Anthropology was located; near Lake Kachess in the Wenatchee National Forest, where the Hendersons' campsite was; and in North Bend, for some of the forest scenes, on the Snoqualmie River.

Chapter 3

The Western States

Montana

One of Montana's more recent movies, *A River Runs Through It* (1992), did more than attract tourists. After the movie opened, the chamber of commerce in Livingston (Missoula in the movie) was actually flooded with requests from people who wanted to move there.

One member of the chamber told a reporter: "The calls came from everywhere—Chicago, New York, Florida, California. You name it. People don't like where they live."

Tourists who visit Livingston might recognize parts of Front Street even though many buildings depicted in the movie had false fronts.

Montana film commissioner Lonie Stimac reports that the movie was filmed at several points along the Yellowstone River, south of Livingston, in an area called Paradise Valley; along the Gallatin River, south of Bozeman; and all along the Boulder River, which is south of the town of Big Timber.

The Tom Cruise–Nicole Kidman feature *Far and Away* (1992) was filmed south of Billings, but the sets are long gone, and all that tourists can see is the general area where the filmmakers re-created the Oklahoma land rush of the 1890s. The area is visible from the Fly Creek exit of I-90 and is south of the freeway.

Tourists can travel over a bridge used in a dramatic shoot-out scene from *The Untouchables* (1987). The scene, which was supposed to have been set on the Canadian border, was where *Untouchables* Kevin Costner and Sean Connery tried to intercept a shipment of Canadian whiskey crossing the border on its way to Al Capone. The bridge, which spans the Missouri River, is located on the Hardy Creek exit of I-15, approximately forty miles south of Great Falls.

Steven Spielberg's romantic comedy *Always* (1989), starring Richard Dreyfuss, Holly Hunter, and John Goodman, was filmed at the Libby Airport in Libby, Montana, which served as the firefighters' air attack base. A scene at the beginning of the movie, in which an airplane flies so low that it causes two fishermen to jump out of their boat, was filmed at Bull Lake, south of Libby (reachable from Highway 2).

Tourists can also visit the Big Sky Ski Resort, south of Bozeman on Highway 191, site of the skiing sequences in *True Colors* (1990); the Old Montana Prison, located in the city of Deer Lodge, where *Diggstown* (1992), starring Louis Gossett Jr., and James Woods, was shot; and Virginia City, Montana, site of the filming of *Little Big Man* (1970) with Dustin Hoffman, and *Missouri Breaks* (1976), with Marlon Brando and Jack Nicholson.

The River Wild (1994), starring Meryl Streep in her first action picture, was filmed on the Kootenai River near Libby and on Middle Fork of the Flathead River in the Kalispell area, where scenes from *Heaven's Gate* (1980) were also shot. *Holy Matrimony* (1994), a road movie directed by Leonard Nimoy, was filmed at the Montana State Fair in Great Falls, which stood in as the Iowa State Fair.

Wyoming

Wyoming's most famous attraction is Devil's Tower National Monument, an eerie mountain shaped like a tree stump. In Steven Spielberg's *Close Encounters of the Third Kind* (1977), space aliens land there and make their first contact with the people of Earth.

The mountain, which still draws visitors from all around the world, is located in the far northeastern corner of the state, about forty miles from Wyoming's common border with Montana and South Dakota. To get there from Gillette, go east on I-90 for thirty miles until you reach the Moorcroft exit, then go north on Highway 14 approximately twenty miles.

Other Wyoming film locations include Jackson Hole, the setting for Clint Eastwood's *Any Which Way You Can* (1982) and for George Stevens's *Shane* (1953). Tourists often drive by the dilapidated *Shane* cabin, in the Bridger-Teton National Forest, where the boy, played by Brandon DeWilde, lived. The cabin is on Gros Ventre Road, immediately west of Kelly and north of Jackson. (Go north on U.S. 187 six miles, turn right on Gros Ventre, then continue past Kelly for five miles.)

Bridger-Teton National Forest also became Siberia in *Rocky IV* (1985). While training for his fight with the Russian superfighter, played by Dolph Lundgren, Sylvester Stallone runs up Rendezvous Peak to do the same triumphant dance he did on the steps of Philadelphia's Museum of Art. The mountain peak is visible from the Jackson Hole tram. It is also possible to hike the two miles to the peak.

The scene in which Brad Pitt goes over the falls in *A River Runs Through It* was filmed at Granite Falls, also in the Bridger-Teton National Forest. To reach the falls from Jackson Hole, go south on U.S. 187 to Hoback Junction. Continue past U.S. 187 about eight or nine miles to Granite Canyon Road, and then go another eight to ten miles until you reach the falls.

The opening scene of *The Vanishing*, in which Kiefer Sutherland's car stalls and Sandra Bullock goes looking for gas, was filmed at a three thousand-foot tunnel leading to Yellowstone Park on Highway 14/16/20, six miles west of Cody. Wishing to convey a foreboding sense of danger, production designer Jeannine C. Opperwall scouted for tunnels in three states before finding the one most useful for her purposes.

The Big Trail (1930), with John Wayne in his first starring role, was filmed at Dead Man's Bar, located about twenty-five miles north of Jackson on U.S. 187.

Spencer's Mountain (1963), a comedy–action feature that starred Henry Fonda, Maureen O'Hara, James MacArthur, and Wally Cox, was filmed at Triangle X Ranch. The guest ranch is located thirty miles north of Jackson on U.S. 187 and is reachable from the Triangle X entry road.

Devil's Tower, Close Encounters of the Third Kind *(courtesy Wyoming Division of Tourism)*

Utah

Greater Moab

The opening scenes of *Indiana Jones and the Last Crusade* (1988), in which an adventurous young Indie (River Phoenix) rescues an artifact from treasure hunters, were filmed near the Double Arch in Arches National Park, located four miles north of Moab on Highway 191.

The park—and the area surrounding Moab—have, in fact, been filmed so often that the Moab Visitor Center (Center and Main streets, Moab, Utah, 84532) furnishes a brochure, *Moab Area Movie Locations Auto Tour*, which includes a list of movie sites tourists can visit. The fifty-one movies filmed in the area include *Wagon Master* (1950), *Rio Grande* (1950), *Taza, Son of Cochise* (1953), *Warlock* (1958), *Ten Who Dared* (1959), *The Comancheros* (1961), *Cheyenne Autumn* (1963), *The Greatest Story Ever Told* (1963), *Rio Conchos* (1964), *Blue* (1967), *Against a Crooked Sky* (1975), *Space Hunter* (1982), *Choke Canyon* (1984), *Sundown* (1988), the aforementioned *Indiana Jones and the Last Crusade* (1988), and *Thelma and Louise* (1991). Since the brochure was published, *Geronimo* (1993) and *City Slickers II* (1994) were also filmed in the area.

Thelma and Louise Point
on the Shafer Trail, south of Dead Horse State Park

One of the most asked about locations on the Moab auto tour is *Thelma and Louise* Point, the site of Susan Sarandon and Geena Davis's dramatic drive off a cliff to elude capture by the police. The movie identifies the cliff as being in the Grand Canyon, but the point is actually on the Shafer Trail, an unpaved road off Route 279, ten miles into the Shafer Trail (also known as Potash Road), which is located nineteen miles south of Moab.

Thelma and Louise *Point*
(courtesy Diane Nagel)

(*Note:* Moab is also the home of the Hollywood Stuntmen's Hall of Fame and Museum, located at 100 East 100 North. For further information write the Hall of Fame at P.O. Box 277, Moab, Utah, 84532.)

Monument Valley Navajo Tribal Park
four miles southeast of U.S. 63, between Kayenta, Arizona, and Mexican Hat, Utah

"Think of Stonehenge on a massive scale," author John Gregory Dunne has written, and you have Monument Valley—a park replete with breathtaking red-sandstone mesas towering over the desert floor; some more than one thousand feet tall. Locals rightly call Monument Valley one of nature's most artistic creations. It is located in the Four Corners area, where Colorado, New Mexico, Arizona, and Utah come together (but primarily in Utah and Arizona)

Monument Valley (courtesy Utah Travel Council)

and was made famous by director John Ford, who made six Westerns here, including *My Darling Clementine* (1946), *Fort Apache* (1948), *She Wore a Yellow Ribbon* (1949), and *The Searchers* (1956).

Today, filmmakers often pay homage to Ford by shooting at some of the locations he used. For example, in *Back to the Future III* (1990), director Robert Zemeckis chose an area between two mesas, the East and West Mittens, to build the drive-in where Michael J. Fox is transported back to 1885. In an industry in-joke, Fox's arrival was greeted by Indians, who were followed by the cavalry. The drive-in was dismantled after those scenes were filmed.

Monument Valley's long list of movie credits also includes *How the West Was Won* (1962), *2001: A Space Odyssey* (1969), *Easy Rider* (1969), *The Legend of the Lone Ranger* (1981), *National Lampoon's Vacation* (1983), *Over the Top* (1986), *Pontiac Moon* (1994), and *Forrest Gump* (1994). Tom Hanks (as Gump) ended his three-year run across country here.

Hiking, rock climbing, and off-road driving is forbidden in the park, but tourists can take the seventeen-mile unpaved loop around the park or tour by horseback. The park is open daily from 8:00 A.M. to 6:00 P.M.

Kanab

The town of Kanab, located on Highway 89 in southwestern Utah, near the Arizona border, is another area where dozens of movies and television episodes have been filmed. A few of the sets are still standing, including some buildings from a western main street in Old Paria, a ghost town located thirty-four miles east of Kanab on Highway 89. The sets were constructed for the Sinatra movie *Sergeants Three* (1962).

Main Street in Dodge City—the set from the long-running *Gunsmoke* (1955–75)—still exists in Johnson Canyon, about nine miles east of Kanab. Although the set is on private property, it can be viewed from a distance from the Johnson Canyon Road, off Highway 89.

Nearby, in Kanab Canyon, about five miles north of Kanab, is the area where such television series as *The Lone Ranger*, *Death Valley Days*, and *Daniel Boone* were filmed.

For further information and maps contact the Kane County Travel Council, 41 South 100 East, Kanab, Utah, 84741.

Other Movies Filmed in Utah

• Two features starring Robert Redford, *The Electric Horseman* (1979) and *Butch Cassidy and the Sundance Kid* (1969), were filmed in Grafton, a ghost town in southwestern Utah, about three miles west of Rockville. The famous scene in which Paul Newman rides Katharine Ross on the bicycle handlebars to the tune of "Raindrops Keep Falling on My Head" was filmed there.

• *Footloose* (1984), starring Kevin Bacon, was filmed in various locations in Provo, American Fork, Payson, and in Lehi at the Lehi Roller Mills, a flower mill visible from the Lehi exit of I-15. Bacon's famous dance sequences were filmed at the mill.

• *Three O'Clock High* (1987) was filmed at Ogden High School in Ogden. Ogden was also a major location for *Melvin and Howard* (1980), a comedy about Utah gas station attendant Melvin Dummar (Paul LeMat) and his legendary encounter with eccentric billionaire Howard Hughes (Jason Robards). Dummar's Chevron station in Willard, a small community ten miles north of Ogden, was also used.

• *Ski Patrol* (1989) was filmed in Park City; *Better Off Dead* (1985), in Alta and Brighton.

• *A Home of Our Own* (1993), starring Kathy Bates and Edward Furlong, was filmed in Heber City and in Wasatch Mountain State Park, where Bates's family house was constructed and later dismantled. Other scenes were also filmed in downtown Midvale, which was also used as a location for both *The Stand* (1994) and *The Sandlot* (1993).

• *Jeremiah Johnson* (1972) was shot on the Alpine Loop and in Provo Canyon, in what is now Robert Redford's Sundance Resort.

• *Josh and S.A.M.* (1993) was also filmed at Arches National Park. The actors who played the title role, Jacob Tierney and Noah Fleiss, pick up Martha Plimpton hitchhiking there.

Colorado

Highland Lake Congregational Church
on Weld County Road 5, Mead

In *Die Hard II* (1990), William Sadler, playing the diabolical Colonel Stuart, commandeers this church while trying to liberate a South American strongman being extradited to the United States on drug charges, crippling a Washington, D.C., airport in the process.

Since the front of the church faces Highland Lake and the script called for Stuart's men to make a getaway through the back door and engage in a gunfight with Bruce Willis and the U.S. Army, the filmmakers used the back door as the front and outfitted the church with a false front and steeple.

The building, erected in 1896, is used for weddings and town meetings and holds services about once a year. There is no signage on the church identifying it. The church is located one mile north and one mile west of Mead, a small farming community about fifty minutes northwest of Boulder. From Exit 245 of State Highway 125, go west two miles and then north on County Road 5.

(*Note: Die Hard II* was set in Washington, D.C., and the Virginia suburbs but was shot at several locations, including several airports in Colorado and Washington State. Denver's Stapleton International Airport was used for some of the runway scenes and one in which Bruce Willis's car, left on the lower-level arrival concourse, is towed by airport police.)

House at 1619 Pine Street
Boulder

Robin Williams and Pam Dawber supposedly lived in this house in *Mork and Mindy*, an ABC sitcom about a free-spirited alien who lands in Boulder to learn about the backward ways of earthlings. The series aired from 1978 to 1982.

A prominent location of the show was the New York Deli, located at 1117 Pearl Street on the Pearl Street Mall. According to current owner Warren Tepper, Mindy's father owned a music store, identified as McConnell's Music Store, two doors down from the restaurant at what is actually Frank Shorter's Sporting Goods.

Jay Thomas and Gina Hecht starred as Remo and Jean DaVinci, Mork and Mindy's friends who owned the deli. The deli still attracts tourists and sells *Mork and Mindy* souvenirs.

Lowenstein Theater
Colfax and Elizabeth, Denver

The courtroom scenes in the two-hour *Perry Mason* movies, which aired from 1985 to 1993, were filmed in this theater in Denver's Capitol Hill area. The original series, which starred Raymond Burr, aired from 1957 to 1966 and was filmed in Los Angeles. When the show was revived, the producers transplanted the show to Denver, filming first at the City and County Courthouse Building and

later at the Lowenstein (formerly the Bonfils) Theater, where they
built their own courtroom sets.

Two streets just outside the theater were renamed Perry Mason
Court and Della Street in their honor.

Church of the Annunciation
3621 Humboldt

This is the church seen in the *Father Dowling Mysteries*, which
starred Tom Bosley as Father Frank Dowling, the pastor of St.
Michael's Parish in Chicago. Seventeen episodes of the mystery
series aired on ABC between 1989 and 1992.

St. Luke's Hospital
17th and Pearl streets, 19th and Pennsylvania

Diagnosis: Murder, a lighthearted CBS mystery series starring
Dick Van Dyke as a crime-solving doctor, used this vacant hospital
as the Community General Hospital, where Van Dyke and Scott
Baio practiced. Although only the first eight episodes of the series
were filmed in Denver (in 1993, the series moved to Los Angeles
to accommodate Van Dyke), the series continued to show St. Luke's
exterior as the façade of the hospital.

Stanley Hotel
333 Wonderview Avenue, Estes Park

Jim Carrey and Jeff Daniels stayed at this grand hotel in *Dumb
and Dumber* (1994). Built in 1906 and located about 65 miles northwest of Denver, the hotel also inspired Stephen King to write his
novel *The Shining*. The 1980 film version, however, was filmed in
Oregon.

Dumb and Dumber also shot at the Copper Mountain Resort in
Breckenridge—where Daniels's frozen tongue was stuck to a ski
lift—and on the streets of Breckenridge and Park City, Utah.

Buckskin Joe

Buckskin Joe is the actual name of a restored mining town located about eight miles west of Canon City. The town was assembled
from Old West buildings, some dating back to the late 1850s, and
is now a theme park and a popular Colorado tourist attraction.

Movies are occasionally filmed in Buckskin Joe. Its main streets are where John Wayne, in *True Grit* (1969), plays a hard-drinking old marshal who is asked to help a young girl who wants to avenge the death of her father. *Cat Ballou* (1965), a Western spoof that starred Jane Fonda and Lee Marvin, was also filmed there, as was *Lightning Jack* (1994), which starred Australia's Paul Hogan.

The park is open between Memorial Day and Labor Day. For hours and prices write to the Buckskin Joe Park and Railroad, P.O. Box 1387, Canon City, Colorado, 81215.

Buckskin Joe, Colorado (courtesy Greg and Judy Tabuteau)

Southwestern Colorado

Between 1949 and the early 1970s, quite a few Westerns were filmed in the small towns of Durango, Ridgway, Gunnison, Silverton, and Grand Junction. Probably the most popular of these was *Butch Cassidy and the Sundance Kid*. The scene in which Robert Redford and Paul Newman, cornered by lawmen, make their famous leap off a cliff, was filmed by a gorge over the Animas River, which is located on a county road about twenty miles north of Durango. According to Tony Schweikle, former director of the Southwest Colorado Film Commission, the jump was shot in three cuts. The first shot shows Newman and Redford about to jump off the rocks above the gorge (which in real life is only about thirty feet above the river). Then we see the stuntmen fly through the air. The third cut shows Newman and Redford landing in water somewhere in California.

To reach the site of the famous jump, from Durango take U.S. 550 north to County Road 250 and then go down a hill. When you see a KOA campground pointing to the left, go to the right another half mile. There are no identifying markers, but the site of the jump is by Baker's Bridge.

The movie that Billy Crystal jokingly referred to as his "coming of middle age" movie, *City Slickers* (1991), was also filmed near Durango, on Steward's Ranch, a privately owned ranch on Lightner Creek. In the movie, Crystal and his friends decide to relive their youths by playing cowboys at a Southwest dude ranch. The movie's cattle drive ends at Steward's Ranch.

Fans of these and other Westerns who plan to visit the area can obtain a map of movie locations from the Southwest Colorado Film Commission (P.O. Box 543, Durango, Colorado, 81302) by sending a self-addressed stamped envelope. The commission also sells a video, *Travel the Movie Trail*, hosted by Western star Jack Elam, which shows the locations of a number of features, including *True Grit* (1969), *The Searchers* (1956), *Cheyenne Autumn* (1964), *How The West Was Won* (1962), *Around the World in 80 Days* (1956), *National Lampoon's Vacation* (1983), *The Unsinkable Molly Brown* (1964), *The Cowboys* (1972), *The Tracker* (1988), *A Ticket to Tomahawk* (1949), *Butch Cassidy and the Sundance Kid* (1969), *Support Your Local Gunfighter* (1971), *Viva Zapata!* (1952), *City Slickers* (1991), *Snowball Expresss* (1972), *When Legends Die* (1972), and *Then Came Bronson* (1968). The video, which sells for $9.95 plus $2.50 shipping and handling, includes clips from the features and interviews with actors, directors, and locals who helped in the making of the films.

Other Movies Filmed in Colorado

• Some of the road scenes in *Thelma and Louise* (1991) were filmed on Unaweep Canyon (Highway 141), between Grand Junction and Utah. Geena Davis and Susan Sarandon stop at the Bedrock General Store in the small town of Bedrock, where Sarandon phones an FBI agent, who says he is trying to help them. The scenes in which the police chase them were filmed just west of there, near Cisco, Utah.

• One of Kevin Costner's early movies, *American Flyers* (1985), was also filmed outside Grand Junction, at the Colorado National Monument in the Grand Mesa National Forest and at the Ramada

Inn of Grand Junction, on 2790 Crossroads Boulevard.

• *Flashback* (1989), a buddy film which starred Kiefer Sutherland as an FBI agent who escorts ex-sixties radical Dennis Hopper to prison, was filmed at the train depot in Glenwood Springs and aboard the Rio Grande Ski Train. What was supposed to be the train station in Oakland was actually Denver's Union Pacific Train Station.

• *National Lampoon's Christmas Vacation* (1989) was filmed at Summit County High School and a Wal-Mart in the town of Breckenridge.

• Woody Allen's science-fiction spoof *Sleeper* (1974) was filmed at the I. M. Pei–designed National Center for Atmospheric Research, on West Table Mesa Drive, and at a privately owned futuristic home just west of Denver on I-70 at Genessee Mountain.

Idaho

Pale Rider (1985), *Heaven's Gate* (1980), *Bronco Billy* (1980), and *Bus Stop* (1956) were all filmed in Idaho. However, the Idaho Film Commission said there were no major film sites still in existence that tourists would be interested in visiting.

As we go to press, the first television series to be based in Idaho is airing on NBC. *Amazing Grace*, a one-hour drama starring Patty Duke as a nurse turned minister, was filmed in the area of Coeur d'Alene, where Duke has lived in recent years.

Chapter 4

The Southwest

Nevada

Las Vegas

Las Vegas has appeared in more than thirty movies over the past twenty years. As one might expect, virtually all of them were filmed in or just outside the casinos on Las Vegas Boulevard, the city's famous "Glitter Gulch."

Caesars Palace has received the most exposure, having appeared in four movies. In *Rain Man* (1988), Dustin Hoffman, playing an autistic savant named Raymond (or "Rain Man," as his cinematic brother, Tom Cruise, calls him), counts cards and beats the house playing blackjack in a former casino pit area near the Cafe Roma. Hoffman and Cruise stayed in a VIP suite, but a spokeswoman for the hotel would not identify the suite, saying it is off limits to the general public. She did say that other scenes were filmed in Cuzzens, a men's clothing store where Cruise goes shopping, and Cleopatra's Salon, where Hoffman receives a makeover.

In *The Electric Horseman* (1979), Robert Redford rides an electrified horse out of Caesars, up the main Vegas Strip, and on to Utah.

Caesars Galleria Bar was also the site of the poker scenes of *Oh, God, You Devil* (1984). Mel Brooks's *History of the World, Part I* (1981) made use of the Palace's fountains.

The fight in *Rocky V* (1990), was supposed to have taken place at the Palace, but was actually filmed elsewhere.

Elsewhere on the Strip, *Honeymoon in Vegas* (1992), starring Nicolas Cage, Sarah Jessica Parker, and James Caan, was filmed at Bally's Casino Resort. The opening sequence of *Rocky IV* (1985), which features a fight between Carl Weathers, who plays Apollo Creed, and Dolph Lundgren, who plays the Russian superfighter Drago, was filmed at the MGM Grand.

In *Indecent Proposal* (1993), Robert Redford's offer to Demi Moore and Woody Harrelson to sleep with Demi for $1 million is made while the couple is staying at the Las Vegas Hilton. The Hilton was also featured in *Diamonds Are Forever* (1971), one of the last James Bond movies starring Sean Connery, and in Sylvester Stallone's *Over the Top* (1987). Stallone participates in the International Arm Wrestling Championships in the Hilton Center.

Bugsy (1991) was set, but not filmed, at the Flamingo Hilton, the first major hotel built in Vegas. Since the movie was a period piece and Vegas no longer looks as it did when Benjamin "Bugsy" Siegel built the Flamingo in the 1940s, the producers re-created the hotel on a set in the Palm Desert. (In fact, most of the original buildings of the Flamingo have been torn down.)

Other movies filmed in Las Vegas include *I Love Trouble* (1994), *City Slickers II* (1994), *Another Stakeout* (1993), *Honey, I Blew Up the Kid* (1992), *Lost in America* (1985), *Fever Pitch* (1985), *Oxford Blues* (1984), *Starman* (1984), *Cannonball Run II* (1983), *The Gauntlet* (1977), *Viva Las Vegas* (1964), and *Ocean's Eleven* (1960).

Vegas was also the setting of the popular ABC-TV series *Vega$*, which aired from 1978 to 1981. Robert Urich played a detective who operated out of the Desert Inn.

The denouement of *Midnight Run* (1988), in which bounty hunter Robert De Niro exchanges his charge, Charles Grodin, for incriminating disks, was filmed in the main terminal of Vegas's McCarren Airport. And the courtroom scenes in *Melvin and Howard* (1980) were shot in the Clark County District Courthouse. Melvin is gas station owner Melvin Dummar, who claims that he picked up the eccentric billionaire Howard Hughes hitchhiking and that Hughes thanked him by including him in his final will.

Valley of Fire State Park
fourteen miles southwest of State Route 169

Patrick Stewart called this state park "a God-awful place" after filming the climax of *Star Trek: Generations* (1994) in sweltering conditions, sometimes reaching 118 degrees. High winds also slowed down the filming of the scenes in which Malcolm McDowell kills William Shatner (Capt. James T. Kirk) while Shatner helps Stewart save the galaxy.

The scenes were filmed on a mountaintop about one-quarter of a mile from the parking lot at the end of Fire Canyon. The park is located fifty-five miles northwest of Las Vegas.

The spectacular desert driving scenes from *The Good Son* (1993) were also filmed at the park, on both State Route 169 and Mouse's Tank Road.

Iron Eagle (1986), *Father Hood* (1993), *The Legend of the Lone Ranger* (1980), *The Professionals* (1966), and *One Million B.C.* (1940) were also filmed at various locations in the park.

Reno

In downtown Reno several movies were shot within a radius of about one mile. The most famous recent film, *Sister Act* (1992), begins and ends at Fitzgerald's Club, on 255 North Virginia Street. Whoopi Goldberg plays a lounge singer at the casino who witnesses her mobster-boyfriend (Harvey Keitel) murder an informant. While Keitel awaits trial, Goldberg hides in a San Francisco church, but Keitel finds her there and brings her back to Reno. The nuns Whoopi befriends at the convent then fly to Reno for the rescue.

Also seen in *Sister Act* (and all the other movies filmed in Reno) is Reno's famous neon arch, situated between Fitzergald's and Harold's Casino, welcoming visitors to Reno, "the Biggest Little City in the World."

Sister Act was also filmed at the Reno Post Office, 50 South Virginia Street, which served as the police station, and at St. Thomas Aquinas Church, 310 West Second Street, the Catholic school that a wisecracking young Whoopi attends.

Blind Fury (1988), starring Rutger Hauer, and *Desert Hearts* (1985), a lesbian love story, was filmed a few blocks away at the Riverside Casino, on 17 South Virginia Street. Marilyn Monroe also stayed there while filming her last film, *The Misfits* (1961).

Down the street, at 345 North Virginia Street, is the Eldorado Hotel and Casino. In *Pink Cadillac* (1989), a stunt was staged in which Clint Eastwood hangs on to the hood of a car, which smashes through the casino's glass doors.

Other Reno locations include:

• The Mapes Casino on South Virginia Street, kitty-corner from the Riverside, a now-closed casino where Monroe and Clark Gable gamble in *The Misfits*. The casino also appeared in *Desert Hearts*.

• The Greyhound Bus Station at the corner of Second and Grant Street, four blocks west of downtown. In *Melvin and Howard*, the real Melvin Dummar, who claims to have inherited millions from Howard Hughes, has a cameo scene here with Mary Steenburgen (who received an Oscar for Best Supporting Actress, playing Dummar's wife.)

• The Reno Wedding Chapel, at 655 North Virginia, site of Kiefer Sutherland and Meg Ryan's marriage in *Promised Land* (1987).

• The Reno train depot at East Commercial Road and Lake; the Park Wedding Chapel, at 136 South Virginia; and Parkers Western Wear, at 151 North Virginia, were all featured in *Desert Hearts*.

The ranch seen in *Desert Hearts*, the privately owned Quail Canyon Ranch off Pyramid Highway outside Reno, was also used as a location in *The Misfits*.

Pyramid Lake

Nevada's largest natural lake, located in the desert about thirty-five miles northeast of Reno on State Road 445, is a popular camping and boating site. Director George Stevens chose it as the Holy Land in *The Greatest Story Ever Told* (1963). According to the July-August 1984 issue of *Nevada* magazine: "When the Inbal Dancing Troupe from Israel arrived at Pyramid Lake to appear in the film, the members were stunned to find that the terrain not only looked like the Holy Land but conveyed its mood as well. An expansive replica of the city of Capernaum was built on the lake's shore, thousands of extras were hired, and Max Von Sydow as Christ led an all-star cast that included Charlton Heston and John Wayne."

William Hurt and Elizabeth Perkins also dance by the sand dunes on the east side of the lake in *The Doctor* (1991), the story of a doctor's eye-opening bout with throat cancer. Perkins, a fellow cancer patient, helps humanize Hurt by teaching him what it is like to be a patient.

The Nevada Film Commission says the exact location where *The Doctor* was shot is up a dirt road about one-quarter mile south of the lake's namesake pyramid formation, but tourists who want to get a general feel of the area can drive up Pyramid Highway, past the town of Nixon. At the summit of the road there is a sign that reads: Pyramid Lake Reservation Fishing Area. Turn left on a dirt road and drive fifteen to twenty minutes until you see the sand dunes. For driving in this area, dune buggies are recommended.

Nevada State Penitentiary
3301 East Fifth Street, Carson City

The exteriors of this state prison were seen in *An Innocent Man* (1989), starring Tom Selleck as an airport maintenance man wrongly accused of drug sales. (The interior scenes were filmed at Cincinnati's Old Workhouse.)

To make the prison look even more ominous, the filmmakers added barbed wire, cyclone fencing, additional sperimeters, and two guard towers. Prison authorities liked the improvements so much that they decided to keep them after the filming ceased.

You can drive by the prison, but tourists are not permitted.

House at 500 Mountain Street
Carson City

This was Lauren Bacall's boarding lodge in *The Shootist* (1976), John Wayne's final movie.

The Shootist was also filmed at the Washoe Lake State Park, on Highway 395, just north of Carson City, where Wayne takes Bacall for a buggy ride.

Fuji Park
Clear Creek Road (off Highway 395), Carson City

In *Pink Cadillac* (1989), the park was transformed into an active rodeo where Clint Eastwood played a clown.

Ponderosa Ranch
100 Ponderosa Ranch Road (on State Road 28), Incline Village

Every year, up to a quarter of a million people visit this Western amusement park, which features the original Cartwright ranch depicted in *Bonanza*, one of the most popular Westerns of all time.

Ponderosa Ranch, Bonanza *(courtesy William A. Anderson Ponderosa Ranch)*

Interestingly, the ranch did not exist when *Bonanza* first aired in 1959. Fans of the show kept coming to Bill and Joyce Anderson's property on Lake Tahoe's north shore, thinking that the real Ponderosa was nearby. The Ponderosa, of course, was fictitious, but the opening credits of the show had shown the Ponderosa's supposed location on a flaming map.

Anderson sensed an opportunity and approached NBC with the idea of building a ranch and a theme park on the land, which was built in 1967. The show ran until 1973.

The ranch is open from mid-April to October. Tourists can see it, watch stunt shows, and even get married at the town's Church of the Ponderosa.

Genoa Country Store
2299 Main Street, Genoa

Misery (1990), Rob Reiner's film about a popular romance novelist (James Caan) held captive by his "number-one fan" (Kathy Bates), was set in the Colorado Rockies but was actually filmed near Lake Tahoe.

The Silver Creek Lodge where Caan finishes his novel is a Forest Service lodge inaccessible to the public, but tourists can go to the country store seen in the movie and the post office next door. These buildings are on Main Street in Genoa, a small town about forty-five minutes south of Reno on I-395 (off the Jack's Valley Road exit).

The country store is just down the street from the Genoa Courthouse Museum at 191 First Street, which was transformed into the bank Walter Matthau robs in *Charley Varrick* (1973).

(Incidentally, the treacherous mountain road where James Caan crashes his car in *Misery* is the Old Donner Pass, about thirty minutes west of Reno, just over the California border. To get there, take I-80 to the Donner exit. Drive west past Donner Lake, and when the lake ends, head up Donner Pass into the town of Soda Springs. The road, which is about three miles long and is elevated several thousand feet, provides a beautiful vista of the area around Donner Lake.)

Lake Tahoe

Francis Ford Coppola used several mansions as the Corleone family's Lake Tahoe estate in *The Godfather Part II* (1974). The two most important ones, the Whittel mansion, on the east side of the lake, near Skunk Harbor, and the former Henry T. Kaiser estate, on the west side, near Homewood, on the California side, are both only visible from a distance. Some of the tour boats operating in Lake Tahoe pass by the estate and point it out.

The Kaiser estate, where the christening of Al Pacino's son takes place, is near Homewood, and is the only house on the lake with a lighthouse.

Also on Lake Tahoe is the Cal-Neva Lodge Resort, Number 2 Stateline Road, in Crystal Bay. The exterior of the Cal-Neva was used as the Galaxy Hotel in *Things Change* (1989), where Joe Mantegna takes Don Ameche for one last fling after coaching him into giving a phony confession.

The hotel's showroom was also featured in *Cobb* (1994), with Tommy Lee Jones, for a scene in which Cobb interrupts a show of performer Louis Prima and launches into a racist harangue onstage.

On the southern edge of Lake Tahoe is a lakeside cabin by Fallen Leaf Lake, where Kevin Costner tries to hide Whitney Houston from an attempted assassin in *The Bodyguard* (1992). The cabin is privately owned and not easily accessible, but hikers and joggers can visit the general area where the movie was filmed. The lake is off Highway 89, near Camp Richardson. Fallen Leaf Lake Road provides the same spectacular vista of the lake and surrounding mountains.

Other Nevada Filming Sites

• *Top Gun* (1986) filmed many of its flight sequences in the skies above Fallon Air Force, north of Las Vegas. Similarly, *Iron Eagle* (1986) was filmed above Nellis Air Force in Las Vegas.

• *The Misfits* (1961), the last film of both Clark Gable and Marilyn Monroe, was shot on the main street of the small town of Dayton, located about fifteen miles east of Carson City on Highway 50. The Washoe County Courthouse and Mia's Restaurant are featured in the movie. Clint Eastwood also filmed *Honkytonk Man* (1982) in Dayton.

• Hoover Dam was featured in *Father Hood* (1993), where a car is driven off a cliff.

Arizona

Monument Valley Navajo Tribal Park
(See page 68)

Grand Canyon

Lawrence Kasdan's *Grand Canyon* (1992) concerns six Los Angeles residents from different social classes and how their lives intersect, sometimes through capricious acts of violence. The title, *New Republic* columnist Milton Kondracke wrote, "was used as a metaphor for the gulf which separates upscale white America from the slum. . . . Half the movie is about the gulf, the rage, and the violence that result, and half is about the efforts of decent people to do something about it."

At the end of the movie the six main characters (Danny Glover, Kevin Kline, Steve Martin, Mary McDonnell, Mary-Louise Parker, and Alfre Woodard) visit the Grand Canyon together, presumably, as another critic put it, to feel "minute and transitory together."

Several other movies have been filmed here, including *Over the Top* (1986), starring Sylvester Stallone, and *National Lampoon's Vacation* (1983). Chevy Chase was photographed in front of the El Tovar Hotel on the Canyon's south rim.

Grand Canyon North Rim, Grand Canyon *(courtesy Arizona Office of Tourism)*

Meteor Crater
near Winslow

Approximately fifty thousand years ago, a giant meteorite crashed into the Arizona desert, about nineteen miles west of what is now Winslow. In 1984, Meteor Crater was selected as the site where an alien, played by Jeff Bridges, is stranded on Earth and rendezvous with his spaceship in *Starman*.

Damnation Alley (1977), with Jan-Michael Vincent and George Peppard, was also filmed at the crater.

Meteor Crater, Starman *(courtesy Arizona Office of Tourism)*

Prescott

A good portion of the 1994 version of *The Getaway* was filmed in Prescott, a city of twenty-eight thousand located about ninety miles northwest of Phoenix. The movie's chase scenes were filmed within a six-block radius downtown, and several stunts were staged with the police in pursuit of Kim Basinger and Alec Baldwin in a cab on Union Street, one-half block east of the Yavapai County Courthouse.

Other locations included the Dinner Bell Cafe at 321 West Gurley, the restaurant where Basinger and Baldwin stop to eat and are spotted by customers when Baldwin's WANTED photo is flashed on TV; Bucky O'Neill's gun shop at 231 North Cortez, where Baldwin relieves the proprietor of some weapons at gunpoint; and the alley behind Murphy's Restaurant, at 201 North Cortez, where Baldwin and Basinger re-create the classic dumpster scene from the original version of *The Getaway*, starring Ali MacGraw and Steve McQueen.

Billy Jack (1971) was also filmed in downtown Prescott, on the courthouse square, at the corner of Gurley and Montezuma. Tom Laughlin was beat up in one infamous scene; another scene, in which bullies pour flour on Indian youngsters to make them look white, was filmed at Kendall's Famous Burgers at 113 South Cortez, across the street from the courthouse.

Phoenix

For some reason, Phoenix has attracted more movies-of-the-week than full-length feature films. Still, Phoenix has had plenty of feature action. Locations include:

• The parking lot of the Phoenix Greyhound Park, at 3801 East Washington, where a gasoline tanker is blown up after a heist in *The Getaway* (1994);

• The Maricopa County Jail, on Madison Street, where Alec Baldwin springs a prisoner; and the Frank Lloyd Wright–inspired Arizona Biltmore Hotel, 24th Street and Missouri Avenue, where Kim Basinger seeks James Woods's help to get Baldwin out of a Mexican jail;

• The Phoenix International Raceway, on 1313 North Second Street, where scenes from Tom Cruise's *Days of Thunder* (1990) were filmed;

• The Sky Harbor Airport and the Turf Paradise Race Horse Track, 19th Avenue and Bell Road, featured in *The Grifters* (1989);

• The former East High School, on 52nd Street between McDowell and Van Buren, and the Metro Center Mall, in *Bill and Ted's Excellent Adventure* (1987);

• A private home at Lawrence and Seventh avenues, seen in *Private Lessons* (1980);

• The city courthouse, on Washington between First and Second streets, seen in the 1980 film *Used Cars* (the car lot itself was specifically built for the movie in Mesa and then dismantled after filming);

• Tempe Stadium, at Arizona State University, where Barbra Streisand performed in *A Star is Born* (1976);

• The former site of the bus terminal (at the time, at Central and Van Buren) seen in *Bus Stop* (1956), starring Marilyn Monroe;

• The Reata Pass Steakhouse, on 27500 North Alma School Parkway, in suburban Scottsdale, which was turned into the bank robbed by John Goodman and William Forsythe in *Raising Arizona* (1987).

• The City of Phoenix Squaw Peak Water Treatment at 20th and Maryland, which became the prison Goodman and Forsythe break out of; and

• The Home Depot, on Cave Creek and Cactus, which became the store Unpainted Arizona owned by Trey Wilson, whose son is kidnapped by Nicolas Cage and Holly Hunter. Interior scenes for the film, including Cage and Hunter's house, were filmed at the Jokake Inn, part of the Phoenician Resort, 6000 East Camelback Road, Phoenix, and at the Old City Hall at 17th and Second Avenue.

Murphy's
301 North Main Street, Florence

Murphy's Drugstore, the primary setting of *Murphy's Romance* (1985), starring James Garner and Sally Field, still exists but is now a soup and salad restaurant.

The building was a drugstore in the 1930s but was used for storage at the time the movie was filmed.

Tucson

A Star Is Born (1976), starring Barbra Streisand and Kris Kristofferson, was filmed in Tucson, but the sets no longer exist; and neither does John Larroquette and Kirstie Alley's house in *Madhouse* (1990). Although the movie was supposedly set in Santa Monica, California, the house was built specifically for the movie on Third Avenue by the University of Arizona and dismantled after filming.

Revenge of the Nerds was filmed at the University of Arizona in 1984, and *Can't Buy Me Love*, a 1987 film in which Patrick Dempsey plays a nerdy high school senior who hires a cheerleader (Amanda Peterson) to be his girlfriend, was shot at Tucson High School on Sixth Street and at the Pima Air Museum, on 6000 East Valencia Road.

The opening scenes of *Major League* (1988) were filmed at Hi Corbett Field, the spring-training home of the real Cleveland Indians.

Old Tucson Studios
201 South Kinney Road, Tucson

Old Tucson Studios was created by Columbia Pictures in 1939 for the filming of the epic *Arizona*, starring William Holden and Jean Arthur. Since then, more than three hundred motion pictures, television programs, music videos, and commercials have been filmed there.

In addition to being Arizona's largest production facility, Old Tucson is also a Western theme park. Visitors can watch gunfights, stunt demonstrations, and special-effects shows, ride in stagecoaches, and shop for souvenirs. Occasionally, tourists can see productions being filmed. *Tombstone* (1993) and *Lightning Jack* (1993) are two of the more recent movies filmed at the studios.

The park is open daily.

Old Tucson Studios, photo of Western buildings (courtesy Old Tucson Studios)

Yuma

Most of the estimated forty feature movies that have been shot in the Yuma area were filmed in the Algonbones Sand Dunes, about seventeen miles west of Yuma, on I-8, just over the border into California. The dunes, which are accessible by dune buggies, have often doubled for the Sahara Desert.

In *Return of the Jedi* (1982), director Richard Marquand transformed the dunes for the arid planet of Tatooine, where Jabba the Hut has a sand barge and Carrie Fisher (Princess Leia) and Harrison Ford (Han Solo) are rescued. The dunes also substituted for Afghanistan in Stallone's *Rambo III* (1988) and as the bizarre planet James Spader and Kurt Russell lead an expedition to in *Stargate* (1994).

Occasionally, filming takes place in Yuma itself. In *The Getaway* (1994), the abandoned Del Sol Hotel, at 300 South Gila Street, was featured prominently as the site of the El Paso hotel where Alec Baldwin and Kim Basinger have their final bloody showdown with Michael Madsen and James Woods's cohorts.

Other Arizona Filming Sites

• *The Karate Kid* (1984) was shot in uptown Sedona, and a major police car chase in *Midnight Run* (1988) was filmed twelve miles west of Sedona, on Highway 89. *Midnight Run* was also filmed at the Flagstaff train station and on the roads outside Williams.

• The mysterious "power spot" seen in the opening sequence of *Poltergeist II* (1986) was filmed at Spider Rock in the Canyon de Chelly National Park in northeastern Arizona.

• Lake Powell, which straddles the Arizona-Utah border, has been featured in several movies, including *Tall Tales* (1994), *Lightning Jack* (1994), and *Maverick* (1994), where an entire Western street was built on the north shore. The sets, however, were removed after the filming.

• The short-lived CBS-TV series *Harts of the West* was filmed in downtown Mayer, a small town outside Prescott.

• Finally, although several features have been set in Tombstone (including the 1993 feature *Tombstone* and 1994's *Wyatt Earp*), the city has never hosted a major film production.

Maverick *set at Lake Powell (courtesy Utah Film Commission)*

New Mexico

The Plaza
Santa Fe

The Plaza, located in the heart of downtown Santa Fe, was where Arnold Schwarzenegger and Danny DeVito buy identical clothes in *Twins* (1989) and Tom Laughlin defends Mexican schoolchildren, eating at a lunch counter, from racists (at the Plaza Cafe) in *Billy Jack* (1971).

Just off the Plaza's southeast corner, at 100 East San Francisco Street, is the La Fonda Hotel, where Willem Dafoe, playing a sheriff investigating a murder, first meets his suspect, gunrunner Mickey Rourke in *White Sands* (1991).

Randall Davey Audubon Center
1800 Upper Canyon Road, Santa Fe

This historic estate, once owned by the artist Randall Davey and now a wildlife sanctuary and education center for the Audubon Society, was one of the two estates used as Whispering Pines, the artists' colony in *Twins*. The colony was where "twin" brothers Arnold Schwarzenegger and Danny DeVito search for their mother, played by Bonnie Bartlett.

And God Created Woman (1987) was also filmed at the center. Rebecca DeMornay's husband (Victor Spano) works at the center's museum in the film, and the two are caught in bed at the studio when a tour group comes through.

Ghost Ranch
off Highway 84 (twelve miles north of Abiquiu)

The Ghost Ranch Conference Center is a Presbyterian retreat and conference center northwest of Santa Fe that sometimes rents out its ranch land to filmmakers. The cattle drive in *City Slickers* (1991), starring Billy Crystal, Jack Palance, Bruno Kirby, and Daniel Stern, was shot there, but none of the sets are left. *Wyatt Earp* (1994), *The Groove Tube* (1973), and *Running Wild* (1973) were also filmed at Ghost Ranch.

Mabel Dodge Luhan House
240 Morada Road, Taos

This is the other house depicted as Whispering Pines in *Twins*. It was used for the exterior scenes in which Schwarzenegger and DeVito and their girlfriends, Kelly Preston and Chloe Webb, climb over the wall to get in.

The exterior of this privately owned educational learning center, once owned by artist Mabel Dodge and in the early 1970s by actor Dennis Hopper, also served as Mary Elizabeth Mastrantonio's home in *White Sands*. Tours of the house are available, and visitors to Taos can stay overnight. For further information write P.O. Box 3400, Taos, New Mexico, 87571.

Memorial Middle School
Las Vegas

This school was the main location in director John Milius's *Red Dawn* (1983), a violent right-wing fantasy about teenagers who defend their homeland from invading Russians. When the invasion begins, paratroopers jump out of a DC-3 onto the school's football field.

Many of the other buildings seen in the movie were built by the production for the purpose of destroying them, but visitors to Las Vegas can drive by the Castaneda Hotel downtown. A former luxury railroad house, the Castaneda was transformed into the occupying army's headquarters. Other film sites included the local Masonic Lodge, which served as the police station in the fictional town of Calumet, Colorado, and an abandoned Safeway store. The town's firehouse is where Jack Nicholson hits the road with Peter Fonda and Dennis Hopper in *Easy Rider* (1969).

Castaneda Hotel
Railroad Avenue, Las Vegas

The Castaneda also served as the hotel where Michael Keaton and Geena Davis, playing speechwriters for opposing political campaigns, meet in the comedy *Speechless* (1994).

White Sands National Monument
fifteen miles southwest of Alamogordo on U.S. 70/82

The unusual snow-white dunes of this national park were featured prominently in the 1991 mystery thriller *White Sands*. Willem Dafoe plays a deputy sheriff who investigates the death of a man found in the park's ruins with a .38 special nearby and a briefcase with half a million dollars in cash. Dafoe's undercover brushes with military gunrunners and the climactic scenes with Mickey Rourke, Samuel Jackson, and Mary Elizabeth Mastrantonio were also filmed in the park.

Tourists who wish to see White Sands can take a sixteen-mile tour daily from 7:00 A.M. to sunset, daily except Christmas Day.

White Sands, White Sands (*courtesy* New Mexico *magazine*)

Other New Mexico Locations

• The opening sequence of *Indiana Jones and the Last Crusade* (1988), in which young Indie (River Phoenix) is chased by outlaws atop a moving circus train, was filmed on the Cumbres and Toltec Scenic Railroad, between the Antonito, Colorado, and Chama, New Mexico, stations. The railroad, a popular Colorado-New Mexico tourist attraction, was also the site of train scenes in *Butch Cassidy and the Sundance Kid* and *Wyatt Earp*.

• In *Natural Born Killers* (1994), Woody Harrelson and Juliette Lewis are "married" on the Taos Gorge Bridge. The drugstore in which they are captured was the old Phar-Mor Grocery off Coors Road in Rio Rancho.

• *Silkwood* (1983), *Wrong Is Right* (1981), and *Outrageous Fortune* (1986) were all filmed at the Albuquerque airport.

• *Outrageous Fortune*, which starred Bette Midler and Shelley Long as aspiring actresses in pursuit of their mysterious Romeo (Peter Coyote), was also filmed in Cerrillos and atop limestone cliffs in an area near Abiquiu known as Plaza Blanca. The cliff areas, however, are on private property that is inaccessible to the public.

• The Jules Verne fantasy *Journey to the Center of the Earth* (1959), starring James Mason, Pat Boone, and Arlene Dahl, was filmed at Carlsbad Caverns (as was the 1950 feature *King Solomon's Mines*).

• NBC's sci-fi series *Earth 2* filmed in various locations outside Santa Fe, including the Santa Fe National Forest.

• *Silverado* (1985), *Young Guns II* (1990), and *Wyatt Earp* (1994) are among the many westerns filmed at the Silverado movie set, built specifically for *Silverado* and used for later westerns. The set is located on the Cook Ranch, outside Santa Fe. The ranch, however, does not offer tours to the public.

• Also in Santa Fe—and closed to the public—is the Eaves Movie Ranch, used for the filming of *The Comeback Trail* (1974) and *Lust in the Dust* (1984).

Cumbres and Coltec Scenic Railroad, Indiana Jones and the Last Crusade, Butch Cassidy and the Sundance Kid *(courtesy* New Mexico *magazine)*

Chapter 5

The Plains States

Note: Return of a Man Called Horse (1976) and some wheatfield scenes in *Kansas* (1987) are North Dakota's only known credits. The North Dakota Film Commission hopes to attract filmmakers to the state in the future.

South Dakota

Grubl-McNenny Ranch
thirty-one miles north of Rapid City

The primary location for *Dances With Wolves* (1990) was the Sioux Indians' summer camp, and that was filmed along two square miles of ranch land along the Belle Fourche River, thirty-one miles north of I-90. The owners of the ranch erected tepees on the original site and for a while offered two-and-a-half-hour guided tours of the ranch, but the tours were discontinued (at least temporarily) when interest began to wane in 1995.

Spearfish Canyon, Black Hills National Forest

It is possible to visit the site of the Indian Winter Camp, which is located in Spearfish Canyon in the Black Hills National Forest, just south and west of the Latchstring Inn and Roughlock Falls. In *Dances with Wolves*, the cavalry tracks Kevin Costner, playing Lt. John Dunbar, in the snow along the meadow and the stream, Little Spearfish Creek. This is also where Rodney A. Grant (Wind in His Hair), on a thousand-foot-high sandstone cliff, bids farewell to Costner and Mary McDonnell (Stands With a Fist) as they leave the tribe at the end of the film.

There used to be signs in the forest identifying the exact filming spots, but *Dances With Wolves* fans have taken them as souvenirs.

Fort Hays Film Set
four miles south of Rapid City

Fort Hays, the military fort where Costner receives his orders to go to Fort Segdewick, was filmed on a private ranch located about thirteen miles east of Rapid City. Two of the original Fort Hays buildings, the major's house and the blacksmith's shop, have since been moved and can be seen from the Moon Meadows Road exit of U.S. 16A, between Rapid City and the Mount Rushmore National Gardens (near Reptile Gardens). The major's house is now a gift shop and seasonal chuck-wagon supper business, open Memorial Day through Labor Day.

There is no charge to stop at the buildings, which continuously show home videos of Costner working on the movie and excerpts from the movie itself. Tourists who wish to dine at the chuck wagon can make reservations by writing to the Fort Hays Movie Set, 3023 Tomahawk Drive, Rapid City, South Dakota, 57702.

Badlands National Park

In *Dances With Wolves*, the erosion-carved formations of this national park were the backdrop of the wagon-travel scene between Fort Hays and Fort Sedgewick. The scenes were filmed in the park's Sage Creek Wilderness Area.

Thunderheart, a 1991 feature that tells the story of an FBI agent (Val Kilmer) sent to investigate a murder on the Pine Ridge Indian Reservation, was also filmed extensively in the Badlands.

(*Note:* The South Dakota Department of Tourism offers visitors a complete list of on-location sites from *Dances With Wolves*, including sites that are inaccessible to the public. Write to 711 East Wells Avenue, Pierre, South Dakota, 57501).

Badlands, Dances With Wolves, Thunderheart *(courtesy South Dakota Department of Tourism)*

Pine Ridge Reservation, Thunderheart *(courtesy South Dakota Department of Tourism)*

Mount Rushmore National Memorial
two miles south of Keystone

The climax of Hitchcock's classic *North by Northwest* (1959) was filmed in part at the Shrine of Democracy (as the mountainside carvings of the presidents are called). Moviegoers saw Cary Grant and Eva Marie Saint escape from a spy ring led by James Mason by climbing down the sixty-foot faces of presidents George Washington and Thomas Jefferson.

Although most viewers would never know it, Hitchcock's crew only spent one day filming at Mount Rushmore, and the scenes running down the faces of the presidents were actually filmed on a set re-creating the memorial at MGM. The memorial's superintendent, Leon Evans, would not give Hitchcock permission to film any acts of violence in the park. Evans later felt Hitchcock broke the spirit of his promise by filming the death scenes on the MGM soundstage.

Mt. Rushmore, North by Northwest *(courtesy South Dakota Department of Tourism)*

Nebraska

Architectural Hall, University of Nebraska
14th and R streets

In *Terms of Endearment* (1983), the scenes in which Debra Winger confronts her philandering husband, Jeff Daniels, were filmed outside the University of Nebraska's Architectural Hall. A room inside the building was also turned into the doctor's office where Winger first learns she has cancer.

Terms of Endearment was also filmed at Leon's Food Mart, at 32nd and South Lincoln, where John Lithgow bails out Winger, who is short of cash; Lincoln General Hospital, on 2300 South 16th Street, where Winger is hospitalized; the Lincoln Municipal Airport at 2400 West Adams; and at a rundown house at 847 14th Street, where Winger and Daniels live.

Father Flanagan's Boys Town
ten miles west of Omaha just off I-680

The 1938 film *Boys Town*, starring Spencer Tracy and Mickey Rooney, and the 1941 sequel, *Men of Boys Town*, were filmed at this village, which has been home to hundreds of abused, abandoned, and neglected children from across the United States.

The visitors center is open daily except Thanksgiving, Christmas, New Year's Day, and Good Friday afternoon. There is no charge for admission or tours. Spencer Tracy's *Boys Town* Oscar is displayed in the Hall of History.

Kansas

The most famous film associated with Kansas, the 1939 classic *The Wizard of Oz*, never left an MGM soundstage. However, Lawrence, Kansas, was the primary location of *The Day After*, the highest-rated TV movie of all time.

That film depicts the aftermath of a catastrophic nuclear attack on Kansas City and the nearby college town of Lawrence. It aired on ABC-TV on November 20, 1983, at a time of heightened fears of nuclear war during Ronald Reagan's administration. The movie, now available on video, was filmed at several locations in Lawrence, including the University of Kansas's Allen Field House, Lawrence Memorial Hospital, and a Kansas River bank, which was the scene of mass graves and people living in tents.

Kansas (1988), which starred Matt Dillon and Andrew McCarthy as drifters who take refuge in a small town after a bank heist, was filmed in Topeka and in several towns (Lawrence, Edgerton, Gardner, and Linwood), but primarily in Valley Falls, where the town's main street and its United Methodist Church provided a backdrop to a visit by the governor of Kansas and his family.

Bad Company (1972), starring Jeff Bridges and Barry Brown as Civil War–era outlaws, was filmed in Severy, about 175 miles southwest of the real St. Joseph, Missouri, where the film was based; Neosho Falls; and Flint Hills.

Paper Moon (1973), with Ryan O'Neal as a Depression-era con man–Bible salesman, was filmed in McCracken (at the McCracken Hotel) and in several small towns, including Hays.

American Flyers (1985) filmed scenes in Salina, McPherson, and Lindsborg; and *In Cold Blood* (1967), based on the famous Truman Capote novel, filmed in Garden City, Holcomb, Olathe, Emporia, Pawnee Rock and Leavenworth.

Oklahoma

Big 8's Motel
1705 East 66th Highway, El Reno

During their cross-country trek in *Rain Man* (1988), Tom Cruise and Dustin Hoffman stayed overnight in this motel, located thirty miles east of Oklahoma City. It is here, after Cruise tries to run a hot bath and Hoffman has one of his fits, that Cruise realizes Hoffman was institutionalized after scalding Cruise in the bathtub as a child.

Owner Kneeles Reeves, who plays the motel's night clerk, reports that thousands of European tourists have asked to stay in room 117, where the Cruise-Hoffman scenes were filmed.

Other Oklahoma Locations

• *Rain Man* was also filmed in downtown Guthrie, where a DON'T WALK sign so confuses Hoffman that he stops in the middle of an intersection and has to be rescued by Cruise, and in a farmhouse outside Hinton, where Cruise talks the lady of the house into letting Hoffman watch *The People's Court* with her children.

• The tiny television station that "Weird Al" Yankovic wins in a poker game in *UHF* (1989) was filmed in a newly constructed and not-yet-occupied wing of the Kensington Mall in Tulsa.

• Tulsa was also the location of two Francis Ford Coppola features released in 1983, *The Outsiders* and *Rumble Fish*. In the latter, the fish are released into the Arkansas River, at the 21st Street Bridge.

• *Fandango* (1984), one of Kevin Costner's first films, was also shot in Tulsa. The stunts, in which airplanes land on an expressway, were filmed at the Utica exit on the Broken Arrow Expressway (Highway 51).

• *Tex* (1982), a Disney coming-of-age movie starring Matt Dillon, Meg Tilly, and Emilio Estevez, was filmed at Broken Arrow High School gymnasium in the city of Broken Arrow; at Bixby High School in Bixby; and in a park area along the Arkansas River in Tulsa (the setting of a big motorcycle chase scene).

• Pauly Shore and Andy Dick undergo basic training at Fort Still in *In the Army Now* (1994).

Iowa

Field of Dreams Baseball Field
three miles northeast of Dyersville on U.S. 20

There is a scene in *Field of Dreams* (1989) in which James Earl Jones predicts: "People will come, Ray. They'll come to Iowa for reasons they can't even fathom. They'll turn up in your driveway, not knowing for sure why they're doing it. They'll arrive at your door as innocent as children."

Since the movie's release an average of forty thousand people a year have come to see the field. "We kept expecting the numbers to drop off, but they just keep coming," Jacques Rahe of the Dyersville Chamber of Commerce told a reporter. "One couple came and got married here. Someone held a christening of their baby here, and a man scattered the ashes of his deceased father here, too."

What dreams these tourists are pursuing are sometimes difficult to fathom, but in the movie Kevin Costner builds the field in the hopes of bringing "Shoeless" Joe Jackson back from the dead to play baseball again. Jackson was one of the members of the 1919 White Sox team that threw the World Series.

Costner hears a heavenly whisper: "If you build it, he will come." As it turns out, when the field is built, not only does Jackson emerge from the cornfields, but so does his team and Costner's dead father.

Visitors to the field are encouraged to bring their baseballs and gloves. Games are played on the field throughout the day. The field is open from 10:00 A.M. to 6:00 P.M. daily, from April 1 to the end of October.

To reach the field from U.S. 20, go north on SR 136 until the N.E. Third Avenue exit and then take Dyersville Road to Lansing Road. There is no charge for admission. The owners make their money off two souvenir stands on the property.

For more information contact the Dyersville Chamber of Commerce, P.O. Box 187, Dyersville, Iowa, 52040.

Field of Dreams baseball field (courtesy Iowa Film Office)

Hillcrest Dormitory, University of Iowa
Iowa City

The shot that is used to depict the office of Craig T. Nelson (Coach Hayden Fox) in ABC's *Coach* (1989–), is actually a ground-level dormitory room at the University of Iowa, the alma mater of Barry Kemp, the show's creator. Shots of a footbridge that crosses a river in front of the Memorial Student Building and of the university's Kinnick Stadium have also been used, but *Coach*, which is taped in front of an audience at Universal Studios in Los Angeles, has never been filmed on the campus.

Other Movies Filmed In Iowa

• Meryl Streep's farmhouse in *The Bridges of Madison County* (1995) was an abandoned structure on a gravel road two miles west of I-35 and eight miles southwest of Des Moines. Other locations include the Winterset Town Square and Madison County's Roseman and Holliwell bridges. To obtain a map to the bridges, write to the Madison County Chamber of Commerce, P.O. Box 55, Winterset, Iowa, 50273.

• *Take This Job and Shove It* (1981) and *F.I.S.T.* (1978) were both filmed in Dubuque; the former at the Dubuque Brewering Bottling Company at 500 East Fourth Street.

• James Earl Jones's Boston apartment in *Field of Dreams* (1989) was on Dubuque's Central Avenue.

• Although much of the action in *Robert A. Heinlein's The Puppet Masters* (1994) supposedly took place at Des Moines City Hall, the filmmakers used the city hall in Fresno, California. Only second-unit shots—those of a helicopter commandeered by Donald Sutherland through Des Moines's downtown—were filmed in the city.

The Roseman Bridge in Madison County (courtesy Iowa Film Office)

Missouri

White Knight Cafe
1801 Olive Street, St. Louis

Susan Sarandon plays a forty-three-year-old working-class wait-ress at this burger joint in *White Palace* (1990), the story of her unlikely romance with a widowed twenty-seven-year-old yuppie played by James Spader. Both the movie and Glenn Savan's novel, which inspired it, identified the shop as "the White Knight."

The movie's bachelor party was filmed at the Lemp mansion, at 3322 DeMenil Place. An office in the Laclede's Landing area on the St. Louis riverfront doubled as the advertising agency; and Duff's Restaurant at 392 North Euclid Avenue in St. Louis's Central West End was used as the New York restaurant where Sarandon and Spader reunite at the movie's end.

White Knight Cafe, White Palace *(courtesy Jeff Keisker/White Knight Cafe)*

Kiel Center
14th and Market streets, St. Louis

Stephen Soderbergh's highly regarded follow-up to *sex, lies and videotape* (1989), *King of the Hill* (1993), was primarily filmed here. The Kiel Center, the new home of the St. Louis Blues hockey team, is the site of the former Kiel auditorium (vacant at the time of filming and dismantled shortly thereafter). The set of the Empire Hotel, a once fine hotel that fell on hard times during the Depression and housed transients and call girls, was created on this site. The movie chronicled the coming-of-age of a twelve-year-old boy (played by James Bradford) who has to survive at the hotel on his own after his family breaks up.

Other *King of the Hill* locations include the vacant Lister Building at the corner of North Taylor Avenue and Olive Street (the hotel's exterior); the New City School at Lake and Waterman in the Central West End, which became the Dewey School; the Sheldon Concert Hall at 3648 Washington, which was the auditorium where Bradford's character graduates; Soulard Market, at South Eighth Street and Lafayette, which doubled as a bus station when Bradford's young brother is sent away; Normandie Park Public Golf Course; and Portland Place, in St. Louis's West End, where the wealthy neighborhood was located.

Hyatt Regency St. Louis at Union Station
One St. Louis Union Station, St. Louis

This majestic structure, now housing a multimillion-dollar festival marketplace–hotel complex, was vacant for much of the 1960s and 1970s. The Grand Hall of the train station was the site of the fight scene in John Carpenter's *Escape From New York* (1981). The futuristic action-fantasy, set in 1997, when Manhattan has been transformed into a maximum-security prison for the United States, focuses around the attempt of a master criminal (Kurt Russell) to rescue the President of the United States (Donald Pleasence), whose plane has crashed inside New York City on the way to a world summit conference. All the Manhattan locations were filmed in St. Louis.

The movie also features St. Louis's Chain of Rocks Bridge, which became New York's 59th Street Bridge (where Russell and Pleasence are ultimately rescued); the Fox Theater at Grand Avenue and Washington, where Russell searches for Pleasence, and meets "Cabby" (played by Ernest Borgnine); and the Civil Courts

Building at 12th and Market (the character Brain's hideout). The wreckage of the plane crash was at the corner of Broadway and St. Charles Street downtown.

Other Missouri Film Locations

• *Planes, Trains and Automobiles* (1987) and *Manhunter* (1986) were filmed in part at St. Louis's Lambert International Airport.

• Part of the bicycle race in *American Flyers* (1985) was filmed by St. Louis's famous Gateway Arch and Laclede's Landing.

• *Mr. and Mrs. Bridge* (1990), which followed the course of Paul Newman and Joanne Woodward's screen marriage, was shot primarily at a private residence in Kansas City's country club district.

• *Article 99* (1991), a drama about medical renegades in a veterans hospital, was filmed at an older wing of Kansas City's Trinity Lutheran Hospital.

Chapter 6

Texas

Royal Theater
115 East Main Street, Archer City

Even though more than two decades have passed since *The Last Picture Show* (1971) was released, thousands of fans still descend on this small Texas town every year to see the remains of the burned-down Royal Theater. Ironically, the movie, which was about stifled dreams and the dreariness of growing up in a small Texas town, has led to a revitalization of this town of eighteen hundred. As Fran Lobpries of the Archer Area Fund put it: "People here hated [the movie] because it [gave Archer] a bad image." But attitudes have changed in recent years, and Archer City has learned to use the exposure to attract tourists.

The sequel, *Texasville* (1990), was also filmed in Archer City. Part of the whorehouse was later built into a wall of the meeting room at the city library on Center Street, and the hotel at 110 North Center Street, is now a bed-and-breakfast, the Spur Hotel.

The Archer City Chamber of Commerce sponsors walking tours, which note the downtown sites seen in both movies. For further information, contact the Archer Area Fund, P.O. Box 877, Archer City, Texas, 76351.

Remains of The Last Picture Show's *Royal Theater (courtesy Archer Area Fund of Communities of Texas)*

Southfork Ranch
3700 Hogge Road, Parker (thirty miles north of Dallas)

For $3,500, you and your friends can stay overnight at the ranch where J. R. Ewing and his family lived in *Dallas*, which aired on CBS from 1978 to 1990. If that is a little steep for your budget, you can always tour the complex for six dollars. It includes the ranch, a gift shop, a clothing store, Miss Ellie's Deli, and a museum.

As many as five hundred thousand people tour the mansion each year. It is also rented for private parties, conferences, and special events.

The tours are offered daily, year-round. For hours and prices write to P.O. Box 516009, Dallas, Texas, 75251.

Southfork Ranch, Dallas *(courtesy Dallas Convention and Visitors Bureau)*

Dealey Plaza
Dallas

With the cooperation of Dallas officials, Oliver Stone was able to re-create the events surrounding the assassination of President John F. Kennedy—where it actually happened—in his controversial *JFK* (1991). To lend authenticity to the look of the film, the exterior of the School Book Depository Building (now the Dallas County Administration Building), at 411 Elm Street, where Lee Harvey Oswald allegedly shot Kennedy, was returned to its original look. Railroad tracks were reinstalled in the area behind the grassy knoll and the picket fence; and trees, which are now far larger than they were three decades ago, were trimmed to match photos from the period.

Stone was also allowed to film at Old Dallas City Jail, at the corner of Main and Harwood, where nightclub owner Jack Ruby fatally shot Oswald; at the Texas Theater, on 231 West Jefferson Street, where police took Oswald into custody; and at St. Joseph's Hospital, on 5909 Harry Hines Boulevard, which represents Parkland Hospital, where Kennedy was pronounced dead. The Venetian Room of the Fairmont Hotel, 1717 North Akard Street, substitutes for Jack Ruby's Carousel Club strip club.

Oliver Stone in front of the School Book Depository building, directing JFK *(courtesy Roger Burke, Dallas/Fort Worth Regional Film Commission)*

More than sixteen blocks near Dealey Plaza were shut down during the filming, requiring more than twenty-one thousand commuters to take another route to work. The city, however, received few complaints, as *JFK* pumped nearly $10 million into the Dallas economy.

Downtown Dallas

Downtown Dallas also doubled as "New Detroit" in *Robocop* (1987). However, the set designers made so many alterations in Dallas's downtown skyscrapers that the buildings would be unrecognizable to the casual tourist.

For example, matte artists added a seventy-story extension to the city's ultramodern city hall, at 1500 Marilla. The building served as the headquarters of Omnicorp, headed by Ronny Cox.

The Plaza of the Americas Atrium, at 650 North Pearl, and the Renaissance Tower, on 1201 Elm Street, were also disguised for the movie. The drug lab scenes were filmed at the Bomb Factory, 2713 Canton Street, a former warehouse and current concert venue, and the Sons of Herman Hall, 3414 Elm Street, served as the Detroit Police Station.

South Edgefield Avenue
Dallas

While preparing for the filming of Oliver Stone's *Born on the Fourth of July* (1989), a team of set designers, carpenters, painters, and other workers transformed several blocks of Dallas's South Edgefield Avenue into 1957 Massapequa, New York, to film the movie's parade sequences. Massapequa was the home of Ron Kovic, the paralyzed Vietnam vet turned antiwar activist, played by Tom Cruise. The street was later updated to shoot a 1969 Fourth of July parade and then returned to normal after filming was complete.

Other Dallas locations for *Born on the Fourth of July* include the former site of Parkland Memorial Hospital, at 3423 Maple, which stood in for the Bronx Veteran Hospital, where Kovic is rehabilitated in 1969; Dallas Hall, at Southern Methodist University, where Abbie Hoffman leads an anti-Vietnam protest after the killings at Kent State; the Dallas Convention Center, which doubled as the Chicago Convention Center; a house on Creekside Drive, where the Kovic family live; Margaret B. Henderson Elementary School in Edgefield, Kovic's high school; and Dallas's Kimball High School on Westmoreland, where Kovic's high school wrestling scenes were filmed.

Problem Child Orphanage
3300 Hemphill Street, Fort Worth

In *Problem Child* (1990), this eighty-year-old Gothic building was used as the St. Brutus orphanage where John Ritter and Amy Yasbeck adopt their problem child, played by Michael Oliver. Two hundred local elementary school children were hired as extras for a scene celebrating Junior's release from St. Brutus by dumping boxes of confetti and releasing hundreds of balloons. At the time of the filming, the building was owned by Our Lady of Victory Catholic Board School, which has since sold the building.

Other *Problem Child* locations include the Old City Jail, at Main and Harwood, where Lee Harvey Oswald was once incarcerated. Michael Richards plays a prisoner there in the movie. The carnival scene was filmed at Fair Park–Dallas, 1300 Robert B. Cullum Boulevard.

The Studios at Las Colinas
6301 North O'Connor Road, Irving

Texas's largest motion-picture and television studio offers a one-and-a-half hour tour of the soundstages that hosted the interior shoots for *Silkwood* (1983), *The Trip to Bountiful* (1985), *Robocop* (1987), *Talk Radio* (1988), *Problem Child* (1990), *JFK* (1991), and *Leap of Faith* (1992) as well as many commercials, music videos, and television productions. The tour includes the makeup and special rooms, which house the miniature models used in box-office hits like *The Hunt for Red October* (1990), *Star Wars* (1977) and *JFK* (Dealey Plaza). Also on the tour is a full-scale replica of the Oval Office seen in *JFK*. On occasion, visitors can see movies being filmed.

The tour is offered daily.

Other Locations in the Dallas–Fort Worth Area

• *Bonnie and Clyde* (1967) was filmed in a series of small towns near Dallas, including Rowlett, Maypearl, Venus, Ponder, Pilot Point, and Garland. A few of the banks Warren Beatty and Faye Dunaway rob in the movie were the same banks the real Bonnie and Clyde robbed, including the long-closed Farmers and Merchants Bank of Pilot Point.

• *Necessary Roughness* (1991), a football comedy, used the University of North Texas's Fouts Field, located in Denton, about thirty-five miles north of Dallas.

• *Hexed*, a 1993 comedy filmed extensively at the Ramada Inn at 1701 Commerce Street, across from Fort Worth's Convention Center.

• Chuck Norris's office in the CBS-TV series *Walker, Texas Ranger* (1992–) was initially filmed at the Tarrant County Courthouse in downtown Fort Worth. The producers later built a set to match the interior of the courthouse.

Waxahachie

The town of Waxahachie, located thirty miles south of Dallas, calls itself "the Hollywood of Texas," and with good reason. Since the early 1970s, Waxahachie has hosted over thirty television productions and the motion pictures, including *Bonnie and Clyde* (1967), *Tender Mercies* (1982), *Places in the Heart* (1984), *The Trip to Bountiful* (1985), and *Daddy's Dyin', Who's Got the Will?* (1990).

Waxahachie's Victorian homes and main town square make the town perfect for turn-of-the-century period pieces. *Dallas* magazine notes: "The same classic architecture that has attracted film crews to Waxahachie has made the Gingerbread Trail one of the state's top events for the past two decades." The Gingerbread Trail is a tour of the city's attractions offered each June. For further information about the tour or to obtain a listing of the movie sites write to the Waxahachie Chamber of Commerce, P.O. Box 187, Waxahachie, Texas, 75165.

Austin

The greater Austin area has appeared in several cult classics, including *The Texas Chainsaw Massacre* (1974), which was filmed in the fields of Round Rock, about thirty miles north of Austin, and *Blood Simple* (1984), the first movie of Ethan and Joel Coen, University of Texas at Austin graduates who went on to film *Raising Arizona* (1987) and *Miller's Crossing* (1991).

Another University of Texas graduate, Richard Linklater, gained notoriety for his low-budget experimental comedy *Slacker* (1991), which was filmed in the coffeehouses, clubs, bars, apartments, and the streets around the university's campus.

Linklater went on to film the critically acclaimed *Dazed and Confused* (1993), which captures the last day of a typical high school in

1976. Austin's Bedichek Junior High School, on 6800 Bill Hughes Road, served as Linklater's Robert E. Lee High. Another principal location in *Dazed and Confused* was the Top-Notch burger drive-in at 7525 Burnet Road, the teen hangout.

Austin's best-known feature film is probably *A Perfect World* (1993), starring Kevin Costner and Clint Eastwood and directed by Eastwood. In *A Perfect World*, primarily a road movie, Costner plays an escaped con who becomes a father figure to a young boy he kidnaps. Most of the movie was filmed on the roads and in the area surrounding Austin. The kidnapping occurs on Austin's Columbus Street, off Bouldin Avenue, and other crucial scenes were filmed in Martindale, which production designer Henry Bumstead transformed into the fictional town of Noodle. It was on Martindale's Main Street that Costner holds up a dry goods store called Friendly's and the boy, played by J. T. Lowther, makes the decision to stay with Costner instead of leaving him and possibly being arrested for stealing a Caspar the Friendly Ghost suit.

Heartbreak Hotel (1988), about an Ohio teenager who kidnaps Elvis Presley as a birthday gift to his mom, was filmed both in Austin and in Taylor. A popular Austin restaurant, the Green Pastures Restaurant, on 811 West Live Oak Street, doubled as the inn owned by star Tuesday Weld, and Austin's Palmer Auditorium was used for the concert scene.

Nadine (1987), a comedy starring Kim Basinger and Jeff Bridges, was shot extensively on Sixth Street, in downtown Austin. Tourists would not recognize the area, though, since street scenes were changed to resemble 1954.

The turn-of-the-century farmhouse that served as Dolly Parton's Chicken Ranch in *The Best Little Whorehouse in Texas* (1982) and later as Sissy Spacek's house in *Hard Promises* (1991) is located outside Pflugerville, a town twenty miles north of Austin. (*Whorehouse* also used Austin's Capitol, which was later used as a backdrop for Clint Eastwood's trailer scenes in *A Perfect World*.)

And on a farm-to-market street between Pflugerville and Hutto, Farm-to-Market Road 685, sits the Victorian farmhouse where Meg Ryan's parents are killed in *Flesh and Bone* (1993). The movie also starred her real-life husband Dennis Quaid, who witnesses the multiple murders and returns to the home with Ryan three decades later.

The Hot Spot (1990), directed by Dennis Hopper, was filmed in downtown Taylor. The movie starred Don Johnson as a car salesman and bank robber who seduces Virginia Madsen, who plays his boss's wife. The title refers to not only the blistering Texas setting but the dangerous predicaments in which Johnson always finds himself.

Finally, *What's Eating Gilbert Grape?* (1993), a comedy-drama set in the fictional Iowa city of Endora, was filmed in Manor, another small town just east of Austin. The Grape family house, which burns to the ground, was on Hodde Lane outside Pflugerville, and the picturesque town square scene was filmed just southeast of Manor in the town of Lockhart.

Mack's Squat and Gobble Barbeque
4010 Farm-to-Market Road 2673, Canyon Lake

This small diner, located west of Highway 35, which connects Austin and San Antonio, was where fugitive Kevin Costner and T. J. Lowther, who plays Phillip, the boy he kidnaps, stop to eat in *A Perfect World*. Called Dottie's Squat and Gobble (one of critic Roger Ebert's all-time favorite names), it was here that a waitress, played by Linda Hart, seduces Costner while Phillip waits outside.

The barbeque is open seven days a week during the spring and summer and on Fridays, Saturdays, and Sunday during the winter months. From Highway 35 go west on 306 until you reach Farm-to-Market Road 2673. The restaurant is two miles west of the town of Sattler and on the south side of Canyon Lake.

San Antonio

San Antonio's most famous landmark, the Alamo, has been highlighted in at least a dozen features, but since Texans consider it a shrine, filming inside has very rarely been allowed. *Cloak and Dagger* (1984) had to re-create the Alamo tour on a Universal Studios soundstage. And the tour in *Pee-wee's Big Adventure* (1985) was filmed at the San Fernando Mission north of Los Angeles.

Since 1911 the story of the siege and fall of the Alamo has been told several times. Ironically, the most famous version, John Wayne's *The Alamo* (1960), was not filmed there but in a re-created Alamo Village in Brackettville (see below).

No major feature has tried to tell the Alamo story since *Viva Max!*, a 1969 spoof, but the Alamo has served as a backdrop in *Wrong Is Right* (1982), where Sean Connery tries to protect a politician giving a speech from assassins. And although the Alamo itself did not appear in *Toy Soldiers* (1991), the post office across the street was transformed into Colombia's Palace of Justice, where convicted drug smugglers, trying to free a drug lord, mercilessly kill hostages.

San Antonio's other primary attraction, its river walk, was featured extensively in *Cloak and Dagger* and in the original 1972 version of *The Getaway*. In *Cloak and Dagger*, Henry Thomas, in his first feature role after playing Elliot in *E.T. The Extraterrestrial*, plays a youngster who likes to play spy games and becomes involved with real-life spies, who chase him through the walk. One of the dramatic confrontations between Thomas, his friend (played by Christina Nigra), and the spies was filmed at the sunken gardens of Brackenridge Park. Thomas's first imaginary spy adventure was filmed at the Tower Life Building in downtown San Antonio.

Eight Seconds (1994), Luke Perry's rodeo movie, was also filmed in the San Antonio area, but primarily on private ranches not accessible to the general public.

Alamo Village
seven miles north of Brackettville on Farm-to-Market Road 674

This western town and movie set, located 120 miles west of San Antonio, includes a full-scale replica of the Alamo and the village of San Antonio in 1836, built for the John Wayne 1960 epic *The Alamo*. Since 1982, over thirty productions have been filmed here,

Alamo Village, The Alamo *(courtesy Alamo Village)*

including *Barbarosa* (1982), the television miniseries *Lonesome Dove* and *Texas*, *Bad Girls* (1994), and *The Good Old Boys* (1995).

For hours and prices write to Alamo Village, Box 528, Brackettville, Texas, 78832.

Houston

In the 1980s one of the Houston area's most popular attractions was Gilley's, the enormous honky-tonk featured in *Urban Cowboy* (1980), starring John Travolta and Debra Winger. The building, at 4500 Spencer Highway in suburban Pasadena, burned down in 1990, and the Pasadena Chamber of Commerce reports that "all, except the memory, is gone."

Terms of Endearment, which was voted Best Picture of 1983 and earned Academy Awards for James L. Brooks (Best Director), Shirley MacLaine (Best Actress), and Jack Nicholson (Best Supporting Actor), was filmed in several locations, including two houses on Locke Lane in the Avalon section of Houston, where MacLaine and Nicholson live as neighbors.

The beach scenes, in which a drunken Nicholson takes MacLaine on their first date (after lunching at Brennan's Restaurant at 3300 Smith Street), were filmed on the East Beach on Galveston. It was here that Nicholson shows MacLaine how to drive with his feet (in *Terms of Endearment*) and both end up in the gulf.

Robocop 2 (1990), ranked by the National Committee on Television Violence as the fifth most violent film of all time, was filmed in several locations in downtown Houston, which served as "Old Detroit." (Dallas had that distinction for the first *Robocop*.) The locations include the Wortham Theater Center, at 500 Texas Avenue, and the George R. Brown Convention Center, on 1001 Avenue of the Americas, which were used for the exteriors and interiors of the "Civic Centrum," where Robocop has a shoot-out with his mechanical counterpart; the Cullen Center at 1600 Smith, where the fictional corporation OCP's "Old Man's" offices were installed; and the abandoned Jefferson Davis Hospital on the Allen Parkway, which served as the illicit drug factory. A number of downtown Houston street scenes were also featured in the movie.

Blind Fury (1988), an action-adventure that stars Rutger Hauer as a blind martial arts expert who takes on drug dealers, was also filmed in Houston (which doubled as Miami and Reno), but the Houston Film Commission could not recall any clearly identifiable locations tourists might be interested in.

Rush (1991) was also shot in greater Houston, but the Houston Film Commission was equally hard-pressed to think of locations tourists would want to see, with the possible exception of the Swinging Door, a restaurant and honky-tonk in rural Richmond, about twenty-five miles from downtown Houston. News articles have identified some locations: the Houston Ship Channel, refineries in suburban Pasadena, and the Watergate Yachting Center in League City.

Sidekicks (1993), an action-comedy starring Beau Bridges, Joe Piscopo, and Chuck Norris, and *Reality Bites* (1994) were filmed in Tranquility Park, downtown. And Houston's most famous attraction, the Astrodome, was featured in *The Bad News Bears* (1976) and *Brewster McCloud* (1970).

Figure 3 Ranch
Claude

The closing scenes of *Indiana Jones and the Last Crusade* (1988), in which Harrison Ford and Sean Connery ride off into the sunset in a blaze of glory, were filmed on this guest ranch, located off I-27, about a one-hour-and-fifteen-minute drive south of Amarillo. Advertising itself as an opportunity to get a taste of what the Old West was like, the ranch offers a cowboy breakfast or dinner at a campsite that is accessible after a twenty-minute ride across the prairie on mule-drawn wagons.

The ranch is open between April and October. Write to Cowboy Morning/Evening, Route 1, Box 69, Claude, Texas, 79019-9712.

Other Texas Location Sites

• *A Perfect World* was also filmed at the state penitentiary in Huntsville, the prison from which Kevin Costner escapes. The denouement was filmed on a private ranch in Bastrop County.

• *Leap of Faith* (1992), which starred Steve Martin as a con artist–faith healer who undergoes a renewal of faith, was filmed in downtown Plainview. The Quik Lunch Cafe, at 108 East Seventh, was one of the Plainview sites. Many of the scenes of fictional Rustwater, Kansas, were filmed on Broadway in the downtown area of Groom, an Amarillo suburb. Martin's enormous revival tent was also constructed in Groom.

• *Fandango* (1984) was filmed in Presidio and Marfa, which was also the site of *Giant* (1956).

• The Lavaca County Courthouse served as they mythical Lanville County Courthouse in *The Best Little Whorehouse in Texas* (1982).

Chapter 7

The Upper Midwest

Minnesota

Jim's Coffee Shop and Bakery
328 Central Avenue East, Minneapolis

Marisa Tomei and Rosie Perez play waitresses, and Christian Slater a reclusive busboy, at this coffee shop in the old-fashioned love story *Untamed Heart* (1993). The movie centers around Tomei and Slater's relationship, which begins after Slater rescues her from would-be rapists in a park on Main Street along Minneapolis's Riverplace.

Jim's Coffee Shop, Untamed Heart *(courtesy Minnesota Film Board)*

IDS Crystal Court
corner of Seventh Street and Nicollet Avenue, Minneapolis

The opening scenes of the *Mary Tyler Moore Show* (1970–77), in which a jubilant Moore flings her beret into the air, were filmed outside this fifty-seven-story skyscraper in downtown Minneapolis. The series, of course, was filmed on a Los Angeles soundstage, and officials of the Minnesota Film Board suspect that this may have been one of the few times Moore actually came to town.

The Victorian mansion where Moore and Valerie Harper (who plays Rhoda Morgenstern) live is located on the southwest corner of Kenwood Parkway and West 22nd Street, near Lake of the Isles. In later seasons, Moore moves out of the house and into an apartment building at Cedar Riverside, close to the University of Minnesota campus.

1100 Block of Hyacinth Street
East Saint Paul

In *Grumpy Old Men* (1993), Walter Matthau and Jack Lemmon play two codgers and next-door neighbors who have been fighting with each other for more than fifty years. When a free-spirited widow, Ann-Margret, moves into the neighborhood, Matthau and Lemmon find themselves competing for her affections.

The story is set in Wabasha, Minnesota, but the movie was not filmed there. Matthau's, Lemmon's, and Ann-Margret's homes were located on the 1100 block of East St. Paul's Hyacinth Street; and Lemmon and Matthau's ice shanties were on Lake Rebecca, a regional park about a forty-five-minute drive from Minneapolis. (In real life, shanties are not permitted on the lake.)

Interior scenes were filmed at Paisley Park, Prince's recording and movie studio in Minneapolis. The nearby town of Faribault was used for the downtown Wabasha scenes, and Memorial Lutheran Church, 1212 Earl Street, Center City, was the site of the wedding at the movie's end.

Palisade Head
located off Highway 61, just northeast of Silver Bay

The climax of *The Good Son* (1993), in which Wendy Crewson is forced to choose between her own son, the evil Macauley Culkin, and her nephew, Elijah Wood, was filmed on these cliffs in the southern end of Tettegouche State Park, overlooking Lake Superior. The wilderness site, called Palisade Head, is accessible to tourists. To reach Palisade Head from Duluth, take Highway 61 north about sixty miles to Silver Bay. Continue past Silver Bay about two miles until you reach the Palisade Head exit. There is an access road to the right that will take you up to the top of the cliff.

Palisade Head, The Good Son *(courtesy Minnesota Department of Tourism)*

Other Minnesota Filming Sites

• *The Mighty Ducks* (1992), which starred Emilio Estevez as a trial lawyer sentenced to coach peewee hockey, was filmed at Peavey Park, an ice rink in South Minneapolis, St. Paul's Rice Park, the Minneapolis Skyways, the IDS Building, the Met Center (Bloomington's sports arena), and in Elliot Park, an inner-city neighborhood in Minneapolis. *Mighty Ducks 2* (1994) used four community ice rinks, including the New Hope Ice Area, at 4949 Louisiana Avenue North, in New Hope, and Parade Ice Garden, on 600 Kenwood Parkway, Minneapolis (also used in the original), and the Mall of America, the country's largest mall.

• *Iron Will* (1994), the story of a 1917 dogsled race from Winnipeg to St. Paul, filmed its wilderness scenes on the north shore of Lake Superior and Gooseberry Falls State Park. Other locations include old Central High School (now the Central Administration Building), 200 East Second Street, Duluth, which served as Winnipeg City Hall; the former Greasolon Plaza Hotel in Duluth; and the Two Harbor Depot, which served as the St. Paul finish line.

• *Airport* (1970) was filmed at the Minneapolis–St. Paul International Airport.

• *Purple Rain* (1984) was shot at thirty-two locations in and around Minneapolis, including Prince's motion picture and recording studio, Paisley Park. Paisley Park, located in suburban Chanhassen, does not offer tours.

• *Little Big League* (1994), the story of a twelve-year-old baseball fan (played by Luke Edwards) who inherits the Minnesota Twins from his grandfather (Jason Robards), was filmed at the bridge over Minnehaha Creek, in Minnehaha Park in Minneapolis, where Edwards and his friends fished; in Groveland Park Elementary School, on St. Clair Avenue in St. Paul; at the Valley Fair Amusement Park in suburban Shakopee; and at the Twins' stadium, the HHH Metrodome.

Wisconsin

University of Wisconsin
Madison

In *Back to School* (1986), Rodney Dangerfield plays a self-made millionaire who goes back to school to set an example for his son (Keith Gordon), who is contemplating dropping out. Most of the scenes of the fictional Grand Lakes University were filmed on the Madison campus, although the dorms, classrooms, and natatorium were filmed in Los Angeles.

The university's Bascom Hill also appeared briefly in *For Keeps* (1988), which starred Molly Ringwald as a pregnant teenager who attends classes at Wisconsin.

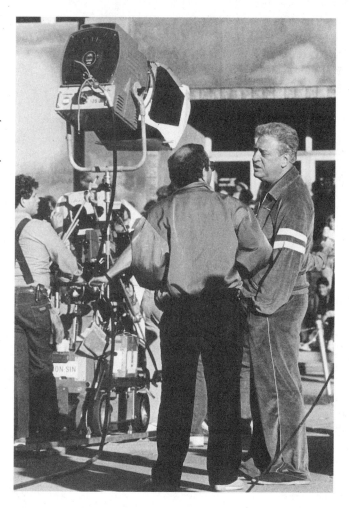

Rodney Dangerfield at the University of Wisconsin, during the filming of Back to School *(courtesy University of Wisconsin)*

County Stadium
Milwaukee

Major League (1989), a fantasy about a Cleveland Indians team winning a pennant, was filmed at Milwaukee's County Stadium, primarily because Cleveland's own stadium at the time was not cozy enough for the filmmaker's needs.

Other Movies Filmed in Wisconsin

• *Mrs. Soffel* (1984), starring Diane Keaton as a prison warden's wife who aids the escape of two criminals, was shot at the Mid-Continent Railroad Museum near Baraboo.

• *I Love Trouble* (1994), a romantic comedy starring Julia Roberts and Nick Nolte as rival newspaper reporters, was filmed at the state Capitol in Madison and a block away on King Street, where a car tries to run them over. Roberts's skinny-dipping scenes were filmed at Devil's Lake State Park in Baraboo.

• Parts of the dogsled race in *Iron Will* (1994) were filmed in the Superior Brute River Forest.

• *Meet the Applegates* (1991) was filmed in Appleton.

• *The Betsy* (1977) was shot at the former American Motors Plant, now a strip mall on Capitol Drive in Milwaukee.

• *Winning*, a 1969 melodrama starring Paul Newman as a race-car driver, was filmed at Elcarte Lake.

Michigan

Detroit

Hoffa (1992), starring Jack Nicholson in the title role and Danny DeVito as Bobby Ciaro, Hoffa's fictitious right-hand man, was filmed at several locations around Detroit, including Cobo Arena, where the 1957 teamsters convention that elected Hoffa was re-created; the Detroit Public Library, which was portrayed as the Washington Senate Office Building in Washington; the Detroit Produce Terminal, where a clash between pro-union and anti-union forces was staged; a newsroom of the *Detroit News*, on 615 West Lafayette Boulevard; and the Kroeger Warehouse, on the waterfront, where several laundry buildings were built under the Ambassador Bridge.

DeVito, who also directed *Hoffa*, returned to Detroit for Penny Marshall's *Renaissance Man* (1994), this time playing an advertising executive who is fired after he is caught in a huge traffic jam on Jefferson Avenue and offends an important client. DeVito's advertising office was at the Renaissance Center, a huge office building, hotel, and shopping complex on East Jefferson. Other scenes were filmed at the Olde Brokerage on Griswold and Lafayette, which served as DeVito's unemployment office, and at Tiger Stadium (which was also seen briefly in the 1994 biopic *Cobb*).

Harrison Ford's trial in *Presumed Innocent* (1990) was filmed inside the Wayne County Building, at 600 Randolph, which was also briefly featured as the site of Christian Slater and Patricia Arquette's wedding in *True Romance* (1993). In that movie, Slater and Arquette play lovers who find themselves in unexpected possession of a suitcase of Mob contraband. Additional scenes were shot at the downtown police station, at 1300 Beaubien, and at the old Packard Plant, on East Grand Boulevard and Mount Elliot, where Dennis Hopper, who plays Slater's father, works. The trailer park on the Detroit River, where Hopper lives, was created specially for the movie.

Roger and Me (1989), Michael Moore's comedic documentary about the suffering of Flint residents when General Motors closed its plants, filmed in both Flint and in Detroit at GM headquarters, on 3044 West Grand Boulevard at Woodward.

Parts of *Beverly Hills Cop* (1984), *Beverly Hills Cop 2* (1987), and *Action Jackson* (1988) were also filmed in Detroit.

Other Movies Filmed in Michigan

• The railroad station in Niles, on 598 Dey Street, was used for both the ending of *Only the Lonely* (1989)—in which John Candy stops a train bound for New York with Ally Sheedy aboard and finally commits to her—and for a scene in *Midnight Run* (1988) in which FBI agent Yaphet Kotto boarded the train in search of Robert De Niro and Charles Grodin, who have disembarked a few stops earlier.

• *Somewhere in Time* (1980), a fantasy about a playwright who travels back in time to see a lost love, was filmed at the Grand Hotel on Mackinac Island.

• The plane crash in *Die Hard II* (1990) was staged on the tarmac of the Alpena airport.

• *Prancer* (1969) was shot in the little town of Three Oaks.

Chapter 8

The Midwest

Illinois

Chicago

Loyola University of Chicago
6525 North Sheridan Road

The Jesuit Residence on the Loyola campus served as the university hospital in the 1990 drama *Flatliners*. The movie begins with a helicopter shot showing Kiefer Sutherland at the southeast end of Cudahy Library, proclaiming, "It's a great day to die," and goes on to show how medical students Sutherland, Julia Roberts, Kevin Bacon, William Baldwin, and Oliver Platt deliberately kill themselves, then bring themselves back to life at the last minute so they can experience the afterlife.

(*Note:* The scenes depicting a wild party on the hospital steps were filmed at Chicago's Museum of Science and Industry, on 5700 South Lake Shore Drive.)

Wrigley Field
1060 West Addison Street

Wrigley Field played itself in *Rookie of the Year* (1993), a baseball fantasy about a klutzy twelve-year-old (Thomas Ian Nicholas) who, after an arm injury heals improperly, is able to throw a 120-mile-per-hour fastball and land a contract with the Chicago Cubs.

Wrigley also played itself in *The Babe* (1993). John Goodman, as Babe Ruth, re-creates the Bambino's "called" home-run shot in the 1932 World Series here. The stadium was also dressed up to appear as both New York's Polo Grounds and Yankee Stadium, where Ruth primarily played.

The tryouts in *A League of Their Own* (1992) were also filmed at Wrigley, and the park has appeared in several other movies, including *Opportunity Knocks* (1990), *Uncle Buck* (1989), *Ferris Bueller's Day Off* (1986), and *About Last Night* (1986). Movie characters sometimes conveniently reside in the apartments across the street, where they watch games from rooftops. Kathleen Turner, playing the title character in *V. I. Warshawski* (1992), lived in an apartment on Sheffield, as did Aidan Quinn in *Blink* (1994), and Kevin Meaney in the short-lived TV series *Uncle Buck*, based on the movie of the same name.

Bento Restaurant
3369 North Clark

For *Only the Lonely* (1991), Bento was transformed into O'Neils, the Irish hangout where Maureen O'Hara toasts Ally Sheedy and John Candy's friends bring a corpse in for one last celebration. Bento is located at the corner of Roscoe Street, directly across the street from the site of the killing of a little girl in *The Untouchables* (1987).

Candy and O'Hara's house in *Only the Lonely* was just around the corner from the bar—at 930 West Roscoe. *Only the Lonely* also holds the distinction of being the last movie to film at old Comiskey Park—just a few days before it was demolished to build a new stadium.

The Pump Room
1301 North State Parkway

This swanky supper club, often frequented by Chicago celebrities, was where John Candy introduces his girlfriend, Ally Sheedy, to his domineering mother, Maureen O'Hara, in *Only the Lonely* and where Dolly Parton and James Woods have their first date in *Straight Talk* (1992).

The Pump Room is located in the Omni Ambassador East Hotel, which was the home of a privileged high school sophomore (played by Chris Makepeace) in *My Bodyguard* (1980) and one of the locations in the Hitchcock classic *North by Northwest* (1959). In that movie, Cary Grant visits Eva Marie Saint, who is staying at the hotel. The Omni also doubled as the Los Angeles hotel where the Chicago Cubs stayed in *Rookie of the Year*.

Mother's
26 West Division Street

Rob Lowe, Demi Moore, Jim Belushi, and Elizabeth Perkins hung out at this nightclub in *About Last Night*, a comedy-drama based on David Mamet's play *Sexual Perversity in Chicago*. It was also where Jackie Gleason drinks in *Nothing in Common* (1986).

Drake Hotel
140 East Walton Place

Key scenes in *Hero* (1992), starring Dustin Hoffman, Geena Davis, and Andy Garcia, were filmed on the roof and both inside and on the ledge outside Suite 1030, where Hoffman convinces Garcia not to commit suicide. The contemporary comedy meditates on the meaning of heroism, and in an intriguing role reversal, Hoffman plays a petty crook who heroically saves several passengers aboard a crashed airliner, while Garcia, a onetime war hero and now a drifter, steals the credit.

The Drake also appeared in *The Blues Brothers* (1980) and in *Risky Business* (1983), which was filmed in the hotel's Palm Court and Gold Coast Room.

Drake Hotel, Hero
(courtesy The Drake)

Water Tower Place
835 North Michigan Avenue

In *Class* (1983), Jacqueline Bisset seduces her son's prep-school roommate (Andrew McCarthy) in the Water Tower Place's glass elevator.

Merchandise Mart
between Wells and Orleans streets

The mart, which is one of the world's largest commercial buildings—it spans two square city blocks—was used for the exterior shots of Hudsucker Industries in *The Hudsucker Proxy* (1994).

Wrigley Building
400 North Michigan Avenue

Tom Hanks's office in *Nothing in Common* was in the Wrigley Building. Across the street from the Tribune Tower, it is also near the Michigan Avenue bridge over the Chicago River, where Kevin Costner asks Sean Connery to join him in *The Untouchables*. It is two blocks from the Irv Kupcinet Bridge on Wabash (named for the former *Chicago Sun-Times* columnist), where Dolly Parton has her happy reunion with James Woods at the conclusion of *Straight Talk*.

Navy Pier
600 East Grand Avenue

The auditorium in this popular Chicago attraction was transformed into the Atlantic City casino where Tom Cruise wins the major pool tournament in *The Color of Money* (1986).

Leo Burnett Building
35 West Wacker (at Dearborn)

In *Curly Sue* (1991), Kelly Lynch's law practice was in this building, as was Kevin Bacon's advertising office in *She's Having a Baby* (1988).

(*Note:* A few blocks west of here, at the intersection of Wacker and Wabash, was the site of the *Red Heat* (1988) bus-crash scene, in which Arnold Schwarzenegger and James Belushi, in pursuit of a Russian drug dealer in a "borrowed" bus, crash through a fountain and then drive into a building by Dearborn and Jackson.)

Chicago Theater
175 North State Street (at Lake Street)

In *Midnight Run* (1988), FBI agents take Charles Grodin and Robert De Niro into custody as they exit a bus across the street from the Chicago Theater, only to lose them when mob snipers, positioned on the theater's roof, start firing at Grodin.

The lavishly decorated interior of the theater served as the interior of the Lexington Hotel, where De Niro, playing Al Capone, lived in *The Untouchables*.

James R. Thompson Center
(formerly State of Illinois Center)
100 West Randolph Street

This immense glass-and-steel building, which houses Illinois government offices, served as the site of the climactic shoot-out in *Running Scared* (1986), which starred Billy Crystal and Gregory Hines; and the offices of the federal prosecutors in *The Music Box* (1989). In the latter movie, Jessica Lange plays a Chicago lawyer who defends her father against charges he was a Nazi war criminal.

City Hall
121 North LaSalle (or 112 North Clark Street)

Opportunity Knocks (1990), *Continental Divide* (1981), *The Untouchables* (1987), *Curly Sue* (1991), and *Backdraft* (1991) were all filmed in Chicago City Hall, but the building may be most famous for the dramatic scenes in *The Fugitive* (1993), in which Harrison Ford, searching for the one-armed man, is unexpectedly spotted by Tommy Lee Jones. Ford makes his escape by merging with the crowd at a St. Patrick's Day parade being held on a three-block stretch of Dearborn. (The same parade, by the way, was filmed for *Blink*, released in 1994.)

The German-American Day parade in *Ferris Bueller's Day Off* (1986) and the parade honoring a firefighter who loses his life in *Backdraft* were also held in the same general area.

Richard J. Daley Civic Center
50 West Washington (at Dearborn)

Directly across the street from City Hall is the thirty-one-story Daley Civic Center, home of many municipal courts and offices. In

The Blues Brothers (1980), Dan Aykroyd and John Belushi drive their Bluesmobile through the building's plate-glass window, across the lobby, and out another window before screaming to a stop in front of the Cook County Building, where they pay an overdue tax assessor's bill.

Chicago Cultural Center
78 East Washington (at Randolph)

The center's rooftop was the setting of the deadly confrontation between Kevin Costner (Eliot Ness) and Billy Drago (Frank Nitti, Al Capone's number-one killer) in *The Untouchables*. The center also served as the exterior of the courthouse in *Natural Born Killers* (1994) and as the setting of an elegant party in *The Babe* (1993).

One South Wacker Building
at Madison

Alec Baldwin had an office here in *Prelude to a Kiss* (1992).

Rookery Building
LaSalle and Adams streets

The exterior of this Chicago landmark served as the exterior of Chicago police headquarters in *The Untouchables* and Eddie Bracken's toy store in *Home Alone II* (1992).

Union Station
210 South Canal Street

At least six movies set in Chicago—*The Sting* (1973), *Code of Silence* (1985), *Raw Deal* (1986), *The Package* (1989), *Things Change* (1989), and *I Love Trouble* (1994)—were filmed here, but Union Station is memorable primarily for two films. In *Silver Streak* (1976), the train, called the "Silver Streak," was supposed to have crashed through the station (although the crash was actually staged in an airplane hangar at Lockheed Aircraft in Los Angeles). More memorably, Brian DePalma filmed the climactic scene in *The Untouchables* here, with a teetering baby carriage caught in the crossfire between "the Untouchables" and Al Capone's men.

Roosevelt University
430 South Michigan Avenue

The university was used as the façade and lobby of Al Capone's main residence, the Lexington Hotel, in *The Untouchables*. The real Lexington had deteriorated to such an extent that it could not be used.

Buckingham Memorial Fountain
on Congress Street in Grant Park

This is the fountain seen in the opening credits of the Fox comedy *Married . . . With Children*. It was modeled after the Latona Fountain at Versailles but is twice its size.

(*Note:* Just south of the fountain, in Grant Park, is the diamond where James Belushi and Rob Lowe play softball in *About Last Night*.)

Chicago Hilton and Towers
720 South Michigan Avenue

The climax of *The Fugitive* was filmed here, and Carol Gifford, the hotel's director of public relations informs us: "Just about every square foot of the Chicago Hilton was on film—from the promenade roof overlooking the city to the Versailles-inspired Grand Ballroom to the state-of-the-art laundry facility. The end result was that the Chicago Hilton [was] featured on the silver screen for the last twenty-five minutes of the fast action-packed drama and chase scenes, and most importantly, 'the Fugitive' was caught in the hotel's laundry department!"

The Conrad Hilton Suite of the hotel also served as Macauley Culkin and his family's New York Plaza Hotel room in *Home Alone II*. At the end of the movie, Culkin and his siblings wake up on Christmas day and receive toys from Eddie Bracken.

The hotel's grand ballroom was also used for a presidential banquet in *The Package* (1989), and a demonstration against a visiting Soviet premier was staged across the street at the edge of Grant Park, the same location as the infamous riots during the 1968 Democratic Convention.

The Chicago Hilton, courtesy the Chicago Hilton

Blackstone Hotel
636 South Michigan Avenue

The hotel, which is across the street from the Hilton, doubled as Tom Cruise's Atlantic City hotel in *The Color of Money*. Scenes from *The Hudsucker Proxy* (1994) were also filmed in the hotel's Crystal Ballroom.

Field Museum of Natural History
1200 South Lake Shore Drive

The museum served as Gene Hackman's Washington, D.C., government offices in *The Package* (1989). Is also appeared in some of the walk-and-talk scenes in *She's Having a Baby* (1988).

Maxwell Precinct Station
corner of 14th and Morgan

The exterior of this police station was the *Hill Street Blues* station, the popular NBC cop show that aired from 1981 to 1987.

Hill Street Blues *police station*

University of Chicago

In *When Harry Met Sally* (1989), Billy Crystal meets Meg Ryan in the main quadrangle off University Avenue at 58th Avenue. It was by that gate that Ryan gives him a ride to New York.

The John Crerar Library, at the university's medical center, was also featured briefly in *The Fugitive*. The hospital was identified as Chicago Memorial Hospital and was where Harrison Ford had his practice.

Other Chicago Locations

• The Art Institute of Chicago, on South Michigan Avenue doubled as the fictional Cole's Department store in the 1994 remake of *Miracle on 34th Street*.

• In *The Untouchables*, the home of Kevin Costner (Elliot Ness) was on 22nd Place and Hoyne. Sean Connery's apartment was on the corner of Racine and Harrison.

• Madeline Stowe's apartment in *Blink* (1994), the Flat Iron Building near the intersection of Milwaukee North and Damen avenues, is an office building in real life. The Illinois Masonic Hospital, where she is cured of her blindness, is at 836 West Wellington.

• Jessica Lange's apartment in *Men Don't Leave* (1990), supposedly in Baltimore, was actually at 510 West Belmont, at the corner of North Sheridan Road.

• Robert De Niro's graystone apartment in *Mad Dog and Glory* (1993) was on the 500 block of West Belden in Lincoln Park.

• The firehouse in *Backdraft* (1991) was located at Archer and Sacramento streets. Robert De Niro's Chinatown firehouse offices were at 22nd and Rinston.

• In *Betrayed* (1988), Debra Winger, thinking she is preventing a political assassination, kills Tom Berenger at a construction site that is now the R. R. Donnelly Building, on 77 Wacker Drive. The bank holdup in the movie was staged at the Midcity Bank on Halsted and Madison.

• In *Risky Business* (1983), the Porsche owned by Tom Cruise's father slips into the marina in Belmont Harbor, where Belmont meets Lake Michigan.

• The football stadium at Lane Technical High, on 2501 West Addison, served as the scene of the climactic game in *Wildcats* (1986), in which Goldie Hawn coaches the football team of an inner-city school (Central High). Lane also became Prescott High, the model suburban school that Hawn leaves. The Central High football field was built on two nearly abandoned city blocks.

• The lobby of 135 South LaSalle Building served as the entry to New York's *Daily News* in *The Public Eye* (1992).

• Tom Selleck's office in *Folks* (1992) was at 190 South La Salle.

• St. Vincent DePaul Church, at 1010 West Webster, and the adjacent parking lot, just south of DePaul University's Alumni Hall, were turned into Babe Ruth's boyhood home, Baltimore's St. Mary's Home for Boys, in *The Babe* (1993).

• Scenes in *The Color of Money* were also shot at St. Paul's Billiards, at 1415 West Fullerton (Tom Cruise is beaten up there); North Center Bowling Alleys, at 4017 North Lincoln (where Forest Whitaker tries to hustle the hustlers and Newman and Cruise get in a fight); Chris' Billiards, at 4637 North Milwaukee; and Fitzgerald's, a bar at 6615 Roosevelt Road in the suburb of Berwyn, where Tom Cruise and Paul Newman first meet. Fitzgerald's was also transformed into the Tear Drop Lounge, where Elisabeth Shue belts out the blues in *Adventures in Babysitting* (1987).

• The Green Mill Lounge, at 4802 North Broadway, a jazz club and popular tourist attraction that was once reportedly Al Capone's favorite meeting place, was the scene of a mob family's meal in *Next of Kin* (1989) and was also featured in *V. I. Warshawski* (1992).

• In *The Package* (1989), the Cermak Road Bridge at Canal Street was transformed into a Berlin exchange point where Tommy Lee Jones is placed in the custody of Gene Hackman.

• The NBC medical drama *ER* uses as its hospital entrance the exterior of the University of Illinois-Chicago Hospital at 1740 West Taylor.

The Chicago Suburbs

The red-brick colonial where Macauley Culkin and his family lived in the 1990 blockbuster *Home Alone* and its 1992 sequel, *Home Alone 2*, has become a Chicago-area tourist attraction in its own right. Located at 671 Lincoln Avenue in Winnetka, the house is in what might be called John Hughes territory. Most of Hughes's films were filmed in Chicago's northside suburbs.

In addition to the house in Winnetka, Hughes has used the Winnetka Congregational Church, at 725 Pine, as the site of Kevin Bacon and Elizabeth McGovern's wedding in *She's Having a Baby* (1988); Old Niles East High School, on Lincoln Avenue in Skokie, as the high school in *Sixteen Candles* (1984); the former Main North High School on Dee Road in Des Plaines (now Central Management Services for the state of Illinois) as the high school in *The Breakfast Club* (1985) and *Ferris Bueller's Day Off* (1986); and New Trier Township High School West, on Happ Road in Northfield, is the school where John Candy drops his brother's children off in *Uncle Buck* (1989). The three gymnasiums inside were also converted into sets for *Uncle Buck*, *Sixteen Candles*, and *Curly Sue* (1991).

Hughes also selected two adjacent houses on Ashland Avenue in Evanston as the Mitchell and Wilson family homes in *Dennis the Menace* (1993). A house on nearby Lincoln Avenue in Evanston was used for the exterior of the Russell family home in *Uncle Buck*.

Other locations in the Chicago suburbs include:

• Northwestern University in Evanston, which has appeared in *Nothing in Common* (1986; Tom Hanks's girlfriend, Bess Armstrong, teaches in Annie May Swift Hall); *Major League* (1989; Tom Berenger does research in the Deering Library); *Dr. Detroit* (1983; Dan Aykroyd teaches in the Technological Institute); and *Class*

(1983; Andrew McCarthy and Rob Lowe's prep school scenes were filmed in Northwestern dorms);

• Evanston High School, where Thomas Ian Nicholas attends junior high in *Rookie of the Year* (1993);

• A house on Linden Street in Highland Park, where Tom Cruise lives in *Risky Business* (1983). The interiors of the house were re-created in the gym of Skokie's Old Niles East High;

• Lake Forest Academy, a private prep school where *Ordinary People*, named the Best Picture in 1980, was filmed extensively. The school also served as the site of the spring training workouts in *The Babe* and the German chalet where the peace terms are negotiated in *The Package*; and,

• Pulaski Woods, a park in Willow Springs, which stood in for West Germany's Black Forest in *The Package*.

In Wheaton, thirty miles west of Chicago, the Cantigny mansion, on One South 151 Winfield Road, the former property of *Chicago Tribune* publisher Robert McCormick, served as both Garry Marshall's estate in *A League of Their Own* (1992) and Lara Flynn Boyle's mansion in *Baby's Day Out* (1994). Nearby, in the town of Glen Ellyn, Glenbard High School served as Corey Haim's high school in *Lucas* (1986).

In Plainfield, thirty-five miles southwest of Chicago, a home on West Ottawa served as the family home Jessica Lange is forced to sell after being widowed in *Men Don't Leave* (1990).

And in Harvey, south of Chicago, the Dixie Mall suffers cosmetic damage when John Belushi and Dan Aykroyd drive their Bluesmobile through it in *The Blues Brothers* (1980).

Cantigny, A League of Their Own, Baby's Day Out *(courtesy DuPage Convention and Visitors Bureau)*

Other Illinois Movie Locations

• *Groundhog Day* (1993), a romantic comedy about a self-centered TV weatherman played by Bill Murray, was filmed in the tiny village of Woodstock, which served as Punxsutawney, Pennsylvania. Punxsutawney's Gobbler's Knob was re-created in the middle of Woodstock's town square.

• The Stateville Correctional Facility, on Highway 53 in Joliet, has been featured in several movies, including *The Blues Brothers* (where John Belushi is released early in the movie and where Belushi and Dan Aykroyd end up performing; *Red Heat*, where it served as a Russian prison in the opening scenes; and *Natural Born Killers*.

• Joliet's Rialto Theater was also transformed in *The Babe* into a luxurious hotel lobby where Babe Ruth gets his first taste of major league life on a Red Sox road trip.

• *The Babe* also filmed at Danville Stadium, which substituted for Pittsburgh's Forbes Field and Boston's Fenway Park. Boston's Green Monster was optically created in the film.

• The Norwood Historical Society served as the interior of Babe and Helen Ruth's country home in *The Babe*.

Indiana

University of Notre Dame
Notre Dame

Rudy (1993) was the story of Daniel "Rudy" Ruettiger, a five-foot-six mediocre student from a working-class background who realizes his lifelong ambition of attending Notre Dame and playing for the school's football team (albeit for twenty-seven seconds). The movie was filmed primarily at the university's Knute Rockne Stadium and at other locations around the campus. *Rudy* also filmed at Holy Cross University in Notre Dame, the junior college where Rudy (played by Sean Astin) is initially enrolled.

Indiana University
Bloomington

Breaking Away (1979), the story of a young cyclist trying to adjust to life after high school, was filmed in and around the Bloomington campus.

Hinckle Fieldhouse
Butler University, Indianapolis

This was the site of the final state playoffs in *Hoosiers* (1986), which was loosely based on the miracle Milan, Indiana, high school team of the 1950s. The movie, which starred Gene Hackman, Barbara Hershey, and Dennis Hopper, was set in the fictional town of Hickory, Indiana, and was filmed in Knightstown and New Richmond. The Knightstown Elementary School doubled as Hickory High's home court.

Bosse Field
in Garvin Park (between North Main and Heidelbach streets)
Evansville

Parts of the World Series in *A League of Their Own* (1992), including the climactic final game, were filmed on Bosse Field, the home of the University of Evansville's baseball team. The comedy-drama, which starred Geena Davis, Tom Hanks, Lori Petty, Madonna, and Rosie O'Donnell, and tells the story of women who play professional baseball during World War II, was based on the short-lived All-American Girls Professional Baseball League.

Huntingburg Stadium
First and Cherry streets, Huntingburg

The stadium, built in 1894 and now one of the oldest baseball stadiums in existence, was the home field of the Rockford Peaches in *A League of Their Own*. Fans trying to figure out which scenes were filmed where should note that Huntingburg Stadium has a wooden fence and dugout, while Bosse Field has a brick wall and brick dugout.

The stadium offers a tour between mid-April and the end of October. For details contact the Huntingburg Chamber of Commerce, 317 Fourth Street, Huntingburg, Indiana, 47542.

Bush Stadium
1501 West 16th Street, Indianapolis

The home of the minor league Indianapolis Indians doubled for both Comiskey Park and Cincinnati's Redland Field in *Eight Men Out* (1988), the story of eight 1919 Chicago White Sox players who take bribes to lose the World Series.

Frankfort Senior High School
One Marsh Road, Frankfort

In *Blue Chips* (1994), an examination of corruption in recruiting for college basketball, Nick Nolte's Western University Dolphins play their games in the school's five thousand-seat Everett Case Arena. In real life, the arena hosts the high school basketball team, the Frankfort Hot Dogs. The school is visible from Highway 28 in Frankfort.

Other Movies Filmed in Indiana

• *Winning* (1969), which starred Paul Newman as race-car driver Frank Capua, was filmed at the Indianapolis Motor Speedway.

• *Prancer* (1969), which starred Rebecca Harrell as a young girl who nurses a wounded reindeer she thinks belongs to Santa Claus, was filmed at director John Hancock's childhood home, the Hancock Fruit Farm in LaPorte.

• The courtroom scenes in which Woody Harrelson is tried as a serial killer in *Natural Born Killers* (1994) were filmed at the Hammond City Court, on 5925 Calumet Avenue in Hammond.

Ohio

Cleveland

The three movies most closely identified with Cleveland— *Howard the Duck* (1986), *Major League* (1989), and its sequel, *Major League II* (1994)—were not actually filmed there. *The Duck* was filmed in the San Francisco Bay area; *Major League*, primarily at Milwaukee's County Stadium, the home of the Milwaukee Brewers—the result of scheduling conflicts between the filmmakers and Municipal Stadium, the former home of the Cleveland Indians. For reasons that remain unclear the sequel was filmed in Baltimore, primarily at the Baltimore Orioles' park, Oriole Park in Camden Yards.

Major League does at least have nice establishing shots of Cleveland and of Municipal Stadium. With its story about an Indians team fighting for the pennant, it also gave long-suffering Cleveland fans something to hope for.

The Russian Orthodox wedding scene in the *Deer Hunter*, which won the Academy Award for Best Picture in 1978, was filmed at St. Theodosius Church, on 733 Starkweather Avenue in downtown Cleveland. Other scenes were filmed at Cleveland's Veterans

Administration Hospital and at LTV's (formerly U.S. Steel's) facility in the industrial Flats area.

Light of Day (1987), which starred Michael J. Fox and Joan Jett as sibling rock and rollers, was filmed at the Euclid Tavern at 11629 Euclid Avenue; at the Marshallan Company, a metal stamping plant in the Flats where Fox works; and at MacNeal Hospital.

A Christmas Story (1983), about an Indiana schoolboy's quest to get a rifle for Christmas, was filmed at a house on West 11th Street directly across from Rowley's Inn, and in Cleveland's Public Square, where a Christmas parade was held.

The sequel, *It Runs in the Family* (1994), which starred Charles Grodin, Kieran Culkin, and Mary Steenburgen, was filmed at the same house, Wilbur Wright Elementary School on Parkhurst Avenue, at Playhouse Square on Euclid Avenue, and on malls A and B, behind the federal courthouse downtown.

Paradise (1991), the story of a ten-year-old (Elijah Wood) who spends the summer with a childless couple (Melanie Griffith and Don Johnson), was filmed at Cleveland's art deco Greyhound Bus Station, at the Mather mansion on the Cleveland State University campus on Euclid Avenue (which served as Elijah Wood's private school), and at an apartment on the 3200 block of Prospect Street (Wood and Griffith's).

Slaughter of the Innocence (1992), which starred Scott Glenn as an FBI agent who enlists his psychic son to track down a killer, was filmed at the North Point Office Building, at the corner of East Ninth and Lakeside (which served as FBI headquarters), Mayfield Cemetery, at the corner of Mayfield Road and Murray Hill (where President McKinley is buried), and at a private home in Shaker Heights.

Double Dragon (1994), which was based on the popular video game, was filmed on the Cuyahoga River downtown, along the Flats, between the mouth of the Cuyahoga River and the LTV plant. In the movie, which starred Robert Patrick and Alyssa Milano, the river doubled as a flooded Hollywood Boulevard after an earthquake destroys Los Angeles in the year 2011.

The Former Ohio State Reformatory
Mansfield

This gloomy Gothic prison, which is halfway between Cleveland and Columbus and visible from Route 30, was used for the filming of *An Innocent Man* (1989), which starred Tom Selleck and F. Murray Abraham, and *The Shawshank Redemption* (1994), in which Tim Robbins plays a mild-mannered banker wrongly accused of killing his wife and her lover. The prison was closed permanently in 1990 after federal courts ruled the facility inhumane.

Cincinnati

Cincinnati's locations include:

• The Greater Cincinnati Airport, where, in *Rain Man* (1988), Dustin Hoffman has a panic attack, forcing Tom Cruise to take him back to Los Angeles by car;

• The lobby of the Dixie Terminal Building (Cincinnati's bus station), on 120 East Fourth Street, which was transformed into Cincinnati Trust, the bank where Cruise learns the identity of the beneficiary of his father's will;

• A house on Beechcrest Lane in suburban East Walnut Hills, where, in *Rain Man*, Cruise's father lives;

• Cincinnati's historic Roebling Suspension Bridge, which fascinates Hoffman and was seen in all the trailers for the movie;

The Roebling Suspension Bridge that fascinated Dustin Hoffman in Rain Man *(courtesy Greater Cincinnati Convention and Visitors Bureau)*

• Tyler Davidson Fountain on Fountain Square, seen in the opening credits of both the original and the reincarnation of the TV sitcom *WKRP in Cincinnati*;

• Cincinnati's former art deco train station, which is now the Museum Center at Union Terminal, on 1301 Western Avenue. In *A Rage in Harlem* (1991), Gregory Hines and Forest Whitaker go there to get money from a locker, and Whitaker gets on a train to follow Robin Givens;

• Washington Park Elementary School, at 13th and Race, where Jodie Foster picks up her son, Adam Hann-Byrd, in *Little Man Tate* (1991); and an apartment on 12th and Vine, where she lives;

• Norwood Middle School gym, site of a fight scene in which Tom Selleck's character kills another inmate in *An Innocent Man*;

• Main Street—in Over-the-Rhine, a section of town between 12th and Liberty—which was used for New York street scenes in both *A Rage in Harlem* and *The Public Eye* (1992) and for Chicago street scenes in *Eight Men Out*;

• Arnold's Bar and Grill on Eighth and Main; Stenger's Cafe on Vine Street; and a private house on Mooney Street in *City of Hope* (1991); and

• Main Street in suburban Lebanon, where, in *Milk Money* (1994), Melanie Griffith tries to hustle customers and Ed Harris later falls in love with her. The climactic 1950s sock hop was filmed in the gymnasium of Kilgour Elementary School in Mount Lookout.

Other Locations in Ohio

• *Teachers* (1984), a black comedy that starred Nick Nolte as a burned-out teacher, was filmed at the now-closed Central High School on Washington Street in Columbus.

• *Little Man Tate* also filmed at several Columbus locations, including the Wexner Center for the Performing Arts on the Ohio State Campus and the Clarion Motel on South High Street (which served as the Florida motel where Jodie Foster and Debi Mazar stay). Additional scenes were shot at Miami University in Oxford, where, in the movie, Adam Hann-Byrd attends classes.

• *Mischief* (1984), a high school comedy that starred Doug McKeon, Catherine Mary Stewart, Kelly Preston, and Chris Nash, filmed at the Nelsonville Public Square. The gym of Columbus's Hamilton High served as Nelsonville High, while the façade of Liberty-Union High in Baltimore, Ohio, was used for exteriors.

• The historic Murphy Theater in Wilmington was where, in *Lost in Yonkers* (1993), David Straithairn works and Mercedes Ruehl goes to escape the severity of life with her steely mother.

Chapter 9

The Southern States

Louisiana

Oak Alley Plantation
3645 Los Angeles Highway 18, Vacherie

The plantation, which was built in 1839 and is noted for its quarter-mile alley of twenty-eight sheltering oaks over 250 years old, served as Brad Pitt's family home in *Interview With the Vampire* (1994). It is also where Ally Sheedy first encounters her future in-laws in *Heart of Dixie* (1989).

The plantation is located halfway between New Orleans and Baton Rouge and is open for tours daily.

Oak Alley Plantation, Interview With the Vampire *(courtesy Oak Alley Plantation)*

Baton Rouge

Baton Rouge film sites include:

- Tiger Stadium at Louisiana State University and Mumford Stadium at Southern University in *Everybody's All American* (1988);
- The thirty-four-story state capitol, where fifteen hundred students carry torches in a 1956 pep rally for that movie and Paul Newman plays Gov. Earl Long in *Blaze*;
- Zeezee Gardens, a bar on Perkins Road in South Baton Rouge, featured in *sex, lies and videotape* (1988); and
- The Charbonnet, an antebellum mansion on Old Perkins Road where Jackie Gleason lives in *The Toy* (1983).

The Long Hot Summer (1958), which starred Orson Welles, Paul Newman, and Joanne Woodward, was filmed in the town of Clinton, about thirty miles north of Baton Rouge. Several scenes were filmed at the East Feliciana Parish courthouse (also seen in the 1971 Cicely Tyson–Paul Winfield film *Sounder*) and at the St. Andrew's Episcopal Church. Orson Welles's home was on False River Road just outside the town of New Roads.

Natchitoches

The Natchitoches Parish Tourist Commission publishes a brochure and map of the seventeen locations seen in *Steel Magnolias* (1989), which starred Sally Field, Dolly Parton, Shirley MacLaine, Daryl Hannah, Olympia Dukakis, and Julia Roberts. Write to the Commission at P.O. Box 411, Natchitoches, Louisiana, 71458.

Jennings and Lake Arthur

The Jeff Davis Parish Tourist Commission also makes available a list of locations in Jennings and Lake Arthur for *Passion Fish* (1992), John Sayles's film about a paralyzed soap opera actress (Mary McDonnell) who is attended by a nurse (Alfre Woodard) with problems of her own. For information send a self-addressed stamped envelope to P.O. Box 1207, Jennings, Louisiana, 70546.

Houmas House Plantation
on the River Road, Burnside

This 1840 Greek Revival mansion, located about an hour's drive west of New Orleans, was the setting for *Hush . . . Hush Sweet Charlotte* (1965), starring Bette Davis and Olivia de Havilland. The plantation is open daily for tours.

New Orleans

Antoine's Restaurant
713 St. Louis Street

Antoine's has appeared in three of New Orleans's biggest movies. In *The Pelican Brief* (1993), Julia Roberts and her lover law-school professor, Sam Shepard, dine at Antoine's just before Shepard is killed in a car explosion outside the restaurant. (The explosion was actually staged in New Orleans's warehouse district.) In *The Big Easy* (1986), Ellen Barkin is eating dinner at Antoine's when she gets the call that her lover, Dennis Quaid, has been arrested for bribery. And in *JFK* (1991), Kevin Costner, playing New Orleans district attorney Jim Garrison, has a memorable confrontation in the restaurant with John Candy, who plays a slimy lawyer.

Gallier Hall
545 St. Charles Avenue (in Lafayette Square)

New Orleans's former city hall, named for the architect who brought the Greek Revival style to the city, was the setting of Caspar's Great Room, where Gabriel Byrne confronts Jon Polito (who plays gangster Johnny Caspar) in *Miller's Crossing* (1989).

The exterior and foyer of Caspar's house were filmed at Louise S. McGehee School, on 2343 Prytania Street.

Maple Leaf Bar
8316 Oak Street

This was the music club where Brownie McGhee, as Toots Sweet, performs in *Angel Heart* (1986). McGhee is subsequently killed at his apartment, the Skyscraper, on Royal and St. Peter streets.

St. Louis Cathedral
Seventh block of Chartres Street, on Jackson Square

This church, one of the oldest in the country and a major land-mark, has been featured in virtually every movie filmed in New Orleans.

Pontalba Buildings
St. Anne's Street (Jackson Square)

This apartment building, built in 1851 and believed to be the old-est in the United States, was used for the exterior shots of Dennis Quaid's apartment building in *The Big Easy*.

Germaine Wells Mansion
corner of Chartres and Esplanade streets

The interiors of Dennis Quaid's apartment in *The Big Easy* were filmed here, as were both the interior and exterior of the apartment owned by Solomon Burke, who plays suspected drug lord Daddy Mention. Burke is killed when Quaid tries to interrogate him, and a major chase scene was filmed at Decatur and Esplanade streets.
(*Note:* On the opposite corner of Chartres and Esplanade is Nastassja Kinski's house in *Cat People* [1982].)

Napoleon House
500 Chartres Street

This European-style cafe is where Dennis Quaid and Kathleen Turner dodge hit men in *Undercover Blues* (1993) and where Kevin Costner learns that President Kennedy has been killed in *JFK*.

Louisiana Supreme Court Building
(formerly the Wildlife and Fisheries Building)
400 Royal Street

Dennis Quaid's trial was staged here in *The Big Easy*. The build-ing also served as Kevin Costner's offices in *JFK*.

Riverwalk Marketplace

In *The Pelican Brief*, Julia Roberts's rendezvous near the market-place's food court with a man she thinks is an FBI agent but who is actually an assassin (Stanley Tucci) ends when the assassin is killed before he has a chance to kill her.

Other New Orleans Locations

• The trial of Tommy Lee Jones (playing Clay Shaw) in *JFK* was filmed at the Criminal Courts Building on Tulane and Broad streets, the same site where the real-life Shaw was tried and acquitted.

• *The Pelican Brief* was also filmed at Tulane University, where Julia Roberts's character is a law student.

• One of the important early scenes in *The Big Easy*, in which Dennis Quaid takes Ellen Barkin to a famous New Orleans dance club called Tipitinas, was actually filmed at a nightclub called Rosie's, which no longer exists.

• Lolita Davidovich's apartment in *Blaze* (1989) is on the 1200 block of Royal.

• Clint Eastwood's shoot-outs in *Tightrope* (1984), in which he plays a New Orleans detective investigating a series of sex murders, were staged at the Dixie Brewery, on 2401 Tulane Avenue, and Jax Brewery on Jackson Square.

• The Columns Hotel, on St. Charles Avenue, was used for the interior scenes of Brooke Shields's brothel in *Pretty Baby* (1978).

• The Beauregard Museum in Chalmette National Historical Park was where Dana Delany is saved in the sex comedy *Exit to Eden* (1994).

Other Louisiana Locations

• The majestic forest in *Miller's Crossing*, the scene of a killing, is visible from Highway 190 one mile west of the community of Robert and four miles west of Hammond. The woods are directly across from Hidden Oaks Camp Ground.

• Hammond also hosted the filming of the television series *In the Heat of the Night* between 1987 and 1989. The police station was on Thomas Street downtown, where the Frame House is now located. *The Pistol* (1989), a biopic about basketball star Pistol Pete Maravich, was filmed in downtown Hammond, at the Columbia Theater, and at Southeastern Louisiana University, which doubled as Maravich's Clemson University.

• *Blaze* also filmed at Earl Long's Pea Patch Farm in Winnifield and at the former site of Clinton High School, which doubled as Mandeville State Hospital, the mental institution where Long is incarcerated near the end of his final term as governor, and the state hospital in Jackson.

• The first Tarzan movie, which starred Elmo Lincoln, was filmed in 1917 in the swamps around Morgan City, Louisiana.

Arkansas

Arkansas's two biggest movies, *A Soldier's Story* (1983) and *Biloxi Blues* (1988), both filmed at Fort Chaffee, an army base located in the northwestern part of the state. Fort Chaffee is an open base, and tourists can drive past the Ninth Street barracks featured in both movies.

A Soldier's Story was about the investigation of a murdered officer at a black military camp during World War II. Its baseball scenes were filmed at Lamar Porter Field, at 3107 West Capitol in Little Rock. Main Street in Clarendon, by way of which Howard E. Rollins Jr., who plays the investigating officer, comes into town, was also featured briefly.

Records were not kept as to the exact site of the murder, but it is known that the scene was filmed on one of the backwoods roads near Frog Bayou Creek in the town of Rudy (population: 45), about twenty miles north of Fort Chaffee.

Biloxi Blues, which was based on Neil Simon's Broadway comedy, centers around the struggles of a Brooklyn boy (Matthew Broderick) and his fellow recruits to survive the rigors of basic training during World War II. When the recruits are granted leave, they go to Main Street in the city of Van Buren (Biloxi, Mississippi, in the movie), where Broderick and his buddies are serviced by a prostitute in the rear of a building at 627 Main Street (now the Art Form Gallery). Broderick also finds a girlfriend at a dance staged at the Barling City Hall. The soda shop scene was filmed at 800 Main Street (now Carolyn's Collectibles).

Jerry Lee Lewis's childhood home in *Great Balls of Fire* (1989) is located at 93 Military Road in Marion. The Blessings Through Faith Temple Congregation, off Highway 70 in West Memphis, was used for the church singing scenes.

Frank and Jesse (1995) starring Rob Lowe and Bill Paxton, was filmed at a number of locations throughout the state, including along the Arkansas-Missouri Railroad, a scenic passenger railroad that runs along Highway 71 between Springdale and Eureka Springs.

The King's Opera House in Van Buren doubled as the Bank of Northfield; Prairie Grove State Park was used for several action scenes, and the Borden house in the park doubled as the house where Jesse James is killed. The James house that burns down in the movie was in the town of Clifty. The city of Chester became Gallatin, Missouri; the city of Winslow became Liberty, Missouri.

CBS's *Evening Shade*, the first network series set in Arkansas, aired between 1990 and 1994 and used Philander Smith College as the Evening Shade High School. Ossie Davis's diner, the Ponder's Barbeque, is actually the Bank of Fayetteville, One South Block Street, on the Fayetteville square.

The house depicted as the Sugarbakers' in the hit CBS-TV comedy *Designing Women* (1986–92) is located at 14th and Scott streets in Little Rock. The Quapaw Quarter Association offers tours Sundays through Fridays.

Designing Women *House (courtesy Quapaw Quarter Association)*

Tennessee

Cotton Exchange Building
65 Union Avenue, Memphis

In *The Firm* (1993), this office building was where Gary Busey has his detective agency and Tom Cruise and Holly Hunter rent an office to copy the files of Cruise's law firm. A plaque in the building's lobby honors John Grisham, the author of the novel on which the movie was based.

A few blocks away, on the corner of Front and Madison streets, the Union Planters Building was used as the exterior of the firm Bendini, Lambert and Locke. Other Memphis locations for *The Firm* include the rooftop of the Peabody Hotel, 149 Union Avenue, where the firm hosts the barbecue party welcoming Cruise and Jeanne Tripplehorn to Memphis; the Blues City Cafe at 138 Beale Street, where Cruise is first approached by an FBI agent, played by Ed Harris; the Front Street Deli, 77 Front Street, where Cruise meets Hunter to plan their way out of the firm's grasp; the Mud Island Monorail and Mississippi River Museum, on 125 Front Street, site of the movie's big chase scenes; and Jake's Place, at 357 North Main, which served as the Boston bar where Cruise waits on tables while attending Harvard.

The William Faulkner Lounge at Memphis State University was used as a Harvard classroom; and Elmwood Cemetery, on 824 South Dudley Avenue, was where the lawyers who buck the firm are laid to rest.

John F. Kennedy Park
4575 Raleigh-LaGrange Road, Memphis

The mob lawyer's suicide that youngsters Brad Renfro and David Speck witness in *The Client* (1994) occurs in this park. Renfro plays an eleven-year-old who learns the whereabouts of a murdered U.S. senator from the man who kills himself.

The Client was also filmed at the Sterick Building, 9 North Third Street, which served as Susan Sarandon's office; Memphis Regional Medical Center, on 877 Jefferson Avenue, which was used for the exterior scenes of St. Peter's Charity Hospital; the Memphis County Courthouse, on 140 Adams Avenue, where Tommy Lee Jones tries to force Renfro to testify; and the Criminal Justice Center, on 201 Poplar Avenue, where young Renfro is locked up overnight.

Arcade Cafe
540 South Main Street, Memphis

The cafe was featured prominently in Jim Jarmusch's *Mystery Train* (1989), although the Arcade Hotel, where the murder takes place, has since been demolished. The hotel also served as a backdrop to a scene in *Great Balls of Fire* (1989) in which Dennis Quaid (playing Jerry Lee Lewis) gives Alec Baldwin (playing Lewis's cousin Jimmy Lee Swaggart) an Oldsmobile during a revival session.

The cafe, located half a block from the National Civil Rights Museum, was also the site where one of Anthony LaPaglia's henchmen hires a thug to spy on, and later tries to kill, Renfro in *The Client*.

Other Movies Filmed in Tennessee

• In Memphis, *Great Balls of Fire* was also filmed in front of Graceland, Elvis Presley's home; at Bruce Elementary School, where Quaid, playing Jerry Lee Lewis, picks up and drops off Winona Ryder, who plays Myra, his thirteen-year-old cousin and wife; and at Sun Studios, on 706 Union Street.

• *Trespass* (1991) was filmed primarily at an old brewery on Tennessee Street on the bluff of the Mississippi River in downtown Memphis.

• The climax of *Nashville* (1975) occurs at the replica of the Parthenon in Centennial Park in downtown Nashville and at Ryman Auditorium, which was also featured in *Coal Miner's Daughter* (1980), the story of Loretta Lynn, and *Sweet Dreams* (1984), the story of Patsy Cline.

• River Phoenix's last movie, *The Thing Called Love* (1992), featured Nashville's famous Bluebird Cafe.

Mississippi

Mississippi has appeared in quite a few television movies but only a few theatrical releases. Of these, the most memorable was probably *Mississippi Burning* (1988), a fictionalized account of the FBI's investigation of the murder of three civil rights workers in the early 1960s. Most of the sixty-two locations for that film were in the small towns outside of Jackson and were usually featured for a few short scenes. Exceptions include the courthouse in Vaiden, which served as the sheriff's office of fictitious Jessup County, and Vicksburg's Cedar Hill Cemetery, which served as the site of the slain men's funeral elegy and procession.

The 1993 version of *The Adventures of Huck Finn*, which starred Elijah Wood in the title role, was filmed in Natchez at the Dunleith, on 84 Homochitto Street, a historic Greek Revival mansion that is now a bed-and-breakfast; the Rosalie mansion, on 100 Orleans Street (where Wood and Jason Robards impersonate relatives of the mansion's owner); Natchez Under-the-Hill; and Historic Jefferson College on U.S. 61 in the town of Washington, six miles east of Natchez. Jefferson College is a onetime boys school (and the first educational institution in the Mississippi territory), which served as a small town Finn travels to.

All these locations are open for tours; contact the Natchez Convention and Visitor Bureau, P.O. Box 1485, Natchez, Mississippi, 39121.

Miss Firecracker (1989), which starred Holly Hunter as an orphan who enters her hometown beauty contest, was filmed in Yazoo City. Much of the action takes place at a house at the corner of Grand Avenue and Canal Street. The Miss Firecracker contest takes place at a carnival that was set up on the south end of Main Street.

Heart of Dixie (1989) and *The Gun in Betty Lou's Handbag* (1992) were filmed at the University of Mississippi campus in Oxford and in the Oxford town square.

Other recent features that have filmed in Mississippi include *Mississippi Masala* (1991), *Crossroads* (1985), and *Ode to Billy Joe* (1976), which were all shot in the Greenwood area.

Alabama

U.S. Space and Rocket Center
just off I-565, Huntsville

In *Space Camp* (1986), youngsters are accidentally launched into space while attending NASA's summer camp at the U.S. Space and Rocket Center. The center is open for tours daily.

Rickwood Field
1137 Second Avenue West, Birmingham

Built in 1910, Rickwood Field holds the distinction of being the oldest baseball park in the country. It is featured as the Detroit, Philadelphia, and Pittsburgh ballparks in *Cobb* (1994), starring Tommy Lee Jones. During baseball's segregation era, Rickwood was home to the Birmingham Black Barons of the Negro Leagues.

Rickwood Field, Cobb *(courtesy Alabama Film Commission)*

Craig Field
Selma

This industrial park, which was once an army base (Craig Airfield), was converted into the fully functional Fort Daly in *Body Snatchers* (1994), the remake of the 1956 and 1978 classic versions of *Invasion of the Body Snatchers. Blue Sky* (1994), which starred Jessica Lange and Tommy Lee Jones, was also filmed here.

Old Courthouse in Monroeville
Courthouse Square, Monroeville

Although *To Kill a Mockingbird* (1962) did not film in Monroeville, tourists from around the world still venture out of their way (some twenty-two miles west of I-65) to see where the movie trial was supposedly held. (Academy Award–winning production designers Henry Bumstead and Alexander Golitzen re-created the courthouse on a studio back lot.)

The courthouse has since been turned into the Monroe County Heritage Museum. Each year the museum presents a stage version of *To Kill a Mockingbird*, adapted from Harper Lee's famous novel.

For tour information, write to the museum at P.O. Box 1637, Monroeville, Alabama, 36461.

USS *Alabama* Battleship Memorial Park
in Mobile Bay

The 1992 thriller *Under Siege*, which starred Steven Seagal as a ship's cook who saves a battleship against military turncoats (Tommy Lee Jones and Gary Busey) trying to steal its nuclear arsenal, was filmed on the USS *Alabama*, a battleship that was decommissioned in the 1950s and that now serves as a museum in Mobile Bay. The memorial park, which also includes the World War II submarine USS *Drum*, honors Alabama veterans of foreign wars and is open to tourists.

Hangars 5 and 6, Building 17, Brookley Field
Old Bay Street, Mobile

Close Encounters of the Third Kind (1977) was filmed in what is believed to have been the largest indoor set in movie history: two former World War II dirigible hangars in a former air force base (now the Brookley Industrial Complex in Mobile). Although one can only see the hangars from behind gates, the site still attracts tourists who want to see where Steven Spielberg had extraterrestrials land on Earth.

Spielberg chose the hangars (the largest being 450 feet long, 250 feet wide, and 90 feet high) because no soundstage in Hollywood was large enough for the spacecraft. The hangars are now owned by Teledyne/Continental. There are no markers in the complex commemorating the site.

Brookley Hanger, Close Encounters of the Third Kind

Other Locations in Alabama

• *Norma Rae* (1979), which starred Sally Field as a Georgia union organizer, was filmed in a textile mill near Opelika. The Georgia textile commission had successfully lobbied against allowing the production to film in Georgia.

• Most of the town scenes in *Mississippi Burning* (1988) were filmed in Lafayette. The courthouse was on the town square.

• *Stroker Ace* (1983) was shot in part at the Alabama International Motor Speedway near Talladega.

• The cult classic *The Heart Is a Lonely Hunter* (1968), which starred Alan Arkin as a deaf mute in a southern town, was filmed at a private house on Mabry Street in Selma and at Old Live Oak Cemetery, an 1830s cemetery on Highway 22 West, in Selma.

Georgia

Driving Miss Daisy House
822 Lullwater Road, Atlanta

This red-brick house in Atlanta's Druid Hills section was where Jessica Tandy lived in the Academy Award–winning film *Driving Miss Daisy* (1989).

The Nations Bank
55 Marietta Street, Atlanta

The interior of this bank was turned into the supposedly impregnable Citizens and Southern National Bank that Kim Basinger breaks into in *The Real McCoy* (1993).

Westin Peachtree Plaza Hotel
210 Peachtree Street, Atlanta

In *Sharky's Machine* (1981), undercover cop Burt Reynolds's criminal nemesis operates from a rooftop Oriental restaurant in the hotel.

Target Store
4000 Covington Highway, Atlanta

This was the principal location of *Career Opportunities* (1991), a teen comedy about a high school student (Frank Whaley) who works as a night watchman at a Target store and the town's beauty (Jennifer Connelly), who falls asleep in the store.

Other Atlanta Locations

• Spike Lee's *School Daze* (1988) was filmed in Harkness Hall, the Quadrangle, and some dormitories at what is now Clark-Atlantic University and at Morehouse College's football stadium.
• *Stroker Ace*, a Burt Reynolds's 1983 race-driving comedy, was filmed at the Atlanta International Raceway.
• *The Slugger's Wife* (1985), a Neil Simon comedy, was shot in Fulton County Stadium.
• *Robocop 3* (1993), *Invasion USA* (1985), and *Love Potion Number 9* (1992) were all filmed in Atlanta's historic Auburn Avenue.
• The homes of the couples in *Consenting Adults* (1992) were in the Atlanta suburbs of Sandy Springs and Alpharetta.
• A mansion at the corner of West Paces Ferry and Castlegate was used as Julian Sands's home in *Boxing Helena* (1993).
• Other movies filmed in Atlanta—for which no records were kept—include *Kalifornia* (1993), *Freejack* (1992), *Not Without My Daughter* (1991), *Love Crimes* (1991) and *1969* (1988). Georgia is one of the states that does not require permits for filming.

Whistle Stop Cafe
McCrackin Road, Juliette

The general store in this small town, which is located about ninety miles south of Atlanta, was turned into a cafe in *Fried Green Tomatoes* (1991). After the movie was released, tourists kept looking for the fictional cafe, so the owners of the store turned it into a real-life Whistle Stop Cafe.

Forsyth Park
Savannah

In *Forrest Gump* (1994), Tom Hanks tells his life story to a succession of strangers on a bus bench in Chippewa Square. The statue of Gen. James Oglethorpe, Savannah's founder, can be seen in the background. The bench, which faced Hull Street, was installed for the movie and later removed.

Other Savannah Locations

Savannah masqueraded as 1860s Boston in *Glory* (1989), the story of the first black regiment that fought in the Civil War:

• Just behind the Cotton Exchange on Savannah's historic River Street, an elaborate set was constructed to resemble the Boston townhomes where the Fifty-fourth Regiment made its first appearance in uniform.
• Battlefield Park, adjacent to the Savannah Visitors Center, was transformed into Massachusetts's Readville Camp.
• The Hugh W. Mercer Home, a private home on Bull Street, became Shaw's mansion (Matthew Broderick).

In the Heat of the Night Locations
Monticello Street, Covington

All but the first six episodes of the television series *In the Heat of the Night*, which began airing in 1988, were filmed in Covington, primarily in the town square. The exterior of the Newton County Sheriff's Office served as the Newman County Sheriff's Department; the Porter Memorial Library at 1174 Monticello Street was the Sparta police station; and Major Appliance, at 1160 Monticello Street, was seen in the show's establishing shots and now sells coffee mugs, T-shirts, and other souvenirs saluting the show.

For a complete list of locations send a self-addressed stamped envelope to the Newton County Chamber of Commerce, P.O. Box 168, Covington, Georgia, 30209.

Other Locations in Georgia

• *Glory* also filmed on Jekyll Island, where the film's climactic battle—a Union assault on Fort Wagner—was re-created, and in a rural area near McDonough, where the Battle of Antietam was staged.

• *Deliverance* (1972), the story of four men who spend a weekend canoeing down a dangerous river, was filmed primarily on the Chattooga River.

• The private school in *Dutch* (1991), where Ed O'Neill picks up his girlfriend's son, played by Ethan Randall, was Berry College in Rome.

• *My Cousin Vinny* (1992) used the courthouse in Monticello for exterior shots of where the trial was held.

• The climactic courtroom scenes in *A Simple Twist of Fate* (1994) were filmed in the historic Madison courthouse.

• The swamps of Savannah doubled for Vietnam in *Flight of the Intruder* (1991).

• Contrary to persistent rumors, there is no Tara mansion from the classic *Gone With the Wind* (1939). The film was shot on the MGM lot. Parts of the door are in storage at the Atlanta History Center, while other pieces of the façade are in the hands of private collectors.

Kentucky

St. Anne's Convent
Highway 8, Melbourne

In *Rain Man* (1988), this convent was transformed into Wallbrooks, the facility for the developmentally disabled, where Tom Cruise discovers he has an autistic brother, Dustin Hoffman.

Pompilios Restaurant
600 Washington, Newport

When Cruise and Hoffman have breakfast here in *Rain Man*, the latter shows off his ability to memorize a phone book (by telling the waitress her home phone number) and takes a quick glance at a toothpick box that has fallen on the floor and accurately counts 246 toothpicks.

Evergreen Cemetery
24 Alexandria Pike, Southgate

Site of the funeral of Cruise and Hoffman's father.

Private Home
corner of Fifth and Main streets, Henderson

The home was used as the boardinghouse where Geena Davis, Rosie O'Donnell, Madonna, and other women professional baseball players stay in *A League of Their Own* (1992).

Other Locations in Kentucky

• The classic James Bond film *Goldfinger* (1963), which was about Goldfinger's quest for the gold at Fort Knox, was not filmed at the U.S. Bullion Depository. The exterior set was built in Pinewood Studios in England, and only a few scenes of Highway 31-A, leading to the depository, appear in the film.

• *Stripes* (1981), a military comedy starring Bill Murray and Harold Ramis, was filmed at the army's Fort Knox base next door. The army offers a tour of the facility but reports that the old barracks are no longer in use or shown on the tour.

• The candy store in *Lost in Yonkers* (1993) was constructed in the parking lot of a Dairy Mart, at the corner of Elm and Kenner in Ludlow, but was torn down after filming was complete. The filmmakers shot in Ludlow because it more closely resembled 1942 Yonkers than the real Yonkers does today.

• *In Country* (1989), the story of a teenage girl trying to learn about her father, who is killed in Vietnam, was filmed at a private home in Mayfield, the Graves County Courthouse, Maplewood Cemetery, Paducah Community College, and the Ballard County Wildlife Management Area, a popular hunting and fishing spot, which doubled for the swamplands in Vietnam. The restaurant, Chuck's, with the plastic chicken on the roof, was a set built specially for the film and was patterned after a Mayfield restaurant, Emma's, that features the same chicken.

• *Eight Men Out* (1988) was filmed at Churchill Downs in Louisville.

• *Next of Kin* (1989) was filmed in Hardburley and Jackson.

Chapter 10

Florida and the Carolinas

Florida

Central Florida Regional Airport
2735 Mellonville Avenue, Sanford

The airplane hijacking in *Passenger 57* (1992), the movie that propelled Wesley Snipes into stardom, was filmed at the airport (as were scenes from *Wilder Napalm* [1993]).

Cafe Jake's
112 East First Street, Sanford

In *My Girl* (1991), Anna Chlumsky and Dan Aykroyd are eating in this downtown cafe when they see Glenda Chism, who plays Macauley Culkin's mother. Earlier in the movie, Chlumsky and Culkin ride their bikes through this section of downtown.

The lake scenes, where Chlumsky and Culkin become "blood brothers" and experiment with their first kiss, were filmed at Mirror Lake in Clermont, another suburb of Orlando.

Sanford Plaza
30th Street, Sanford

Site of the carnival in *Wilder Napalm,* which starred Debra Winger and Dennis Quaid.

Harry P. Leu Botanical Gardens
1730 North Forest Avenue, Orlando

John Ritter and Amy Yasbeck are married here in *Problem Child 2* (1991). The house and garden are open daily for tours.

(*Note:* The movie's food fight takes place at the Bubble Room Restaurant, at 1351 South Orlando Avenue, in nearby Maitland. Michael Oliver's school was the Delaney Street School in downtown Orlando.)

Tinker Field
287 South Tampa Avenue, Orlando

This stadium, which is the home of the minor league Orlando Cubs, doubled as St. Louis's Busch Stadium in the opening scenes of *Parenthood* (1989).

Other locations in the movie included a house on Lakeside Drive, which was used as Steve Martin and Mary Steenburgen's home; an office in the Landmark Center on Robinson, where Martin works; and Howard Middle School, where Rick Moranis sings "Close to You" to his wife.

Sea World of Florida
7007 Sea World Drive, Orlando

In *Jaws 3-D* (1983) the shark somehow manages to infiltrate this Florida theme park.

Universal Studios Florida
1000 Universal Studios Plaza, Orlando

This working studio offers a tour of its back lot, which is patterned after the tour of Universal Studios Hollywood. *Parenthood*, *Oscar* (1991), and *Matinee* (1993) are among the movies that have filmed there since the studios opened in 1989.

The NBC series *seaQuest DVS* began shooting here in 1994, after filming its first season at Universal Studios Hollywood.

Scene from Matinee *being shot at Universal Studios Florida (courtesy MCA Publishing Rights, a division of MCA Inc.)*

Disney-MGM Studios Theme Park
Lake Buena Vista

Built in 1989, the studio is part of the Disney World theme park, which also encompasses Epcot Center, the Magic Kingdom, and other attractions. A tour of the back lot, where *Quick Change* (1990), *Ernest Saves Christmas* (1988), *Honey, I Blew Up the Kid* (1992), and *Passenger 57* were filmed, is included with the price of admission. Several TV shows also tape here, including the Disney Channel's *Mickey Mouse Club* (between April and August only).

Other Orlando Locations

• What is now the plaza in front of Orlando's new city hall on South Orange Avenue downtown is the site of the former Orlando City Hall that was imploded in the opening of *Lethal Weapon III*

(1992). The demolition was not in the original script, but when Orlando officials informed producer Joel Silver that they were looking for a movie company to blow up the building (thus saving Orlando demolition costs), the explosion was incorporated into the script.

• The parking garage next to the Orlando Police Station, on the corner of Church and Hughey streets, is the garage terrorists take over in *Passenger 57*.

• The commune in the Central American jungle where hippies Eric Roberts and Cheech Marin live in *Rude Awakening* (1989) was in Wekiwa Springs State Park, just north of Orlando.

• Barret Oliver's elementary school, identified as the Barketon School in *D.A.R.Y.L.* (1985), was actually Kaley Elementary School on Kaley Avenue.

• The Domirick School, in suburban Maitland was used as the school in *Matinee*.

• The Children's Museum in *Ernest Saves Christmas* was actually the Orlando Science Center, on 810 East Rollins Street.

• *Passenger 57* and *Ernest Saves Christmas* were also filmed at Orlando International Airport.

House at 555 Sanford Street
Bartow

This turn-of-the-century frame house was used for the exterior shots of the Sultenfuss Funeral Parlor—where Dan Aykroyd and Anna Chlumsky live—in *My Girl*. Bartow is halfway between Orlando and Tampa.

The house was used in the original but duplicated on a Los Angeles soundstage for the sequel, *My Girl 2* (1994).

Tampa/St. Petersburg

To satirize conformity in modern suburban life, director Tim Burton picked the Carpenter's Run subdivision outside of Wesley Chapel, about eighteen miles north of Tampa, as the neighborhood where Dianne Wiest brings Johnny Depp home to live with her and her family in *Edward Scissorhands* (1990). In a display of community involvement that would have been unheard of in Los Angeles, forty-four of the fifty homeowners in the four-year-old housing settlement agreed to have their homes repainted in an array of pastel colors—blue, green, pink, and yellow—and allowed realistic-looking shrubs in the shapes of animals to be planted on their front lawns.

The beauty salon where housewife Kathy Baker tries to seduce

Depp was in the Southgate Shopping Center, on 2500 South Florida Avenue, in Lakeland, about twenty-five miles east of Tampa.

Tampa also hosted the Spencer Tracy classic *A Guy Named Joe* (1944), which was filmed at Drew Air Force Base (now Drew Park, an industrial park). *Cop and a Half* (1993), a less-than-classic Burt Reynolds vehicle, also filmed throughout Tampa, highlighting its Port Facilities area, Hispanic Ybor district, shorelines, bridges, parks, and plazas.

Cocoon (1985), a comedy about a group of Florida senior citizens who discover a fountain of youth, was filmed throughout St. Petersburg. According to *Hollywood East*, John Ponti's book on Florida sites: "Wilford Brimley gets rejected for his driver's license at the St. Petersburg Municipal Building, and the whole gang goes ballroom dancing at the St. Petersburg Coliseum on Fourth Ave. In real life, the Coliseum's fine hardwood floor makes it a popular local dance spot."

The Break (1994), which starred Martin Sheen and Vince Van Patten, was shot primarily at St. Petersburg's Pinellas Club. The big playoff game was filmed at the Stouffer Vinoy Hotel.

Burt Reynolds Ranch
16133 Jupiter Farms Road, Jupiter

Reynolds's ranch, located seventeen miles north of Palm Beach, offers tours daily, giving fans the chance to see his property, studios, and sets from the Gator Motel and Everglades Gas Station seen in *Smokey and the Bandit* (1977).

Everglades Gas Station, Smokey and the Bandit (Burt Reynolds Ranch)

Amphitheater
at the end of Lucerne, Lake Worth

William Hurt first spots and tries to pick up Kathleen Turner at a concert at the Amphitheater in *Body Heat* (1981). The movie was filmed throughout the city of Lake Worth, although the house where much of the action takes place (where Turner lives with her husband Richard Crenna) is a private mansion located at the corner of Federal Highway and Hypoluxo Road, in the town of Hypoluxo.

Hurt's office was on Lakeview Street.

The Breakers Hotel
One South County Road, Palm Beach

This posh resort hotel, used for a political fund-raiser sponsored by suspect Lorraine Bracco, was one of several locations in *Traces of Red* (1992), a mystery that starred James Belushi and Tony Goldwyn as Palm Beach detectives investigating the murder of a waitress.

Traces was also filmed at the Twin Lakes High School, which doubled as the Palm Beach sheriff's headquarters; the South County Courthouse in Delray Beach, where Belushi testifies in a murder case; the Squeeze nightclub, 2 South New River Drive, in Fort Lauderdale, where Belushi and Goldwyn track down leads; Monarch Galleries in Fort Lauderdale, where Bracco works; and St. Anthony's Catholic Church, in Fort Lauderdale.

Reed Reef Park
Boca Raton

The climactic scenes in *Whispers in the Dark* (1992), in which Annabella Sciorra kills Alan Alda with a hatchet, occur on this beach.

Briny Breezes Mobile Home Park
Boynton Beach

This was the retirement home of Don Ameche and Anne Jackson, who play Tom Selleck's parents in *Folks* (1992).

Boca Raton Resort Hotel and Club
501 East Camino Real, Boca Raton

Bette Midler and Trini Alvarado vacation here in *Stella* (1990). The hotel was also turned into a swank hospital in *Folks*.

Where the Boys Are Beach
between Las Olas Boulevard and Sunrise Boulevard
Fort Lauderdale

The beachfront in Fort Lauderdale, portrayed in *Where the Boys Are* (1960), no longer looks as it did when the movie was released. And due to a major crackdown on under age twenty-one drinking, the beach is no longer the spring-break mecca it once was. After the movie was released, Fort Lauderdale became the country's most popular spring-break destination, with as many as 350,000 students descending on the city every spring. Today only about ten thousand students visit the beaches during spring break.

The Elbow Room, on Las Olas Boulevard, still exists, although, like the beachfront, it has also been updated.

The beachfront was also the site of *Where the Boys Are '84* and *Spring Break* (1983).

Ocean Hacienda Hotel
1924 North Atlantic Boulevard, Fort Lauderdale

This vintage-1938 hotel, located just north of the public beach on State Road A1A, was converted into the fictional apartment complex, the Lone Palm, where Richard Harris lives in *Wrestling Ernest Hemingway* (1993).

Fort Lauderdale Yacht Basin
2001 S.W. 20th Street, Fort Lauderdale

In *Ace Ventura: Pet Detective* (1994), the basin serves as the hide-out where Jim Carrey rescues Miami Dolphins quarterback Dan Marino and the kidnapped mascot for the team: a dolphin.

Rainbo Cafe
1909 Hollywood Boulevard, Hollywood

In *Cape Fear* (1991), this cafe was transformed into the ice cream shop where Nick Nolte realizes that he is being followed by Robert De Niro, a recently paroled rapist whom Nolte, as a public defender, had less than diligently defended fourteen years earlier. When

Nolte goes to pay his bill, the cashier tells him it has been taken care of, and Nolte looks out the shop's window to see De Niro sitting in a red Mustang convertible, puffing on a cigar.

Other scenes—in which Nolte tries to bribe De Niro into leaving him alone and pushes him when he realizes De Niro is following him again during a Fourth of July parade—were filmed on the Hollywood Boardwalk.

Cape Fear was also filmed at a house on S.W. 29th Terrace in Fort Lauderdale and at the lecture theater on Broward Community College's central campus in suburban Davie, where De Niro lures Nolte's teenage daughter, Juliette Lewis, into the basement and Lewis ends up seductively sucking De Niro's thumb. The denouement was filmed on a specially constructed water stage at Fort Lauderdale Production Central studios.

The Fontainebleau Hilton Resort and Spa
4441 Collins Avenue, Miami

In *Goldfinger* (1964), Sean Connery, playing James Bond, calls the Fontainebleau the best hotel in Miami Beach. He has been sent there to investigate Gert Frobe, who plays Goldfinger, and in one memorable scene catches Frobe cheating at cards by the Fontainebleau's pool deck (which no longer exists). Connery subsequently beds Frobe's companion (Shirley Eaton), and Frobe retaliates by having the poor girl asphyxiated by painting her with gold in one of the hotel's suites.

The Fontainebleau has also appeared in *The Bellboy* (1960). Jerry Lewis plays a hapless bellboy in this comedy, which he also wrote, directed, and produced.

In *The Bodyguard* (1992), Kevin Costner protects Whitney Houston in the presidential suite, and in *Police Academy 5: Assignment in Miami Beach* (1988), the 50th Annual National Police Chiefs Convention was held at the hotel.

Sylvester Stallone and Sharon Stone's steamy shower scene in *The Specialist* (1994) supposedly took place in room 1205, a room which Stallone subsequently blows up, causing it to fall into the Atlantic Ocean.

The Fontainebleau's other credits include Pacino's *Scarface* (1983), *Stick* (1985), with Burt Reynolds, Sinatra's *Tony Rome* (1967), and the 1960s TV detective series *Surfside Six*.

Eden Roc Resort and Spa
4525 Collins Avenue, Miami Beach

Located next to the Fontainebleau, the Eden Roc is the hotel where Blair Underwood kidnaps Sean Connery's wife and daughter (played by Kate Capshaw and Scarlett Johansson) in the 1995 thriller *Just Cause*. Michelle Pfeiffer accompanies Dean Stockwell to the Eden Roc in the 1988 Mafia comedy *Married to the Mob*.

Joe Robbie Stadium
2269 NW 199th Street, Greater Miami North

Ace Ventura: Pet Detective filled the stadium for a scene recreating the Super Bowl halftime show. The stadium is home to the Miami Dolphins and Florida Marlins.

Terremark Building
1220 Brickell Avenue, Miami

The denouement of *True Lies* (1994) was filmed atop this twenty-story skyscraper in the heart of downtown Miami. Arnold Schwarzenegger, piloting a Harrier jet, rescues his daughter (Eliza Dushku) and foils nuclear terrorists.

Harrier Jet atop Miami office building in True Lies *(courtesy Miami Film Office)*

To accommodate the jet and in order to blow out some of the building's windows, the crew built two additional stories on the building's roof, which were dismantled after filming was complete.

Desiree Supper Club
9674 S.W. 24th Street, Miami

Jack Gifford (Bernie) and Elaine Strich (Ruby) have their first date at this supper club in *Cocoon: The Return* (1988). The movie was also filmed at Baptist Hospital, Morningside Park (the site of the spirited basketball sequence), the Miami Seaquarium, the Sunrise Court apartments (which served as the exterior of the senior citizens' bungalows), the Rosensteil School of Marine and Atmospheric Studies (which doubled as the St. Petersburg Oceanographic Institute), and No Name Harbor.

Orange Bowl Stadium
1501 N.W. Third Street, Miami

The Orange Bowl was featured both in the Burt Reynolds movie *Semi-Tough* (1977) and in *Ace Ventura: Pet Detective*, but its most famous movie appearance was in *Black Sunday* (1977). In that movie a Goodyear blimp, hijacked by terrorists, appears over the edge of the stadium, causing fans to run in panic.

Miami Herald
One Herald Plaza, Miami

Both *Absence of Malice* (1981), written by former reporter Kurt Luedtke, and *The Mean Season* (1985) were filmed in the *Herald* offices. *Absence of Malice* tells the story of how the owner of a legitimate wholesale liquor business (Paul Newman) fights back against a reporter (Sally Field) who wrongly assumes he has followed his father's footsteps into organized crime. *The Mean Season* was a thriller about a Miami police reporter (Kurt Russell) who becomes a spokesman for a killer, who later targets the reporter's girlfriend (Mariel Hemingway).

Vizcaya (courtesy The Vizcaya)

Vizcaya Museum and Gardens
3251 South Miami Avenue, Miami

This mansion, which was built by International Harvester magnate James Deering, served as James Stewart's home in *Airport '77* (1977) and as the site of a pivotal scene between Sally Field and Melinda Dillon in *Absence of Malice*, as well as the wedding in *Miami Rhapsody* (1995). The exterior of the mansion, where Jim Carrey and Courteney Cox attend a party, is seen in *Ace Ventura: Pet Detective*. The mansion is now a Dade County museum.

Miami International Airport
Miami

In *Miami Blues* (1990), Alec Baldwin breaks the finger of a Hare Krishna here, causing him to go into shock and die. Fred Ward is called in to handle the investigation.

Biltmore Hotel
1200 Anastasia Avenue, Coral Gables

The hotel's Country Club Ballroom served as the interior of the mansion where Jim Carrey and Courteney Cox attend a party in *Ace Ventura: Pet Detective*. A pool cabana is blown up in *The Specialist*.

Hialeah Park Racetrack
2200 East Fourth Avenue, Hialeah

The park was featured in both *Let It Ride* (1989), which starred Richard Dreyfuss as a compulsive gambler, and *The Champ* (1979), which starred Jon Voight as a washed-up prizefighter.

Grove Towers
7950 N.W. 58th Street, Coconut Grove (or Bay Shore Drive)

Site of a memorable stunt in *Stick* (1985) in which famed stuntman Dar Robinson falls from the twenty-story condominium complex.

Old Seven-Mile Bridge
near Marathon

One of the most harrowing action sequences in *True Lies* was filmed on the Old Seven-Mile Bridge, which parallels the new bridge and is no longer in use today. To stop nuclear terrorists driv-

Seven Mile Bridge, True Lies *(courtesy Stewart Newman Associates)*

ing a truck along the bridge, marines flying Harrier jets fire missiles that destroy a section of the bridge (actually a miniature built in California). Meanwhile, a limousine carrying Jamie Lee Curtis, who is kidnapped by Tia Carrere, careens out of control after a gunshot kills the driver. Arnold Schwarzenegger, dangling from a helicopter, has to grab Curtis from the limousine's sunroof before the limo goes off the bridge. Curtis performed the stunt herself, which took weeks to film. She was never actually in the limo; she hung from the helicopter door, held by wires, with, as she put it, nothing but "lots of water and manta rays" underneath her.

St. Mary's Catholic Church
1010 Windsor Lane, Key West

Timothy Dalton and David Hedison parachute to Hedison's wedding at this church in the opening sequences of *Licence to Kill* (1989), the second thriller in which Dalton plays British secret agent James Bond. Power lines had to be removed from the church for the stunt.

Ernest Hemingway Home and Museum
907 Whitehead Street, Key West

In *Licence*, Dalton's "license to kill" is revoked, and "M" asks for his weapon, on the second-floor veranda of the home. Hemingway wrote some of his most important works here, prompting Dalton to pun: "I guess it's a farewell to arms."

Ernest Hemingway House, Licence to Kill *(courtesy Stewart Newman Associates)*

Other scenes from *Licence to Kill* were filmed on Overseas Highway, where drug smuggler Robert Davi's police escort plunges into the Atlantic Ocean; at the Garrison Bite Marina; and at the Key West Airport, where Dalton learns of Davi's escape.

Mallory Square
Key West

Billy Crystal and Gregory Hines, playing Chicago policemen on forced vacation in *Running Scared* (1986), watch the sunset here and decide they want to retire and buy a bar in Key West.

Eden House Hotel
1015 Fleming Street, Key West

In *CrissCross* (1992), Goldie Hawn, playing a single mother during the turbulent 1960s, and her son, played by David Arnott, live in rooms 203 and 204 of the hotel. Hawn works as a waitress in the hotel's cafe during the day and as a topless dancer elsewhere at night. The modern, European-style hotel was transformed into somewhat of a fleabag hotel for purposes of the movie.

Other Locations in Florida

• *Key Largo* (1948), which starred Humphrey Bogart and Lauren Bacall, was filmed primarily in Los Angeles but included some aerial views of the Key West coastline.

• *Caddyshack* and *Caddyshack 2* (1988) were both filmed at the Rolling Hills Country Club in the city of Davie, located southwest of Fort Lauderdale.

• The House of Hirsch, an antique store at 209 N.E. Cholokka Boulevard, in Micanopy, a suburb of Gainesville, was transformed into the South Carolina hospital where Michael J. Fox works in *Doc Hollywood* (1991).

• The spectacular scene in *Just Cause* (1995) in which Sean Connery chases his wife's kidnapper was filmed on the MacArthur Causeway, which connects Miami to Miami Beach.

• The daydream in *Parenthood* (1989) in which Steve Martin imagines his son turning into a sniper was filmed at Century Tower on the University of Florida's Gainesville campus. The campus also doubled as Harvard in *Just Cause*.

• *Stroker Ace* (1983) and *Days of Thunder* (1990) were filmed at the Daytona International Speedway. *Days of Thunder* was also shot at the Daytona Beach Hilton, Sophie Kay's Restaurant, on 3516

South Atlantic Avenue, and on the beach just north of the Main Street Pier, where Tom Cruise's stuntman, plowing through a flock of seagulls, upset local residents.

• The Cocoa Village Playhouse, on Beard Avenue in Cocoa, was used for the exterior of the Strand Theater in *Matinee* (1993). The interiors were filmed at Universal Studios.

• Melanie Griffith swims at Tallahassee Motor Inn in *Something Wild* (1986).

• *PT 109* (1963) was filmed on what is now Little Palm Island, a resort island located about thirty minutes east of Key West. Photographs of the movie are on display in the dining room.

• *The Greatest Show on Earth*, which won the Academy Award for Best Picture of 1952, was filmed at the Barnum and Bailey headquarters in Saratoga.

• *Jaws 2* (1978) was filmed on Navarre Beach.

• *Creature From the Black Lagoon* (1954) was filmed at Wakulla Springs State Park.

South Carolina

Bay Street Inn
601 Bay Street, Beaufort

This waterfront mansion, built in 1852 and located on the Intracoastal Waterway, served as the home of Kate Nelligan, who plays Nick Nolte's mother, after she marries a wealthy businessman in *The Prince of Tides* (1992). It is now a bed-and-breakfast.

Bay Street Inn, Prince of Tides *(courtesy The Bay Street Inn)*

Rice Hope Plantation
206 Rice Hope Drive, Moncks Corner

This bed-and-breakfast, located about thirty-five miles northeast of Charleston, was the first vacation destination Kevin Kline and Mary Elizabeth Mastrantonio share with Kevin Spacey and Rebecca Miller in *Consenting Adults* (1992), a story of wife swapping, duplicity, and murder.

The couples also stay on John's Island and in Mount Pleasant. The final battle between Kline and Spacey was filmed in a private residence on Sullivans Island.

The Pavilion
on Ocean Boulevard, Myrtle Beach

Shag (1988) is the story of four female friends who go to the beach and catch shag fever. Shag is South Carolina's state dance. The movie was filmed primarily at this 1960s amusement center, with other scenes filmed at the Mount Hope Plantation, a private home in Georgetown County; the Thomas Cafe, at 703 Front Street in Georgetown; and Myrtle Beach's Strand Theater.

Old Grace Memorial Bridge
Charleston

The denouement of *Chasers* (1994), an action-comedy about two navy special policemen (Tom Berenger and William McNamara) assigned to escort a prisoner (Erika Eleniak) to jail, was filmed on this bridge over the Cooper River.

Chasers also filmed at Patriot's Point, which was transformed into a navy base; Wacky Golf, 3900 Highway 17 Street in Myrtle Beach, where Berenger and McNamara slug it out and wreck their car on a volcano (built specially for the movie); and Harold's Garage, a bikers' bar in Yemassee.

Fort Jackson
Columbia

Fort Jackson, the nation's largest army basic-training facility, served as Fort McClane in *Renaissance Man* (1994), the story of Danny DeVito's attempts to teach English to slower learners in the army. The post offers group tours Tuesdays through Fridays. Requests should be made in writing thirty days in advance and sent to Public Affairs Office, Attn.: Community Relations, Fort Jackson,

29207, or can be faxed to (803) 751-2722. Customized tours can incorporate a visit to the forty-foot-tall Victory Tower, a confidence training obstacle, which the out-of-shape DeVito climbs, and rappels down, to show his students what can be done by just trying.

Victory Tower at Fort Jackson, Renaissance Man (*courtesy U.S. Army*)

Williams-Brice Stadium
University of South Carolina
Columbia

The Program (1993), a football story starring James Caan, was filmed extensively at the seventy-eight-thousand–seat stadium. A controversial scene in which players lie down in the middle of the street was filmed at Meeting and State streets in Columbia. After it inspired a copycat incident in real life that led to the death of a young man, the scene was deleted from all prints of the movie.

Other Locations in South Carolina

• Beaufort is also the home of Tidalholm, a nineteenth-century private residence that served as Kevin Kline and Glenn Close's home in *The Big Chill* (1983). The same house also served as Robert Duvall's in *The Great Santini* (1979).

• The oak tree featured in *The War* (1994), where Elijah Wood and friends build a tree house, is located just out of town.

• Tom Hanks's shrimp boat in *Forrest Gump* (1994) is tied up at Lucy Creek, located about fifteen minutes southeast of Beaufort on Ladys Island. The Gump House was actually a set built alongside the Combahee River, on the private Bluff Plantation in Yemassee. The scenes in which Hanks saves his fellow soldiers in Vietnam were filmed on Fripps Island and Hunting Island State Park. Additional scenes, in which a young Forrest Gump, played by Michael Humphreys, grows up in a fictional Alabama town, were filmed on the main street of Varnville.

• Tom Cruise wins his first major race in *Days of Thunder* (1990) at the Darlington raceway. Darlington was also a featured racetrack in *Stroker Ace* (1983), which starred Burt Reynolds.

• The deep-sea environment in *The Abyss* (1989) was created in tanks at the never-completed Cherokee Nuclear Power Plant, outside Gaffney. Twentieth Century-Fox left the sets standing after filming completed, but the plant is closed to the public.

• In *Sleeping With the Enemy* (1990), Julia Roberts seeks refugee from an abusive husband in Abbeville, which was identified in the movie as Cedar Falls, Iowa.

• *Paradise* (1991), which starred Don Johnson and Melanie Griffith as a childless couple whose neighbor (Elijah Wood) comes to visit them, was filmed in the tiny town of McClellanville, off Highway 17 between Charleston and Georgetown. The quaint seaport town located just south of Myrtle Beach—and identified in the movie as Brimley—was actually Georgetown.

• *Coupe de Ville* (1990), a road movie about three brothers who drive a 1963 Cadillac from Michigan to their mother's home in Miami, was filmed on various highways and roads in the Scenic Upstate region of South Carolina, including a small town called Tigerville.

• *Rich in Love* (1993), a family drama starring Albert Finney, Ethan Hawke, and Kyle McLachlan, was filmed throughout the historic section of Charleston; at a private home in Mount Pleasant; in the Steam Room and Oyster Bar of the Fish Market Restaurant, on 12 Cumberland Street, Charleston; at Fishbones Nightclub, on 1658 Snowden Road in Mount Pleasant; and at Wando High School, on 1560 Mathis Ferry Road.

North Carolina

Carolco Studios
1223 North 23rd Street, Wilmington

Although tours are not offered, you can drive past Carolco Studios, which is one of the largest motion-picture and television production facilities east of Hollywood. The lot, Jeffrey Goodall of *Premiere* magazine reports, "isn't exactly a vision of Hollywood glamour. On a road lined with office buildings and industrial warehouses on the outskirts of town, it could easily be mistaken for the local UPS distribution center. It's a place to make movies cheap."

The studio was initially built in 1984 by Italian producer Dino DeLaurentiis, who came to Wilmington to make *Firestarter* (1984). Since then, dozens of films have been shot on the studio's stages and back lots, including *Year of the Dragon* (1985), *No Mercy* (1986), *Teenage Mutant Ninja Turtles* (1990), *Betsy's Wedding* (1990), *Billy Bathgate* (1991), *29th Street* (1991), *The Hudsucker Proxy* (1994), and *The Crow* (1994). During the filming of *The Crow*, actor Brandon Lee was accidentally killed by a prop gun on stage 4.

Wilmington

When Wilmington became a production center, filming also began spilling over to the city itself. Locations in town include:

• The Carolina Apartments, at Fifth Avenue and Market Street, where Isabella Rossellini lives in *Blue Velvet* (1986).

• The Wilmington Police Station and New Hanover High School, seen in the same movie.

• The historical Bellamy mansion, at Fifth Avenue and Market Street, which served as the exterior of the Hillyer Hotel in *Rambling Rose* (1991); and the Graystone Inn, 100 South Third Street, which was used for the hotel's interior.

• The Old Wilmington Light Infantry Armory, at 409 Market Street (now Wilmington city offices), and the Independence Shopping Mall, on Oleander Drive, in *Raw Deal* (1986).

• The Thalian Hall Center for the Performing Arts, on 310 Chestnut Street, which was used as a Broadway theater in *Weeds* (1987); the college theater where Julia Roberts tries on hats in *Sleeping With the Enemy* (1990); and the opening and closing sequence of *Dream a Little Dream* (1989).

• The Kenan House, on 1705 Market Street, and the Wise House, on 1713 Market Street, on the campus of the University of North Carolina at Wilmington. The Kenan House, which is the private home of the chancellor, served as a Saratoga hotel in *Billy Bathgate* and also appeared briefly in *Rambling Rose* and *Betsy's Wedding*.

• The Wise House, which is now the university's alumni office. It was used for interior scenes of Anthony Hopkins's home in *The Road to Wellville* (1994). The television series *Matlock* has also filmed extensively on the campus and all over town.

Other Movies Filmed in Wilmington

• The fabulous home that Julia Roberts shares with Patrick Bergin in *Sleeping With the Enemy*—before she runs away from him—was built specifically for the movie by the production company at the north end of Wrightsville Beach, eight miles east of Wilmington, and torn down after production was complete.

• Similarly, the beach house in *Weekend at Bernie's* (1989) was constructed on the Fort Fisher recreation area, about thirty miles south of Wilmington, and then carted away after filming. The movie also filmed at the Wrightsville Marina; Carolina Beach State Park, south of Wilmington, for the scenes where Bernie was skiing; and at Bald Head Island, which was also featured in *The Butcher's Wife* (1991). That movie used "Captain Charlie's Station," three adjacent seaside homes that were once owned by Capt. Charles Swan, the lighthouse's keeper for five decades.

• Laura Dern's wedding in *Rambling Rose* was filmed at Black River Presbyterian Church in neighboring Ivanhoe.

• *Crimes of the Heart* was filmed at a private home on Caswell Street in Southport.

Orton Plantation
on NC Highway 133, eighteen miles south of Wilmington

This onetime rice plantation, built in 1725 and located between Wilmington and Southport, served as the headquarters of the Shop, a secret government organization that tries to capture Drew Barrymore in *Firestarter*.

In *Crimes of the Heart* (1986) the plantation served as the Botrelle mansion, where Sissy Spacek shoots her husband (Beeson Carroll) after he finds her with a fifteen-year-old black boy.

The mansion and gardens are open daily.

Orton Plantation, Firestarter *(courtesy North Carolina Travel and Tourism/William Russ)*

Durham Athletic Park
428 Morris Street, Durham

Bull Durham (1988) is a comedy about a ditzy schoolteacher (Susan Sarandon) who each year chooses a different member of the minor league Durham Bulls to be her lover. (In the movie, Kevin Costner and Sarandon's real-life husband, Tim Robbins, vie for her affections.) It filmed extensively at the five thousand–seat stadium, which, until 1995, was the home of the Durham Bulls, the Atlanta Braves' Class A ball team.

Duke University
on Chapel Drive, Durham

The library's Gothic Reading Room and several campus buildings were featured in the football film *The Program* (1993). *The Handmaid's Tale* (1990), which starred Natasha Richardson, Robert Duvall, and Faye Dunaway, was also filmed extensively on campus, but no records exist as to which buildings were used.

Other films that used Duke exteriors include *Weeds* (1987) and *Brainstorm* (1983), Natalie Wood's last movie. A very brief scene of

Nicole Kidman swimming underwater in *Billy Bathgate* was filmed at Duke's diving pool.

Winston-Salem

Mr. Destiny (1990), a fantasy in which James Belushi is granted a wish to relive his life as a success, was filmed at the abandoned offices of the R.J. Reynolds tobacco plant on RJR Boulevard, which was turned into the factory and executive offices of Liberty Republic, where Belushi's character works. Additional scenes were filmed at the Grecian Corner, a restaurant at 101 Eden Terrace, where Belushi dines with Linda Hamilton, and at the Cafe Piaf, on 405 West Fourth Street.

The Bedroom Window (1986), in which Steve Guttenberg's married lover witnesses an assault outside the apartment and Guttenberg pretends to be the witness (only to become a suspect himself), was filmed at the Performing Arts Center for the North Carolina School of the Arts.

Critical Condition (1987), a comedy in which Richard Pryor pretends to be a doctor, was filmed in a wing of the High Point Regional Hospital, about thirty minutes southeast of Winston-Salem. The wing no longer exists.

Biltmore Estate
on U.S. 25, Asheville

The 255-room French château, built in 1895 by philanthropist George W. Vanderbilt, is the largest private home in America. It became James Belushi's house in *Mr. Destiny* and Macauley Culkin's in *Richie Rich* (1994), and was where Peter Sellers worked as a gardener in *Being There* (1979). The grounds, which are open to tourists, were also featured in *The Last of the Mohicans*.

Biltmore House and Gardens, Being There, Mr. Destiny *(courtesy North Carolina Travel and Tourism/William Russ)*

Chimney Rock Park
U.S. 74 and 64, twenty-five miles southeast of Asheville

The Last of the Mohicans (1992) was filmed extensively at the park and at least five other sites, including Hickory Nut Falls, where the climactic fight scene was staged, and Inspiration Point, the setting of the love scene between Madeleine Stowe and Daniel Day-Lewis, can be seen or visited by tourists. The park publishes a brochure with a complete list of film sites. Write to Chimney Rock Park, Highway 64-74, Chimney Rock, North Carolina, 28720.

Chimney Rock, Last of the Mohicans (*courtesy North Carolina Travel and Tourism/William Russ*)

The Great Smoky Mountains Railway
Near Dillsboro

The spectacular train-wreck crash in *The Fugitive*, which frees Harrison Ford, playing the prison-bound Dr. Richard Kimble, was staged along a specially built track of the Great Smoky Mountains Railroad, constructed next to existing track. The wreckage is not visible from any highways, but tourists who ride the train between Dillsboro and Bryson City can see the remains of the two engines that were left after the stunt.

The crash involves a bus carrying prisoners and guards tumbling down a mountainside and landing on the railroad track, with Ford escaping just before the train slams into the bus. Since the wreck could only be staged once, the producers spent ten weeks in preparation, and sixteen cameras were set up to capture the action. One camera became embedded in twenty-six feet of dirt, and it took eight hours to dig it out.

To ride the Great Smoky Mountain Railway, write Dillsboro Depot, Box 397, Dillsboro, North Carolina, 28725.

The Fugitive *train engine (courtesy Lavidge & Associates)*

Cheoah Dam
on U.S. 129

The other spectacular stunt in *The Fugitive* was filmed at this hydroelectric dam, located about two miles north of the Tennessee–North Carolina border. Cornered by Tommy Lee Jones (playing Marshal Gerard), Harrison Ford—or at least six Harrison Ford look-alike dummies—plunges 225 feet into the waters below and miraculously survives.

There is a good view of the dam from U.S. 129 River Bridge, which is close to the Rock Trail Head hiking trail. Do not go looking for the subterranean tunnels which Ford runs through: they were built in a Chicago warehouse especially for the movie.

Other Locations in North Carolina

• Jodie Foster's cabin in *Nell* (1994) was built in an isolated area on Fontana Lake in the Nantahala National Forest in Western North Carolina.

• *The Color Purple* (1985) was filmed at a restored antebellum farmhouse near Wadesboro, at the Wadesboro courthouse, and in downtown Marshville.

• *Billy Bathgate* was filmed in the town of Hamlet, primarily at a hotel on Main Street that has since burned down and at the train station. Several storefronts were dressed up to resemble 1930s upstate New York.

• The North Carolina governor's mansion, located at 200 North Blount in Raleigh, was the scene of the wedding reception in *Betsy's Wedding*.

• *The Handmaid's Tale* was also filmed in downtown Raleigh during an arts festival.

• 1963 Dallas was re-created along Rocky Mount's Main Street, and in the cities of Wilson and Elm City for *Love Field* (1992), which starred Michelle Pfeiffer and Dennis Haysbert.

• *Days of Thunder* (1990) and *Stroker Ace* (1983) filmed at Charlotte Motor Speedway.

Chapter 11

The Mid-Atlantic States

Virginia

Hidden Valley Bed and Breakfast
Hidden Valley Road, Warm Springs

This bed-and-breakfast, which was built for Judge John Woods Warwick between 1848 and 1951, was Richard Gere and Jodie Foster's family home in *Sommersby* (1993). The house, formerly known as the Warwickton mansion, is located on National Forest Service property, about fifty-five miles east of Lexington.

Sommersby Home, Hidden Valley, Virginia (courtesy Hidden Valley Bed and Breakfast Warwickton Mansion)

Downtown Lexington

Sommersby was also filmed on Lexington's Main and Washington streets, which were transformed into 1860s Nashville by dressing windows and importing dirt on the two streets. According to Martha Doss, director of the Lexington Visitors Bureau: "The final scene of the movie—the hanging of Richard Gere—was filmed in a parking lot off of Main Street. The sign 'Millinery de Russelot' is still on the wall of a shop called the Victorian Parlor on Main and Washington. Visitors are welcome to walk around the areas where the film was shot."

(*Note:* The courtroom scenes were filmed in the town of Charlotte, about a hundred miles southeast of Lexington.)

Downtown Lexington seen in Sommersby *(copyright 1994 Nathan Beck)*

University of Virginia
Charlottesville

True Colors (1990), the story of two graduates of the University of Virginia law school who are best friends until they go their separate paths, includes some beauty shots of the campus and classroom scenes in Clark Hall, where the university's law school was once located. The movie, which was about the loss of morals to obtain power, starred James Spader as the student who becomes a straight-arrow prosecutor and John Cusack as his onetime friend who betrays everyone as a senator's aide and congressional candidate.

Keswick Hall
701 County Club Drive, Keswick

In *The Four Seasons* (1981), a comedy-drama about a year in the lives of three couples who are friends, the couples (Alan Alda and Carol Burnett; Len Cariou and Sandy Dennis; and Rita Moreno and Jack Weston) vacation in this English country inn, located seven miles east of Charlottesville.

Mountain Lake Hotel
Route 700, Mountain Lake 24136

This hotel, located fifty-five miles west of Roanoke, was turned into Kellerman's, a Catskill resort in *Dirty Dancing* (1987), the movie that helped launch Patrick Swayze and Jennifer Grey's careers. In the movie, Grey and her family stay at the hotel's Virginia Cottage, while Swayze stays in room 232 in real life. The scenes depicting the employee cottages, Grey dancing on a bridge, and the dancing were filmed in another resort that has since closed.

Richmond

Richmond's Capitol, located on Capitol Square, served as the back portico of the White House in *Dave* (1993). The chambers of the House of Representatives were also filmed inside the building, which Thomas Jefferson designed.

My Dinner With Andre (1981) filmed in the Grand Ballroom of the Jefferson Hotel on Franklin and Adams streets, and *Love Field*

(1991) filmed throughout the city, with downtown Richmond serving as Dallas in 1963. For the night scenes, the area adjacent to the State Capitol and Jeb Stuart Circle was adopted to resemble Washington, D.C.

Pentagon
near Washington Boulevard, Arlington

The 1987 thriller *No Way Out* (1987) was filmed in the Pentagon concourse and in a few of its corridors. However, the scenes inside the Pentagon, in which Kevin Costner tries frantically to thwart an investigation that would reveal his affair with Sean Young, the secretary of defense's mistress, was re-created on soundstages at MGM studios in Culver City, California.

Other Locations in Virginia

• The resort town of Smith Mountain Lake played the New Hampshire town of Lake Winnipesaukee in *What About Bob?* (1991), a comedy about a disturbed patient (Bill Murray) who follows his psychiatrist (Richard Dreyfuss) on vacation.

• *Toy Soldiers* (1991), which starred Sean Astin as the leader of some prep-school boys who fight back against terrorists who take over their school, was filmed at the Miller School, off Route 250 in Crozet.

• In *Crazy People* (1990), Dudley Moore is institutionalized at Chatham Hall, a private girl's school in Chatham. Roanoke's Crestar Bank was transformed into the Manhattan advertising agency where Moore and Paul Reiser work.

• The family farmhouse in the 1994 version of *Lassie* was on Floyd Avenue in Tazewell, and the climactic scene, in which Lassie and Thomas Guiry struggle to survive against raging river rapids, was filmed by Samson Falls in Hinton.

• Arlington National Cemetery made appearances in *Gardens of Stone* (1987), *JFK* (1991) and *Clear and Present Danger* (1994).

• Mt. Vernon, George Washington's home, was used for a scene in which Denzel Washington meets his editor, John Lithgow, to discuss his story in *The Pelican Brief* (1993).

• *The Silence of the Lambs* (1990) was filmed at FBI training headquarters in Quantico.

• Some sequences of *Navy SEALS* (1990) was shot along the Virginia Beach shoreline.

West Virginia

West Virginia has hosted three movies. *Reckless* (1984) was filmed at the Lodge on Williams Drive (next to the Williams Country Club). The facility, owned by Weirton Steel and used to house its board members, served as Daryl Hannah's home. Hannah's love scene with Aidan Quinn was filmed in the boiler room of the community center on Main Street. Also featured was Jimmy Carey Stadium, used by the Weir High School.

Sweet Dreams (1985), the screen biography of Patsy Cline (with Jessica Lange), filmed in Martinsburg at the Rainbow Road Club on Route 340 and at the Green Hill Cemetery on East Burke Street. One Martinsburg resident told *People* magazine: "It's the most exciting thing that's happened here since the great train robbery at Warm Springs Crossing forty years ago."

Matewan (1987), John Sayles's film about striking miners fighting union-busting owners, was filmed in Thurmond, which West Virginia officials describe as more or less a ghost town. In the film, Thurmond became a fictional 1920s West Virginia mining town.

District of Columbia

The White House
1600 Pennsylvania Avenue

Since commercial use of the White House is prohibited by law, every Oval Office depicted in the movies is a re-creation. Filmmakers are only allowed to take establishing shots of the White House from a distance, and those scenes, of course, have appeared in practically every movie based in the nation's capital.

The White House (courtesy Washington Convention and Visitors Association)

Lincoln Memorial

In one of the more controversial scenes in *JFK* (1991), Kevin Costner, playing New Orleans district attorney Jim Garrison, visits Washington to investigate the murder of President John F. Kennedy and meets Donald Sutherland at the memorial. Sutherland plays an unidentified chief of the CIA's "black operations" division ("Just call me X") who tells Costner that he was ordered to the South Pole two weeks before the assassination. Had he been in Washington, Sutherland claimed, he would have ordered additional protection for the president. Sutherland called that "the best indication of a massive plot in Dallas," but the story was rather fanciful. In real life the CIA has no responsibility for the protection of presidents, and Sutherland's claim that the telephone lines in Washington were closed down an hour before the assassination so no one could warn Kennedy was also not true.

In *In the Line of Fire* (1993), Clint Eastwood takes fellow Secret Service agent René Russo to the memorial on their first date. Eastwood also expresses regrets that he could not have been there for the assassinated Lincoln.

In *Forrest Gump* (1994), Tom Hanks, who apparently has no idea he is addressing a crowd of antiwar protesters, starts to deliver a speech when a saboteur pulls the plug of the sound system. When his childhood friend, played by Robin Wright, spots Hanks, the two run to each other in the Reflecting Pool. The scene marks the first time the District of Columbia has given permission to film in the pool.

The memorial also made cameo appearances in *The Firm* (1993)—as a backdrop to a scene in which Ed Harris and Steven Hill try to turn Tom Cruise into a Justice Department informer—and in the classic *The Day the Earth Stood Still* (1951). Spaceman Michael Rennie, who is looking for one person on Earth he can reason with to stop its destructive ways, sees the statue of Lincoln and says: "That's the man I'd like to talk to."

Lincoln Memorial, JFK, In the Line of Fire, The Day the Earth Stood Still, Forrest Gump (courtesy Washington Convention and Visitors Association)

Georgetown University Law Center
600 New Jersey Avenue, N.W.

In *The Pelican Brief* (1993), Julia Roberts and Denzel Washington go to the law school trying to find the White and Blazevich lawyer who has learned that a contributor to the president's election campaign has had two Supreme Court justices killed.

Georgetown has also been featured in *The Exorcist* (1973) and *The Exorcist III* (1990), both written, and the latter directed, by Georgetown alumnus William Peter Blatty. *Born Yesterday* (1992) was filmed in Healey Circle, inside the front gates and in Healey Building classroom 104.

Exorcist Steps
from Prospect Street down to M Street, Georgetown

One of the famous scenes in *The Exorcist* involves a possessed Linda Blair running down the long staircase adjacent to her brick house on Prospect Street, to M Street, where it becomes Canal Road.

Riggs National Bank
Pennsylvania Avenue and 15th Street

Julia Roberts goes to this bank in *The Pelican Brief* to pick up the incriminating videotape.

The scenes where she is almost killed in a parking garage after going to the bank were filmed in Bethesda, Maryland.

Willard Intercontinental Hotel
1401 Pennsylvania Avenue, N.W.

The hotel, located a block and a half from the White House, was where John Goodman hires a journalist (Don Johnson) to do an IQ makeover on his Las Vegas showgirl-girlfriend (Melanie Griffith) in *Born Yesterday*.

Washington Post
1150 15th Street, N.W.

Ironically, the *Post* refused to allow filming in its offices for *All the President's Men* (1976), the story of its own reporters' investigation of the Watergate scandal. (The offices were re-created at Burbank Studios.) Yet it did allow cameras in its pressroom for the light 1989 romantic comedy *Chances Are*. In the latter movie Ryan O'Neal plays a *Post* reporter who befriends Robert Downey Jr., a recent Yale graduate who aspires to work for the *Post*. The apparent reason for the *Post*'s change of heart: the screenwriters of *Chances Are*, Perry and Randy Howze, were childhood friends of *Post* editor Ben Bradlee's daughter.

Watergate Building
2650 Virginia Avenue, N.W.

The owners of the Watergate building did allow it to be filmed for the re-creation of the famous bungled burglary in *All the President's Men*.

Omni Shoreham Hotel
2500 Calvert Street, N.W.

In *No Way Out* (1987), Kevin Costner first meets and becomes captivated by Sean Young during a party at the Shoreham Hotel.

St. Elizabeth's Hospital
2700 Martin Luther King Jr. Avenue

The hospital doubled as U.S. Naval Academy grounds in *A Few Good Men* (1992), which starred Tom Cruise, Jack Nicholson, and Demi Moore.

Smithsonian Institute

Cybill Shepherd works as the curator of the Smithsonian's First Ladies' Gowns Exhibit in *Chances Are*.

Georgetown Park Mall
M Street and Wisconsin Avenue

The outrageous men's room shoot-out in *True Lies* (1994) supposedly takes place at this shopping mall. It was, of course, filmed on a set, but the movie did feature scenes in which Arnold Schwarzenegger chases a nuclear terrorist, played by Art Malik, through some of the mall's shops and then onto M Street, where Malik, trying to escape, hijacks a motor scooter, and Schwarzenegger "borrows" a policeman's horse in Franklin Park to continue the pursuit.

Other Locations in Washington, D.C.

• The driving scenes in *No Way Out*—in which Kevin Costner tries to prevent Pentagon goons from killing Sean Young's friend Iman—were filmed on the Whitehurst Freeway in Georgetown.

• *In Country* (1989) was filmed at the Vietnam Memorial.

• Kevin Kline's house in *Dave* (1993) was on Kenyon Street in Mount Pleasant.

• Cher lives in the Adams Morgan section of Washington in *Suspect* (1987), and in *In the Line of Fire*, Eastwood's chase of John Malkovich—and the scenes in which Malkovich kills Eastwood's partner (Dylan McDermott) and saves Eastwood's life—were filmed in Adams Morgan.

Maryland

Ashby Bed-and-Breakfast
27448 Ashby Drive, Easton

This bed-and-breakfast was transformed into the site of a double murder in *Silent Fall* (1994), which starred Richard Dreyfuss as a child psychiatrist hired to solve a murder. Dreyfuss tries to get into the mind of the only witness: the victimized couple's nine-year-old autistic son, plays by Ben Faulkner. Liv Tyler plays Faulkner's teenage sister.

Baltimore

The Bedroom Window Apartment
12 East Mount Vernon Place

In *The Bedroom Window* (1986), Steve Guttenberg is having an affair with his boss's wife (Isabelle Huppert) when she witnesses an assault on Mount Vernon Square from his bedroom window. Guttenberg reports the crime to the police, but to conceal the affair, he pretends that he is the witness. Inconsistencies in Guttenberg's story lead the police to suspect that Guttenberg committed the assault himself, and in order to defend himself, Guttenberg becomes the investigator.

George Peabody Library
17 East Mount Vernon Place

Jessica Lange meets Arliss Howard, who plays a musician, while delivering lunch here in *Men Don't Leave* (1990). The Peabody Library, which is part of Johns Hopkins University but separate from the main campus, is around the corner from *The Bedroom Window* apartment.

B&O Railroad Museum
901 West Pratt Street

This museum was also the scene of an uncomfortable family lunch in *Men Don't Leave.*

Hollywood Diner
400 East Saratoga Street

The diner from director Barry Levinson's *Diner* (1982), located on an empty lot at Boston and Montford streets. At the time of the filming, is now located at the corner of East Saratoga and Holliday streets in downtown Baltimore.

The diner also made appearances in the 1987 film *Tin Men* (Danny DeVito and Richard Dreyfuss eat there), the 1991 film *Homicide*, the NBC series of the same name, and *Sleepless in Seattle* (1993), in which it was called the Capitol Diner. Meg Ryan stops for tea at the diner and hears the waitresses talking about "Sleepless in Seattle" on the radio.

Clarence Mitchell Courthouse
100 North Calvert Street

The courthouse, located a few blocks from the Hollywood Diner, was featured in four of the movies shot in Baltimore: *And Justice for All* (1979), *The Bedroom Window* (1986), *Her Alibi* (1989), and *The Distinguished Gentleman* (1992). In the latter movie, the ceremonial courtroom doubled as the U.S. Senate's Arts Caucus Room.

Broadway Recreation Pier in Fells Point
on Thames Street at Broadway

The pier, which resembles a police station, was used for the exterior of the police station in director Barry Levinson's acclaimed NBC series *Homicide*. Soundstages for the series were built inside.

Parts of Levinson's *Avalon* (1990) were also filmed in this area as well as in the Mount Vernon area and at a house on Cliffmont Avenue, where Armin Mueller-Stahl grows up. That house is also down the street from Danny DeVito's house in the Levinson-directed *Tin Men*, at 3107 Cliffmount.

Belvedere Condominiums
Charles Street at East Chase

The Belvedere Hotel, where Danny DeVito drinks and fights with Richard Dreyfuss in *Tin Men*, is now a condominium complex.

The hotel was also featured briefly in *Clara's Heart* (1988) in a scene in which Kathleen Quinlan goes to a luncheon and sees her husband, Michael Ontkean, with another woman.

Orioles Stadium at Camden Yards

The park doubled as Cleveland's stadium in *Major League II* (1994). It was also featured briefly in *Dave*. Kevin Kline, playing the president, throws out a ceremonial first ball.

Orioles Stadium, Major League *(courtesy Baltimore Orioles)*

Baltimore County Courthouse
400 Washington Avenue, Towson

Director John Waters used the old courthouse, normally reserved for workmen's compensation and zoning hearings, for Kathleen Turner's trial in *Serial Mom* (1994).

The courthouse is located in suburban Towson's town square. Other Towson locations in the movie include the Church of the Good Shepherd, on 1401 Carrolltown Avenue, where Turner barely manages to elude police; a Video America store on Cold Springs Lane; and Hammerjacks (now the Inner Harbor Concert Hall), on 1101 South Howard Street, in Baltimore, near Orioles Stadium. Turner is finally arrested in the dance club while a band and dancers cheer her on.

Other Locations in Baltimore

• Shirley MacLaine's house in *Guarding Tess* (1994), supposedly in Columbus, Ohio, was located on South Road in the Mount Washington section of town.

• *Sleepless in Seattle* was filmed at the offices of the *Baltimore Sun*, where Meg Ryan and Rosie O'Donnell work, and at a rowhouse at 904 South Broadway, which served as Ryan's apartment.

• *The Accidental Tourist* (1988) was filmed primarily in Roland Park.

• *Meteor Man* (1993) was filmed in Reservoir Hill, an inner-city neighborhood in Baltimore.

• *Broadcast News* (1987) was filmed at Baltimore's Trailways Bus Terminal and at BWI Airport, where Holly Hunter refuses to board a plane with William Hurt because he has crossed an ethical line.

• *Avalon* was filmed at the Hollins Market, located on Hollins Street in Union Square; across the street from the market at the 19th Century Shop, a bookstore at 1047 Hollins Street that was transformed into the K and K market appliance store; at the Senator Theater, on 5904 York Road, the site of a street car crash; and at Druid Hill Park on Druid Park Lake Dr. in downtown Baltimore, where the family camps out to escape the heat.

• *Clara's Heart* also filmed at St. Anne's Church, on 528 East 22nd Street, downtown; at the Rusty Scupper restaurant in Harbor Place; and (for the final scene) at Children's Hospital, on 3825 Greenspring Avenue.

• The Baltimore Museum of Art, on Art Museum Drive, was used for the opera house in which Isabelle Huppert is stabbed in

The Bedroom Window and was the site of the cocktail reception for Tom Selleck in *Her Alibi* (1989). Selleck first eyes Paulina Porizkova at the Kelmscott Bookstore, on 32 West 25th Street, and tells his publisher about her at a coffee shop now called Budlows, on 1501 Budlow Street.

• The infamous spot where Divine eats dog feces in *Pink Flamingos* (1972) was in front of 894 Tyson Street.

Other Maryland Locations

• In *Patriot Games* (1992), Harrison Ford defends himself from a revenge-seeking IRA terrorist outside Gate 3 of the U.S. Naval Academy in Annapolis.

• John Malkovich shoots duck hunters in *In the Line of Fire* (1993) at the Isaac Walton League Ponds at Patuxent River Park on Governors Ridge Road in Bowie.

• *Clara's Heart* was filmed primarily at a private estate called Locust Grove in Talbot County, near St Michael's and Easton.

Delaware

St. Andrew's School
Noxontown Pond Road, Middletown

Dead Poets Society (1989), a drama that starred Robin Williams as an unconventional teacher, was filmed at this private prep school. The play was held at Middletown's Everett Theater.

Pennsylvania

Pittsburgh

Pittsburgh's film locations include:

• The Carnegie Institute, on 4400 Forbes Avenue, where in *Flashdance* (1983), Jennifer Beals dances through the Hall of Sculpture;

• The Hall of Dinosaurs at the Carnegie's Museum of Natural History that Jodie Foster walks through in *The Silence of the Lambs* (1990);

• The Music Hall foyer of the Carnegie, where Nick Nolte and Susan Sarandon, after an opera performance, talk to their son's doctor (Peter Ustinov) about a cure in *Lorenzo's Oil* (1991);

• The Soldiers and Sailors Museum, on 4141 Fifth Avenue, which was turned into the Memphis Town Hall—where a caged Anthony Hopkins is interrogated by FBI agent Jodie Foster—in *The Silence of the Lambs*;

• A parking lot at the corner of Tinsbury Street and Hatteras Street in Troy Hill, where an elaborate façade that represents the Teamster Hall was constructed for *Hoffa* (1992);

• The Mellon Institute, on Fifth Avenue, which doubled as the Washington, D.C., courthouse steps in *Hoffa*;

• An apartment on Bayard and Morewood avenues in Shadyside, where Marisa Tomei lives in *Only You* (1994). (Other key locations include the Kennywood Amusement Park, on 4800 Kennywood Boulevard in West Mifflin, and Pittsburgh's new airport);

• The Allegheny Cemetery in Bloomfield, where Ellen Burstyn, Olympia Dukakis, and Diane Ladd attend funerals in *The Cemetery Club* (1992);

• Heinz Hall for the Performing Arts, at 600 Penn Avenue, in *The Cemetery Club*, where Lainie Kazan's many wedding ceremonies and receptions are held;

• Washington's Landing on the Allegheny River, where Bruce Willis docks his houseboat in *Striking Distance* (1993). (Detillo's Roost, the scene of the final shoot-out, was a cabin on Duck Hollow built specifically for the movie. The car explosion in the movie's opening scenes occurred inside the Armstrong Tunnel in downtown Pittsburgh, and the memorable car chase scenes where three police cars chasing a suspect on hills seemingly go airborne, was filmed on Fifth Avenue in suburban Duquesne. Willis's River Rescue station was another set built specifically for the movie atop a barge at the Old River Rescue Center on Pittsburgh's south side);

• The Duquesne Steel Works, a steel mill off Route 837 in Duquesne, where Peter Weller confronts his executioners in *Robocop* (1986). It was also at the abandoned mill, on a paved road gated off to the public, that John Cusack finds $1.2 million in unmarked, untraceable currency that has just fallen off an armored truck in *Money for Nothing* (1993);

• The City/County Building on Grant Street. City Council chambers were turned into a Senate hearing room in *Bob Roberts* (1992);

• WQED-TV, 4802 Fifth Avenue, Pittsburgh's public broadcasting station, where Tim Robbins films *The Cutting Edge* in *Bob Roberts*; and

• Liberty Avenue, where Anthony LaPaglia finally kills Robert Loggia in *Innocent Blood* (1992).

• Pittsburgh also stood in for Washington, D.C., in *Lorenzo's Oil*, the story of a couple's search for a cure for their son's rare genetic disease. Nick Nolte and Susan Sarandon's house was actually a façade built between two existing houses on Dickson Avenue, near the corner of Woodland in Ben Avon, six miles from downtown Pittsburgh. The school Lorenzo (who was played by six different actors) attends burned down while the movie was being filmed, necessitating some on-the-set rewrites.

• *Mrs. Soffel* (1984), which starred Diane Keaton as a prison warden's wife who assists in the escape of two criminals sentenced to hang for the murder of a grocer, and *The Silence of the Lambs* were filmed at the Allegheny County Jail, which is not open to the public.

• Some scenes from *The Deer Hunter* (1978) were shot in Pittsburgh, but the mills are no longer in existence today.

Philadelphia

Thirtieth Street Station
30th Street

The train station has figured prominently in three of Philadelphia's biggest movies. In *Trading Places* (1983), Eddie Murphy, Dan Aykroyd, Jamie Lee Curtis, and Denholm Elliott, dressed in disguises, board a New York–bound train to switch briefcases with the Duke Brothers' bagman. In *Witness* (1985), Lukas Haas, playing a young Amish boy, witnesses a murder while hiding in a rest-room stall. And in *Blow Out* (1980), John Travolta, John Lithgow, and Nancy Allen use the station as a key meeting place.

Arena
46th and Market streets

This now-empty warehouse was the original home of *American Bandstand*, hosted by Dick Clark. Matthew Modine and Nicolas Cage also chase pigeons here in *Birdy* (1984).

2014 Delancey Street
(at 21st Street)

Dan Aykroyd's house in *Trading Places*.

Mellon Bank Center
1735 Market Street

The exterior of the bank served as the "Wheeler Building," Tom Hanks's former law offices, in *Philadelphia* (1993). Directly across the street is the Pickwick Pharmacy, where Denzel Washington fends off advances from a Penn law student who incorrectly assumes that Washington is gay because he is defending a gay man.

Rittenhouse Square

The park is where Eddie Murphy pretends he is a legless veteran while panhandling in the opening scenes of *Trading Places*.

Sylvester Stallone and Talia Shire walk in the park in *Rocky II* (1979); and in *Mannequin* (1987), Andrew McCarthy visits his girlfriend in the nearby Dorchester Apartments on the square.

Academy of Music
Broad and Locust streets

This was the turn-of-the-century New York opera house where Daniel Day-Lewis first sees Michelle Pfeiffer in the opening scenes of *The Age of Innocence* (1993). The Academy of Music is the home of the Philadelphia Orchestra.

Fidelity Bank Building
corner of Broad and Sansom streets

This was the Duke and Duke Bank owned by brothers Don Ameche and Ralph Bellamy in *Trading Places*.

City Hall
at Penn Square, Broad and Market streets

Courtroom number 243 in this extraordinary Greek Revival building was the setting for the courthouse scenes in *Philadelphia*. In *Blow Out*, John Travolta drives a jeep through the concourse of city hall. In *Birdy*, Matthew Modine and Nicolas Cage joke about the statue of William Penn hovering above city hall, some 548 feet above ground. The basement of city hall was also used as the setting for the art thriller *Civil Defense* (1994).

Philadelphia City Hall (courtesy Philadelphia Convention and Visitors Bureau)

John Wanamaker's Department Store
corner of Market and 13th streets (on South Penn Square)

Just east of city hall is the store that was the primary location for both *Mannequin* (1987) and *Mannequin II: On the Move* (1991), in which Kim Cattrall (in the former) and Kristy Swanson (in the latter) play department-store dummies who come to life.

The store also appears in *Blow Out*. John Travolta crashes his jeep into the display window.

Independence National Historic Park
Chestnut Street between Fifth and Sixth streets

The Liberty Bell, Philadelphia's most historic attraction, has been featured in *Trading Places*, *Blow Out*, *Cross Country* (1983), and several TV movies.

Veterans Stadium

Mark Harmon and Harold Ramis relive their high school baseball moments in *Stealing Home* (1988). The stadium is home to the Philadelphia Eagles and Phillies.

Philadelphia Museum of Art
26th Street and Benjamin Franklin Parkway

Sylvester Stallone immortalized the art museum steps by running up them in the *Rocky* movies (and even tells his son he will go inside at the conclusion of *Rocky V*).

The museum itself doubled for the Metropolitan Museum of Art in New York City in *Dressed to Kill* (1980), starring Angie Dickinson.

Philadelphia Museum of Art, Age of Innocence, Rocky *(courtesy Philadelphia Museum of Art)*

Other Philadelphia Locations

• *Philadelphia* was also filmed at the University of Pennsylvania Fine Arts Library on Walnut Street, which served as the law library where Denzel Washington, realizing that Tom Hanks is being discriminated against, finally decides to represent him; a building at 1901 Chestnut Street, which served as Denzel Washington's law office; the Raquet Club, on 215 South 16th Street, where Hanks, Jason Robards, and other members of the law firm enjoy a sauna; the Spectrum, at Broad Street, where Robards and his partners, enjoying a basketball game in the SuperBoxes, are served with a subpoena; 1216 Arch Street, the Action AIDS office where Hanks receives his checkups; and Mt. Sinai Hospital, at Fourth and Reed, where Washington's wife delivers their baby, and Hanks dies.

• Michael Keaton and Kathy Baker meet for a date in *Clean and Sober* (1988) at the Colonial Theater, at 11th and Moyamensing streets.

• Bob's Diner, at Lyceum and Ridge avenues, is where Mark Harmon tells Harold Ramis the truth about a high school romance in *Stealing Home*.

• The murder that John Travolta taped in *Blow Out* occurs when the car crashes into Wissahickon Creek.

• *Taps* (1981) was filmed at the Valley Forge Military Academy and Junior College in Valley Forge, a suburb located twenty-six miles northwest of Philadelphia

• The 600 block of Durfor Street, between Seventh and Eighth streets, and Marshall Street, and the 2300 block of South Eighth Street, between Wolf and Ritner, were transformed into 1933 South Philadelphia in *Two Bits* (1995), starring Al Pacino. Other scenes were filmed in the President's Banquet Room at 2308 Snyder Avenue, which was transformed into the La Paloma Theater; at St. Gabriel's Church, at 29th and Dickenson streets (scene of the simultaneous wedding and funeral), and at Alcorn Elementary school at 32nd and Tasker.

Other Movies Filmed in Pennsylvania

• Johnstown was the setting for *All the Right Moves* (1983), the story of a high school football star (Tom Cruise) who struggles for a scholarship to avoid following his brother and father into steel mills. The Greater Johnstown High School has been torn down, but the practice field, beside the current high school building on Central Avenue, is still used today (as is Point Stadium, where the big football game was filmed).

• *Slap Shot* (1977), a hockey comedy that starred Paul Newman, was also filmed in Johnstown, primarily at the War Memorial Arena downtown.

• The interior of Harrisburg's state Capitol doubled as the U.S. Capitol in the Eddie Murphy comedy *The Distinguished Gentleman* (1992).

• Aerial views of Harrisburg were also seen in opening montage of the ABC-TV soap opera *One Life to Live*.

• Harrisburg's Riverside Stadium, home of the minor league Harrisburg Senators, was transformed into the Cleveland Indians' Winter Haven spring-training home in *Major League II*.

• In *Witness*, Harrison Ford, impersonating a peaceful Amishman, slugs a bully by W. L. Zimmerman & Sons general store in downtown Intercourse.

• The search for Hitler clones brings Gregory Peck to a farm about eleven miles south of New Providence in *The Boys From Brazil* (1978).

New Jersey

Hudson County Courthouse
Pavonia Avenue and Newark Street, Jersey City

In *It Could Happen to You* (1994), Rosie Perez is awarded, during divorce proceedings, $4 million that her ex-husband Nicolas Cage has won in the lottery and has shared with waitress Bridget Fonda as a tip. While the interior courtoom scenes were filmed in Brooklyn, the scenes in which Fonda bolts from the courtroom with Cage in pursuit were filmed in the ornate hallways and rotunda of the Hudson County Courthouse. The courthouse was also where third-generation crook Matthew Broderick is tried for burglary in *Family Business* (1989) and where immigrants are sworn in as citizens in *Moscow on the Hudson* (1994), starring Robin Williams.

Castelo Restaurant
61 Ferry Street, Newark

Mafia boss Dan Hedaya runs his operation out of this restaurant in *Wiseguys* (1986), which starred Danny DeVito and Joe Piscopo as inept hoods in his employ.

The movie was also filmed at the Meadowlands Race Track in East Rutherford, where DeVito and Piscopo bet on the wrong horse, getting them in hot water with Hedaya, and at St. Lucy's Cathedral in Jersey City, where an attempt is made on their lives.

Hartley Dodge Memorial Building
Kings Road and Green Avenue, Madison

Glenn Close, running for governor of New York in *The World According to Garp* (1982), is assassinated in front of Madison's town hall.

Other New Jersey locations for *Garp* include the Lincoln Park airstrip, where, in one of the movie's most memorable scenes, a plane crashes into a house built on the airfield; and Bishop House, a building on the Rutgers University campus.

Ross Dock Park, Palisades Interstate Park
Fort Lee

Big (1988), which starred Tom Hanks as a thirteen-year-old whose wish to grow "big" was granted by a carnival fortune machine, was filmed on the banks of the Hudson River, directly beneath the George Washington Bridge. The filmmakers rented a traveling carnival and constructed the set in the park. Hanks's home was in Cliffside Park.

Woodrow Wilson Hall, Monmouth College
Long Branch

The administration building of Monmouth College, known as Shadow Lawn, served as Daddy Warbucks's Fifth Avenue mansion in *Annie* (1982). The lawn of the college library was used as the White House lawn.

Andy's Tire and Service Center
130 West Broad Street, Hopewell

In *IQ* (1994), this service center was transformed into the gas station where Tim Robbins repairs cars and meets Meg Ryan, who plays the niece of Albert Einstein (Walter Matthau). Major scenes were also filmed outside Fuld Hall at the Institute for Advance Study, in the township of Princeton (where Einstein did his research); the back yard of Einstein's former home at 112 Mercer Street, Princeton (although all interior shots were filmed at the more spacious home next door); Princeton University's Palmer Hall, which was used for the lecture hall scenes; Lawrenceville School, a private prep school which was turned into the hospital where

Matthau recovers from a heart attack; and at Princeton Battlefield State Park on Mercer Boulevard in Princeton Township, which was the movie's "Stargazer Field."

Bowcraft Playland
Route 22, Scotch Plains

This amusement park holds the distinction of appearing in two movies featuring Bruce Willis. In *Mortal Thoughts* (1991), a drunk and drugged-out Willis is killed in the parking lot, leading to an elaborate cover-up by his wife, Glenne Headly, and her best friend, Demi Moore (Willis's wife in real life). And although Willis does not appear in any scenes filmed at Bowcraft in *North* (1994), the park was featured very briefly as a site where John Ritter and Kate Capshaw take Elijah Wood on an outing. Ritter and Capshaw are one of the couples Wood stays with and interviews as prospective adoptive parents after winning free agency from his own parents.

Bridgewater Commons Mall
400 Commons Way, Bridgewater

In *North*, Elijah Wood's secret place where he retreats to when he feels down was, of all places, a furniture store in the mall. It was here where Wood meets Bruce Willis, who plays an Easter bunny and a guardian angel of sorts. The scenes featuring the interior of the store were filmed in Los Angeles.

Other New Jersey Locations

• The docks and warehouses seen in the Academy Award–winning *On the Waterfront* (1954) no longer exist, but fans of that film can still drive past Our Lady of Grace Church, at 400 Willow Avenue in Hoboken, the site of a love scene between Marlon Brando and Eva Marie Saint.

• Newark's City Hall, on 920 Broad Street, was used for the scenes depicting Harrison Ford's office in *Presumed Innocent* (1990).

• *Presumed Innocent* was also filmed at the Essex County Courthouse on Springfield Avenue and Market Street in Newark. The same courthouse was used as a government building in *Jacob's Ladder* (1990).

• Tim Robbins's house in *Jacob's Ladder*—supposedly on Fifth Avenue in New York—was on Ballentine Parkway in Newark.

• *The Color of Money* (1986) was filmed briefly in front of Merv Griffin's Resorts Casino Hotel in Atlantic City. The big pool tournament was supposed to have taken place at the casino; however, the scenes were actually shot at Chicago's Navy Pier.

• *The Pick-up Artist* (1987) and *Wiseguys* (1986) also filmed at the hotel.

• In *Running on Empty* (1988), filmed in Tenafly and Englewood, River Phoenix attends the Dwight Morrow High School at 274 Knickerbocker Road, in Englewood.

• *Something Wild* (1986), a road movie that starred Melanie Griffith, Jeff Daniels, and Ray Liotta, was filmed at Ringwood State Park in Ringwood and on other various New Jersey roads.

• *Lean on Me* (1989), which starred Morgan Freeman as "Crazy Joe" Clark, the controversial bat-wielding principal of Paterson's Eastside High School, filmed at the actual high school at 150 Park Avenue.

• *The Thing Called Love* (1992), River Phoenix's last movie, was filmed at Liberty State Park in Jersey City, as were scenes in *Married to It* (1993).

• The boxing sequence in *A Bronx Tale* (1993) was filmed at the Jersey City Armory.

• *Stealing Home* (1988), which starred Jodie Foster and Mark Harmon was filmed at Island Beach State Park.

• *Ragtime* (1981) and *Stardust Memories* (1980) were filmed among the Victorian houses on Ocean Avenue in Ocean Grove. *Stardust Memories* was also filmed at the Ocean Grove Auditorium.

• *The Lemon Sisters* (1990) was filmed on the boardwalks in Atlantic City and Asbury Park.

Chapter 12

New York City and State

New York City

Manhattan

Statue of Liberty
on Liberty Island

Like Central Park, this symbol of New York has appeared in more movies than anyone can count. Its most memorable recent film appearances include a scene in *Splash* (1984) in which a naked Daryl Hannah swims ashore in search of Tom Hanks and a corny coming-to-life of the statue in *Ghostbusters II* (1989). In their efforts to combat a gigantic slime wall, ghostbusters Bill Murray, Dan Aykroyd, Harold Ramis, and Ernie Hudson take over the statue, a symbol of everything good and decent about America, to mobilize New Yorkers into fighting the feelings of hatred that give the ghosts life.

Battery Park

Rosanna Arquette hits her head on a lamppost in the park, giving her amnesia, in *Desperately Seeking Susan* (1985). The quirky comedy, which also starred Madonna, was shot mostly in the East Village and SoHo.

U.S. Customs House
corner of Whitehall Street and Bowling Green

In *Ghostbusters II*, this beaux arts building was turned into the fictional Manhattan Museum of Art, where Sigourney Weaver works on the Carpathian painting that comes to life. The ghostbusters' triumphant final scenes were filmed on the building's steps.

The building also served as the headquarters of the Trask Company in *Working Girl* (1990). Weaver costarred in that movie with Harrison Ford and Melanie Griffith.

Federal Hall
28 Wall Street

In front of Federal Hall is a statue of George Washington that commemorates the site where Washington was sworn in as the first U.S. president. In *Ghost* (1990), two nuns set up a stand at the base of the statue, and Whoopi Goldberg reluctantly donates to them the blood money Patrick Swayze helps her take out of Tony Goldwyn's bank account.

(*Note: Ghost* was also filmed at a loft at Prince and Green streets in Soho, where Swayze and Demi Moore have their apartment; and at a restaurant, Mezzogiorno, on 195 Spring Street, where Goldberg has her first meeting with Demi Moore. Swayze's death was filmed on Crosby Street, between Prince and Spring.)

World Trade Center
on Church Street between Vesey and Liberty streets

In the 1976 version of *King Kong* the gorilla climbs the towers instead of the Empire State Building, which was scaled in the original.

The lobby of 7 World Trade Center was also one of four buildings filmed as the brokerage house where Sigourney Weaver and Melanie Griffith have their offices in *Working Girl*.

In *Trading Places* (1983), the climax was filmed in Comex, the commodities exchange located in the center. Filing took place over a weekend, with real-life commodities brokers working as extras.

Winter Garden, World Financial Center
200 Liberty Street

The formal party seen in the beginning of *The Bonfire of the Vanities* (1990) was filmed here, as was the party in which Grace Jones makes her spectacular appearance in *Boomerang* (1992). Over thirty thousand people work in the center, located across the West Side Highway from the World Trade Center.

Firehouse at 14 North Moore Street
at Varick Street

The firehouse was used for the exterior shots of Dan Aykroyd, Bill Murray, and Harold Ramis's offices in *Ghostbusters* (1984).

World Trade Center

New York County Courthouse
60 Centre Street

Dozens of movies and television series have been filmed at the courthouse, dating back to *Miracle on 34th Street* (1947). The Macy's Santa Claus (played by Edmund Gwenn) stood trial here. The exterior was also used in John Hughes's 1994 remake of the classic.

Other movies filmed at the courthouse include *12 Angry Men*; *Nuts* (1987), in which the courthouse served as the venue of Barbra Streisand's trial; *The Godfather* (1970), which includes a scene where Richard Conte tumbles down the steps; *GoodFellas* (1990), in which Ray Liotta testifies against fellow mobsters Robert De Niro and Paul Sorvino; *Regarding Henry* (1990), in which Harrison Ford tries a case before being shot; and *Legal Eagles* (1986), in which Robert Redford and Debra Winger defend Daryl Hannah. The courthouse has also appeared in quite a few television detective series, including *Law and Order*, *Kojak*, and *Cagney and Lacey*.

Gus' Pickle Stand
35 Essex Street

Pickle man Peter Riegert works at this stand in *Crossing Delancey* (1988), a comedy that also starred Amy Irving as the object of Riegert's affections.

Puck Building
295 Lafayette Street

This building, where *Spy* magazine was once published, was the site of the New Year's Eve party where Billy Crystal finally commits to Meg Ryan in *When Harry Met Sally* (1989). The wedding of their pals Carrie Fisher and Bruno Kirby was filmed in the Puck's ballroom.

Greenwich Village

Two of television's most popular sitcoms were based in the Village. *Taxi*, which appeared on ABC and NBC between 1978 and 1983, centered around taxi drivers who supposedly operated out of a garage at 534 Hudson Street, at the corner of Charles Street in the Village. *The Cosby Show*, which is widely regarded as the most popular series of the eighties, aired on NBC between 1984 and 1992. Cosby's town house can be found at 10 St. Luke's Place.

In his book *The Movie Lover's Guide to New York*, Richard Alleman identifies a number of other locations in the Village, including Al Pacino's residence in *Serpico* (1973), on 5–7 Minetta Street; the Bleecker Street Cinema, at 144 Bleecker Street, where Aidan Quinn worked as a projectionist in *Desperately Seeking Susan*; and a house at 111 Waverly Place, where Jane Fonda and Robert Redford lived in *Barefoot in the Park* (1967).

The park, of course, is Washington Square Park, which has been seen in dozens of movies, including *The Butcher's Wife* (1991), *Searching for Bobby Fischer* (1993), and *When Harry Met Sally*.

The park is also across from New York University on Fourth Street, where Matthew Broderick attends classes in *The Freshman* (1990).

Farther north in the Village, on the southeast corner of 12th Street and Fifth Avenue, is the building depicted as Paul Reiser and Helen Hunt's apartment in the NBC comedy *Mad About You*.

NYPD Blue Police Station
321 East Fifth Street

The exterior of the Ninth Precinct of the police department is used for what is identified as the 15th Precinct station in the ABC cop drama *NYPD Blue*. It was also the station Telly Savalas supposedly operated out of in *Kojak*.

Interiors for *NYPD Blue* are filmed on a Los Angeles soundstage.

Macy's
151 West 34th Street, Herald Square

Miracle on 34th Street, the 1947 Christmas classic, was filmed here. The 1994 remake, however, was filmed in Chicago. A Macy's spokesman, explaining why the store denied filmmaker John Hughes permission to film there again, said: "We feel the original stands on its own and could not be improved on." *Entertainment Weekly*, however, reported that the real reason permission was denied was because "the plot, in which Kris Kringle (Sir Richard Attenborough) fends off a corporate raider, hit too close to home. (The store went private in a leveraged buyout in 1986.)"

Morgan Court Condominium
211 Madison Avenue

"Sliver" is an architectural term for a tall and slim building on a narrow lot, and this condo was selected for the Sharon Stone–William Baldwin thriller *Sliver* (1993) because it fit the bill perfectly.

Stone supposedly lived on the twenty-fourth floor of the thirty-two-story building, in an apartment that rents for $5,200 a month. That, *Entertainment Weekly* noted, is "two or three times what a book editor like Stone's character could probably afford."

Empire State Building
350 Fifth Avenue

This famous New York skyscraper played a key role in each of the three versions of *Love Affair*. The original was made by director Leo McCarey in 1939 and starred Charles Boyer and Irene Dunne

Empire State Building, An Affair to Remember, King Kong, Sleepless in Seattle *(courtesy Empire State Building, managed by Helmsley-Spear, Inc.)*

as two people who meet and fall in love on a transatlantic crossing, even though they are engaged to others. To see if their love is real, Boyer and Dunne agree to meet three months later on the observation deck of the Empire State Building. Both intend to keep the appointment, but Dunne is struck by a cab on her way to the building, paralyzed, and too ashamed to tell Boyer of her condition.

McCarey remade the romance in 1957 under the title *An Affair to Remember*, with Cary Grant and Deborah Kerr playing the lovers. The updated 1994 version, *Love Affair*, starred real-life marrieds Warren Beatty and Annette Bening.

The 1993 hit *Sleepless in Seattle* also drew heavily on *An Affair to Remember*. Tom Hanks finally meets his soul mate, Meg Ryan, atop the skyscraper's observation deck, after the two almost miss each other. For *Sleepless in Seattle*, only the exteriors and lobby scenes of the building were filmed. Writer-director Nora Ephron could not get access to the observation deck for a long enough period of time to complete the work; so a replica of the deck was built in a hangar at the Sand Point Naval Station in Seattle, with an enormous photograph of the New York skyline built around the stage.

The Empire State Building, is of course, also famous for a love story of another stripe: the gorilla's infatuation with Fay Wray in the original *King Kong* (1933).

Grand Central Terminal
89 East 42nd Street

The climaxes of a number of movies, including *The House on Carroll Street* (1988), *Loose Cannons* (1990), and *Carlito's Way* (1993), were filmed here.

Metropolitan Life Insurance Company
11 Madison Avenue

The building served as Griffin Dunne's office in *After Hours* (1985), as the site where William Hurt witnesses a murder in *Eyewitness* (1981), and as Andrew McCarthy and Jonathan Silverman's offices in *Weekend at Bernie's* (1989).

Daily News Building
220 East 42nd Street

This building was transformed into the *Daily Planet* in *Superman* (1978) and its sequels.

Fred French Building
Fifth Avenue and 45th Street

In *Bright Lights, Big City* (1988), this was the site of the fictional *Gotham* magazine, where Michael J. Fox works as a fact checker.

Waldorf-Astoria
301 Park Avenue

The Waldorf has been featured in at least a dozen movies, including *Scent of a Woman* (1992), in which Chris O'Donnell accompanies a blind Al Pacino in what the latter thinks is his last fling in the big city; *Crimes and Misdemeanors* (1989), in which Woody Allen and Martin Landau philosophize at a wedding about the emotional consequences of getting away with murder; and *The Cowboy Way* (1994), in which Woody Harrelson and Kiefer Sutherland are denied a room and from which they later skip out without paying for dinner.

Other films that have featured the Waldorf include *The Out of Towners* (1970), *Broadway Danny Rose* (1978), *Rich and Famous* (1981), *My Favorite Year* (1982), *Hannah and Her Sisters* (1986), *Coming to America* (1988), and *The Godfather, Part III* (1990).

Seagram Building
375 Park Avenue at 52nd Street

The Seagram Building was turned into the corporate headquarters of the IBC network in *Scrooged* (1988), Diane Keaton's offices in *Baby Boom* (1986), and Michael J. Fox's office in *Life With Mikey* (1993).

NBC Studios
30 Rockefeller Plaza

NBC's *Saturday Night Live* has been taped here since October 1975. The network offers a one-hour tour of its production areas for both its television and radio shows.

Rainbow Room
65th Floor, 30 Rockefeller Plaza

The restaurant was the setting of romantic encounters between psychiatrist Barbra Streisand and Nick Nolte in *The Prince of Tides*

(1991) and Will Smith and Anthony Michael Hall, who dance together in *Six Degrees of Separation* (1993).

Ed Sullivan Theater
1697 Broadway

CBS's *Late Show With David Letterman* is taped in this onetime home to the Ed Sullivan, Jackie Gleason, and Garry Moore variety shows.

Building at 860 Fifth Avenue

The building was used for exteriors of Donald Sutherland and Stockard Channing's apartment in *Six Degrees of Separation*. Interiors were filmed on the sixteenth floor of an apartment at 1049 Fifth Avenue.

Tiffany & Company
727 Fifth Avenue (at 57th Street)

Featured in *Breakfast at Tiffany's* (1961), which starred Audrey Hepburn and George Peppard.

FAO Schwartz Toy Center
767 Fifth Avenue

Big (1988) director Penny Marshall had the run of the toy store for two days and filmed the sequence in which Tom Hanks and Robert Loggia play music with their feet on a giant piano keyboard.

Russian Tea Room
150 West 57th Street

In *Tootsie* (1982), Dustin Hoffman, as a female television soap star, reveals to his agent (played by the film's director, Sidney Pollack) that he is really his client in drag. The restaurant has also been featured in *The Turning Point* (1977), *Manhattan* (1979), and *Unfaithfully Yours* (1983).

Plaza Hotel
at Fifth Avenue and Central Park South

The Plaza has appeared in at least thirty-five movies dating back to the silent era, including the 1959 Hitchcock classic *North by Northwest* (Cary Grant is kidnapped from the hotel's Oak Bar), the 1992 comedy *Home Alone II* (Macauley Culkin lives in a $1,000-a-night suite—room 411—when he is stranded in New York), and *Plaza Suite*, the 1971 Neil Simon comedy about three couples who stay in room 719.

The Plaza was also featured extensively in *Big Business* (1988), which starred Lily Tomlin and Bette Midler as switched-at-birth babies who finally discover each other at the hotel. Other guests have included Jane Fonda and Robert Redford, who honeymoon there in *Barefoot in the Park* (1967); Meg Ryan in *Sleepless in Seattle* (1993), Paul Hogan in both *"Crocodile" Dundee* (1986) and *"Crocodile" Dundee II* (1988); Nicolas Cage and Bridget Fonda in *It Could Happen to You* (1994); and Barbra Streisand, who meets Robert Redford at the hotel in *The Way We Were* (1972).

The Plaza's Oak Room is also featured in *Arthur* (1981). Dudley Moore brings a lady of the evening to the hotel for dinner. In *Regarding Henry* (1991), Annette Bening is offered financial assistance after her husband, Harrison Ford, is shot, and in *Scent of a Woman* Al Pacino and Chris O'Donnell dine there.

The Plaza Hotel (courtesy The Plaza, New York)

Lois Lane's Penthouse Apartment
240 Central Park South

In *Superman*, Margot Kidder, playing Lois Lane, lives in this penthouse apartment, which critics noted she could never afford on a reporter's salary.

Mayflower Hotel on the Park
15 Central Park West (at 61st Street)

In *Wolf* (1994), Jack Nicholson moved into the Mayflower after catching his wife (Kate Nelligan) cheating on him. Only the lobby scenes in which Nelligan asks him to take her back were filmed at the Mayflower. Nicholson's affair with Michelle Pfeiffer and the police interview in room 825 were re-created at Sony Studios.

Central Park

It seems safe to say that just about every movie that has been filmed in Manhattan has featured Central Park, if only in establishing shots.

Ghostbusters Building
55 Central Park West

Sigourney Weaver lived here in *Ghostbusters* (1984).

Tavern on the Green
Central Park at West 67th Street

This upscale restaurant has been featured in over a dozen movies. In *Ghostbusters*, Rick Moranis pounds on the glass walls to get the attention of diners. In *Stella* (1990), Bette Midler stands in the rain and watches her daughter (Trini Alvarado) get married in the Terrace Room. In *Crimes and Misdemeanors* (1989), a reception is held there for Martin Landau. Charlie Sheen walks into the restaurant in *Wall Street* (1987), where it is revealed that he is wired by federal prosecutors and has tape-recorded a conversation with Michael Douglas. And in *Heartburn* (1986), the restaurant is the site of Meryl Streep's first meeting with Jack Nicholson.

*Tavern on the Green
(courtesy Tavern on the
Green)*

The Dakota
One West 72nd Street (at Central Park West)

The apartment building was called the Branford in *Rosemary's Baby* (1968). The Dakota is more widely known as the site where one of its famous residents, John Lennon, was killed by a crazed fan on December 7, 1980.

Ansonia Apartments
at 73rd and Broadway

This famous seventeen-story beaux arts residential complex was selected as Bridget Fonda's apartment in the psychological thriller *Single White Female* (1992). According to Richard Alleman's *Movie Lover's Guide to New York*, it was also Walter Matthau's apartment in *The Sunshine Boys* (1975) and "the location for a dramatic sequence in *Three Days of the Condor* (1975) that finds Robert Redford narrowly escaping being gunned down in the Ansonia's alleyway." Alleman also reports that because of the Ansonia's thick walls, which make the building among the most soundproof in the city, "many famous musicians took up residence in the building, including Enrico Caruso, Lauritz Melchior, Igor Stravinsky, Arturo Toscanini, Ezio Pinza, and Lily Pons." Sarah Bernhardt and Babe Ruth were other former Ansonia residents.

Apthorp Apartments
2207 Broadway

The Apthorp, a twelve-story limestone Renaissance Revival building, has appeared in so many movies (over forty, by the estimate of landlord Milton Kestenberg) that one longtime resident, who was fed up with the disruptions, told a reporter: "Who do you have to screw to get *out* of this movie?"

Alleman reports: "In *Heartburn*, when Meryl Streep escapes from her marital problems in Washington, she finds refuge in her father's Apthorp apartment. . . . The Apthorp also turns up in *Network* (1976) as the love nest shared by TV execs William Holden and Faye Dunaway. On the other hand, in *Eyewitness* (1981), it is a TV newscaster (Sigourney Weaver) who resides in the landmark 1908 building. Other Apthorp feature-film credits include *The Cotton Club* (1984), where mobster 'Dutch' Schultz keeps his moll Diane Lane in grand style at the Apthorp; plus *The Changeling* (1978) [and] *The Money Pit* (1986)." It has appeared in *When Harry Met Sally* (1989).

(*Note:* The Shakespeare & Co. bookstore, two blocks north at 2259 Broadway, is often recognized as the site where Billy Crystal bumps into Meg Ryan and Carrie Fisher in *When Harry Met Sally*.)

American Museum of Natural History
Central Park West at West 79th Street

When Daryl Hannah is exposed as a mermaid in *Splash* and her boyfriend, Tom Hanks, is suspected of being the same, government scientists cart them off to the museum to study them.

Molly Ringwald works as a tour guide here in *The Pick-up Artist* (1987), and just outside the museum is where Christina Vidal tries to pick Michael J. Fox's pockets in *Life With Mikey*.

Denzel Washington and Angela Bassett, playing Malcolm X and Betty Shabazz, have their first date at the Museum in *Malcolm X* (1993). The museum was also the scene of a party in *Rollover* (1981), which starred Jane Fonda and Kris Kristofferson.

American Museum of Natural History

Bloomingdale's
1000 Third Avenue

In *Splash*, Daryl Hannah breaks TV sets with her high-pitched voice when she tries to tell Tom Hanks her name. In *Moscow on the Hudson* (1984), Robin Williams defects in the cosmetics department (re-created on a soundstage).

The Pierre
61st Street and Fifth Avenue

The exterior of the hotel doubled as the Bradbury, where Michael J. Fox worked as a concierge in *For Love or Money* (1993). His costar, Gabrielle Anwar, also tangoed in the hotel's Cotillion Room with Al Pacino in *Scent of a Woman*.

In *Joe vs. the Volcano* (1990), Tom Hanks asks a cabbie to take him to the best hotel in New York and is dropped off at the Pierre.

Diane Keaton has lunch at the Cafe Pierre in *Baby Boom* just after she inherits her cousin's daughter.

The Pierre (courtesy The Pierre, New York)

Metropolitan Museum of Art
1000 Fifth Avenue (at 82nd Street)

Billy Crystal has a date with Meg Ryan here in *When Harry Met Sally*. The museum has also been featured in *Regarding Henry*, *Six Degrees of Separation*, and *Angie* (1993).

Elaine's
1703 Second Avenue

Woody Allen, one of the many celebrities who like to frequent this upper East Side hangout, dines at Elaine's in two of his movies: *Manhattan* (1979) and *Manhattan Murder Mystery* (1993).

Tom's Restaurant
2880 Broadway (at 112th Street)

To avoid paying fees to the restaurant, the producers of the NBC sitcom *Seinfeld* only show the word "restaurant" in their establishing shots designating where Jerry Seinfeld and his pals eat each week. The interior of the diner, which is located a few blocks south of Columbia University's main entrance, does not resemble the stage set used.

Columbia University
between Amsterdam and Broadway (by 116th Street)

The university will not discuss any of the movies filmed on campus (in fact, it does not allow moviemakers to identify Columbia as Columbia), but it is known that Woody Allen taught at the former Barnard College in the 1992 film *Husbands and Wives* (which is where he becomes infatuated with his student Juliette Lewis), and that in *Ghostbusters*, Bill Murray and Dan Aykroyd worked as scientists there before being expelled.

The college was also featured briefly in *Altered States* (1980) and *Punchline* (1988).

Other Locations in Manhattan

• In *Fatal Attraction* (1987), Michael Douglas first meets Glenn Close at a business reception at Mr. Chow of New York, on 324 East 57th Street.

• Lauren Bacall, Betty Grable, and Marilyn Monroe's apartment in *How to Marry A Millionaire* (1953) is at 36 Sutton Place, on the Upper East Side.

• The apartment where Marsha Mason and Richard Dreyfuss live in *The Goodbye Girl* (1977) was on southeast corner of 78th Street and Amsterdam, on New York's Upper West Side.

• Roseanne Arnold and Ed Begley Jr. first meet Meryl Streep at the Solomon R. Guggenheim Museum, on Fifth Avenue at 89th Street, in *She-Devil* (1989).

• Terrorists kidnap passengers aboard the tram that links Roosevelt Island and Manhattan in *Nighthawks* (1981), a Sylvester Stallone–Billy Dee Williams action picture.

• The bank Bill Murray, Randy Quaid, and Geena Davis rob in *Quick Change* (1990) was a closed branch of the Chemical Bank at Park Avenue and 41st Street.

• In the black comedy *After Hours* (1985), Griffin Dunne and Rosanna Arquette meet at the River Diner on Eleventh Avenue and

37th Street. Dunne later meets Teri Garr, who works as a waitress at the Emerald Pub, on 308 Spring Street in Lower Manhattan.

• For *Batteries Not Included* (1987), the producers built their own building on vacant city property on East 8th Street between Avenues C and D.

• Both Michael Douglas's and Charlie Sheen's offices in *Wall Street* (1987) were filmed at a vacant high-rise at 222 Broadway in downtown Manhattan.

• Director Ron Howard set up his *New York Sun* in an office building at 127 John Street for his feature *The Paper* (1994), which depicts twenty-four hours in the life of a New York tabloid.

• O'Neill's Saloon on 61st Street, across from Lincoln Center (where Al Pacino meets women who answer his personal ads) and the Maud Frizon Shoe Store on 57th Street (where Ellen Barkin works) were two of the important locations in *Sea of Love* (1989). Neither business, however, exists today.

• The Hotel Waldron, where Woody Allen and Diane Keaton find a dead body in *Manhattan Murder Mystery*, is actually Hotel 17, on Seventeenth St. between Second and Third in Gramercy Park.

• *Fame* (1989) was filmed at an abandoned high school (Haaren) on Tenth Avenue and 59th Street, not at the former High School of the Performing Arts, which was located at 120 West 44th Street.

• There is no real-life Yvonne's Diner, featured in *It Could Happen to You* (1994). The diner was built especially for the film and later dismantled.

• The climactic chase scene in *The Cowboy Way* (1994), in which Woody Harrelson and Kiefer Sutherland jump from horses onto a subway in pursuit of their friend's abducted daughter (Mia Sara), was filmed on the Manhattan Bridge.

Brooklyn

According to Alleman, Brooklyn's locations include:

• The Brooklyn Bridge, which was featured in *Tarzan's New York Adventure* (1942), *The Wiz* (1978), *Sophie's Choice* (1982), and *Hudson Hawk* (1991). For the latter movie, angry commuters were inconvenienced for a week so that scenes could be shot of Bruce Willis weaving in and out of traffic on a hospital gurney;

• A house at 3 Pierrepont Place in Brooklyn Heights, used as mobster William Hickey's residence in *Prizzi's Honor* (1985);

• Cammareri Brothers Bakery, at 502 Henry Street, where Nicolas Cage works in *Moonstruck* (1987);

• A house at 101 Rugby Road, where Meryl Steep lives with Kevin Kline in *Sophie's Choice*;

• A house at 221 79th Street, where John Travolta lives with his family in *Saturday Night Fever* (1977);

• The Verrazano-Narrows Bridge, where Travolta and his pals scare Donna Pescow by pretending to jump off in the same movie;

• A garage on 10th Street in Flatbush that was converted into the bank Al Pacino robs in *Dog Day Afternoon* (1975); and

• New Utrecht High School, 16th Avenue and 79th Street, seen as James Buchanan School in the TV series *Welcome Back Kotter*.

Queens and Staten Island

The two major studios in Queens, Kaufman-Astoria Studios, at 34-12 36th Street, and Silvercup Studios, at 45-25 21st Street, do not offer tours. However, it is possible to drive by the studios and also see:

• A Wendy's on Queen Boulevard in Queens, which served as the restaurant where Eddie Murphy works and that John Amos owns in *Coming to America* (1988);

• The former site of a Bayer Cadillac dealership on Northern Boulevard in Queens, which was transformed into Turgeon Auto's showroom in *Cadillac Man* (1990);

• The area around Putnam and Forest streets, in the Ridgewood section of Queens, where Melanie Griffith works undercover in a Hassidic community in *A Stranger Among Us* (1993); and

• Seneca Avenue in Ridgewood, which was transformed into a 1930s neighborhood for *Brighton Beach Memoirs* (1986).

• The estate used to represent the house of *The Godfather* in the 1971 classic is located at 110 and 120 Longfellow Road in Staten Island.

New York State

Sands Point Preserve
95 Middleneck Road, Port Washington

The four mansions on this 216-acre public nature preserve, located on the north shore of Long Island, have often been used as movie locations, particularly Hempstead House, an English Tudor that most recently was one of the two mansions depicted as Chris O'Donnell's prep school in *Scent of a Woman* (1992). The wooded area behind Hempstead House was used for River Phoenix and Martha Plimpton's courtship in *Running on Empty* (1988). The mansions have also been used for *New Jack City* (1991) and *The Godfather* (1972), and the shoreline was featured in *Malcolm X* (1993).

Harrison House
Dosoris Lane, Glen Cove

This Georgian manor was turned into the nursing home where George Segal takes Ruth Gordon in the black comedy *Where's Poppa?* (1970). Tourists can drive past the Harrison Conference Center, which serves businesses and associations but it is not open to the public (except on weekends, when weddings are often held). The fifty-five-acre estate is in a residential neighborhood in Glen Cove.

Old Westbury Gardens
71 Old Westbury Road, Old Westbury

In the Hitchcock classic *North by Northwest* (1959), the mansion was used as the Townsend home, James Mason's estate, where Cary Grant is taken after he is kidnapped. In *Wolf* (1994), the mansion served as the estate of Christopher Plummer. Plummer plays a business tycoon who takes over the publishing company where Jack Nicholson works as an editor. Nicholson meets Plummer's daughter, played by Michelle Pfeiffer, here.

Parts of the estate were also used for various scenes in *The Age of Innocence* (1993), *Arthur* (1981), *Love Story* (1970), and *Oliver's Story* (1978). The estate is now a museum and horticultural institution. Tours are offered between April and December.

Old Westbury Gardens, North by Northwest, Wolf (courtesy Len Jenshel)

Office Building at 2 Jericho Plaza
Jericho

This was the building Matthew Broderick is caught breaking into in *Family Business* (1989).

Millbrook School
School Road, Millbrook

This Dutchess County boarding school, located about ninety miles north of New York City, was where Mikki Allen, who plays Harrison Ford and Annette Bening's daughter, attends school in *Regarding Henry* (1991). It also served as the Steering School where Robin Williams spends his formative years in *The World According to Garp* (1982).

National Baseball Hall of Fame and Museum
Main Street, Cooperstown

At the end of Penny Marshall's *A League of Their Own* (1992), Geena Davis and her teammates from the All-American Girls' Professional Baseball League are recognized in baseball's Hall of Fame. The end credits roll with scenes of the women who were actually in the league, now in their sixties and seventies, playing ball at the Abner Doubleday Field by the Hall of Fame.

Baseball Hall of Fame, Cooperstown (courtesy National Baseball Hall of Fame and Museum)

Union College
Schenectady

Union College served as the fictional Wentworth College in *The Way We Were* (1973), the story of Barbra Streisand's three-decades-long romance with, and marriage to, Robert Redford. Several different locations on campus were featured, including Memorial Field House (the site of the prom scene), Nott Memorial, the Chester Arthur Statue, Alumni Gymnasium, and Carnegie Hall.

Downtown Troy

A number of buildings in downtown Troy, all within walking distance of each other, were used in *The Age of Innocence*:

• Rensselaer Polytechnic Institute's Pi Kappa Phi fraternity house on Second Street, which was transformed into the 1870s home of Miriam Margolyes, who plays Mrs. Mignott;

• The Federal Gale House, a Sage College residence hall on First Street, which served as the home of the parents of Daniel Day-Lewis;

• Troy's Washington Park. The park, which was also featured extensively in the 1987 film *Ironweed*, doubled as New York's Gramercy Park; and

• The Rice Building at First and River Streets, which was used as Day-Lewis's law office. River Street was also transformed into New York's Wall Street in the 1870s.

Emma Willard School
285 Pawlings Avenue, Troy

Al Pacino defends Chris O'Donnell during disciplinary hearings filmed at this private prep school in *Scent of a Woman*.

Mohonk Mountain House
1000 Mountain Rest Road, New Paltz

This lakeside hotel resort, located ninety miles north of New York City, was used as Dr. John Harvey Kellogg's Battle Creek, Michigan, clinic in *The Road to Wellville* (1994). The property includes award-winning Victorian show gardens and gazebos and is a national historical landmark.

Mohonk Mountain House, The Road to Wellville

Hurley Mountain Inn
on Old Route 209, Hurley

After he is exposed as a man in *Tootsie* (1982), Dustin Hoffman sits at the inn's bar with Charles Durning and attempts a reconciliation.

Buffalo

The Natural (1984), which starred Robert Redford, was filmed extensively at what was Old Memorial Stadium. At one time, the stadium at Jefferson and Best streets, was the home of the minor league Buffalo Bisons, but most of the grounds have since been torn down and the stadium has been turned into a youth sports complex for the neighborhood.

The Natural was also filmed at the Masten Street Armory; the Old World Cookery, on Allen Street; the Buffalo Psychiatric Center;

the Ellicott Square Office Building (which was used as a Chicago hotel lobby); the field behind Bennett High School (which served as Wrigley Field); the Parkside Candy Store, on Main Street (used as an ice cream parlor in which Redford and Glenn Close meet); and at a farmhouse in suburban South Dayton.

The Natural was directed by Barry Levinson, who also cowrote *Best Friends* (1982), a Burt Reynolds–Goldie Hawn comedy about two married writers who encounter problems when they visit their families. The home of Hawn's parents was on Summit Avenue in North Buffalo.

Hide in Plain Sight (1980), a melodrama that starred James Caan, used the steps of Buffalo's City Hall on Niagara Square and the north part of Delaware Park near the zoo entrance.

Both *Best Friends* and *Superman* also filmed sequences at Niagara Falls. And *Planes, Trains and Automobiles* (1987) filmed at the South Dayton Train Station (also seen in *The Natural*).

Other Locations in New York State

• The private Knole Mansion on Post Road in Old Westbury served as both Dudley Moore's residence in *Arthur* (1981) and the von Bulow estate in *Reversal of Fortune* (1990).

• In *Married to the Mob* (1988), Alec Baldwin and a fellow hit man wait at the Cedarhurst train station to follow their target onto a train. Baldwin's wife, Michelle Pfeiffer, tries to avoid Mercedes Ruehl and other mob wives at a Foodtown at 4938 Merrick Road in Massapequa Park. Ruehl plays Dean Stockwell's wife and suspects Pfieffer of having an affair with her husband.

• *The Godfather, Part III* (1990) was filmed at the private Trevor Mansion in Millneck.

• Glenn Close's feminist halfway house in *The World According to Garp* (1982) was the Wilmerding estate on Fishers Island, a private island inaccessible to tourists.

• The mansion featured in *The Money Pit* (1986) is on Feeks Lane in Lattington.

• The fictitious town of North Bath, depicted in *Nobody's Fool* (1994), was created from bits and pieces of five real Hudson Valley towns: Beacon, Fishkill, Poughkeepsie, Newburgh, and Hudson.

• Rosanna Arquette finds the *Desperately Seeking Susan* (1985) ad while getting a perm at the Nubest & Company Salon, at 1482 Northern Boulevard in Manhasset.

• Suffern High School in Suffern played Ithaca High in *The Manhattan Project* (1986). The town of Haverstraw doubled as Ithaca.

• Woody Allen's *Zelig* (1983) was filmed in part on the boardwalk in Long Beach.

• The former Lido Beach Hotel, now a condominium complex at Maple Boulevard and Broadway in Long Beach, was used as the nursing home in *Raging Bull* (1980).

• Two homes served as Michael Douglas and Anne Archer's country home in *Fatal Attraction* (1987). The exterior was the former Irene Selznick estate in Bedford, and the interior was a private home in Mount Kisco. When Glenn Close kidnaps their daughter, the two go on a roller-coaster ride at Playland Amusement Park, a 1923 art deco park in Playland Parkway in Rye.

Chapter 13

New England

Connecticut

Former Gilbert and Bennett Manufacturing Plant
off Route 107, Georgetown

This wire mill plant was featured as New England Wire and Cable, the company Danny DeVito tries to take over in *Other People's Money* (1990). Although it is on private property, it is possible to see it from a distance.

Interiors were filmed at Seymour Specialty Wire, a fully functioning copper-and-brass mill in Seymour, Connecticut.

Stamford Town Center
Atlantic Street, Stamford

Scenes From a Mall (1991), which starred Woody Allen and Bette Midler, was filmed for two weeks, with the mall doubling as Los Angeles's Beverly Center. Since the filmmakers could not use the mall indefinitely, the crew also designed a two-story replica mall at New York's Kaufman Astoria Studios.

Former Waterbury Company Building
835 South Main Street, Waterbury

This abandoned manufacturing plant (which has since been converted into office space) was transformed into the Nevins and Davis Bakery, where Jane Fonda and Robert De Niro work in the working-class love story *Stanley and Iris* (1988). The movie was set in the fictitious community of Laurel, Connecticut. Other locations include a house at 40 Sycamore Lane, where Fonda (Iris) lives, and a house at 46 Pond Street, where De Niro (Stanley) resides.

Other Locations in Connecticut

• Although there is a real-life Mystic Pizza House in Mystic (which inspired the 1988 movie *Mystic Pizza*), the pizza parlor was actually filmed at the former Garbo Lobster Company (now Anguilla Gallery, an antiques store) on Water Street in nearby Stonington.

• *Everybody Wins* (1990), a detective story starring Debra Winger and Nick Nolte, was filmed at Norwich's city hall, and at private homes on Washington Street and Broadway.

Massachusetts

Bull and Finch Pub
84 Beacon Street, Boston

The pub, located across from the Boston Common and beneath the Hampshire House restaurant, was used for the opening shots of *Cheers*, the popular NBC sitcom that aired between 1982 and 1993. Souvenirs are sold on the premises.

Bull and Finch Bar,
Cheers *(courtesy Greater Boston Convention and Visitors Bureau)*

Copley Square
Boston

A police car was blown off the ground during one of the more spectacular explosions in *Blown Away* (1994), an action thriller that starred Jeff Bridges as a former IRA bomber turned Boston bomb-squad expert and Tommy Lee Jones as his crazed nemesis. *Blown Away* also filmed at the Hatch Memorial Shell at the Esplanade on the Charles River, where Bridges races to saves his wife (Suzi Amis), a violinist with the Boston Pops, from one of Jones's bombs; the MIT Computer Lab, where Bridges saves another day; and the East Boston Harbor, where a spectacular explosion during the filming did not go as planned. Windows were shattered and plaster cracked in surrounding neighborhoods, causing an estimated $20,000 in damage.

Massachusetts State House
Beacon Street, Boston

Paul Newman's office was located here in *The Verdict* (1982). The State House, which was built in 1795 and is a popular Boston tourist attraction, is on Beacon Hill.

Widener Library, Harvard University
Cambridge

In *With Honors* (1994), Brendan Fraser plays a Harvard under-graduate student who accidentally loses his senior thesis under a sidewalk grate at the Widener Library, where a homeless man (Joe Pesci) finds it and uses part of it as fuel for a fire. Fraser works out a deal to get the rest of his thesis back, and that begins an unusual relationship between them in which Pesci eventually moves into Fraser's house and teaches Fraser and his roommates what honor really means.

The real Widener Library was featured briefly in the movie, but the interior scenes were filmed at the Boston Athanaeum, the old-est and most distinguished independent library in America. Most of the exteriors were shot at the University of Minnesota's performing arts center, Nothrop Auditorium. The house Fraser shares with three roommates was in Chicago.

Other movies featuring Harvard include *Love Story* (1970), which was filmed in Harvard Yard and at the Tercentury Theater; the end-of-the-1960s comedy *A Small Circle of Friends* (1980), in which students take over Memorial Hall, which doubled as Harvard's administration building; *The Paper Chase* (1973), which was filmed outside Langville Hall, Harvard Law School's main building, and *The River Wild* (1994), in which Meryl Streep trains at the Weld Boat House on the Charles River. One of Harvard's gates was also featured briefly in *The Firm* (1993), a movie in which Tom Cruise plays a recent Harvard Law graduate.

Middlesex School
1400 Lowell Road, Concord

School Ties (1992), a drama that starred Brendan Fraser as a star quarterback at a prep school rife with anti-Semitism in the 1950s, was filmed at this private prep school.

First Parish Unitarian Church
23 North Main Street, Cohasset

This was the church featured in *The Witches of Eastwick* (1987).

Tom Nevers Field
Airport Road, Nantucket Island

The opening credits of the NBC sitcom *Wings* (1990–) shows the Nantucket airport, where brothers Timothy Daly and Steven Weber operate Sandpiper Air, their one-plane airline. The show is filmed at Paramount Studios in front of an audience.

Castle Hill
290 Argilla Road, Ipswich

The mansion, located about thirty miles north of Boston, served as Jack Nicholson's mansion in *The Witches of Eastwick*. Tours are offered from May through October.

Castle Hill, The Witches of Eastwick *(courtesy The Trustee of Reservations)*

Smith College
Northampton

In *Malice* (1993), the scenes in which Bill Pullman plays a college dean at the fictional Westerly College were filmed in Campus Hall. Smith has also hosted *Who's Afraid of Virginia Woolf?* (1967). Elizabeth Taylor and Richard Burton lived in the university's Tyler Annex.

Other Locations in Massachusetts

• The building identified as St. Eligius Hospital in the long-running NBC drama *St. Elsewhere* (1982–88) is actually an apartment building on Tremont Street in Boston, near the border of Roxbury.

• *Starting Over* (1979) and *The Brink's Job* (1978) included beauty shots of Boston, but no records of specific locations for these movies exist.

• The press kit for *Coma* (1977) indicates that some filming was done at Boston City Hospital. The principal hospital, however, was built on MGM soundstages.

• *Field of Dreams* (1989), *Little Big League* (1994), and *Blown Away* were all filmed at Fenway Park.

• *Charly* (1968), which earned Cliff Robertson an Academy Award, was filmed throughout South Boston, at Faneuil Hall, and the town of Nahant.

• *Once Around* (1991) was filmed on the Boston Commons and at Boston Public Gardens.

• *The Bostonians* (1986), which starred Christopher Reeve and Vanessa Redgrave, was filmed in and around Beacon Hill.

• *Mermaids* (1989), which starred Cher and Winona Ryder as her daughter, was filmed extensively on Rockport's Main Street.

• *Housesitter* (1991), a comedy that united Steve Martin and Goldie Hawn, was filmed in Concord and Cohasset, which served as the fictional town of Dobbs Mills. The house which Martin builds for his former girlfriend, Dana Delaney, was a show house that was dismantled after filming.

• The original *Jaws* (1975) and the sequels *Jaws 2* (1978) and the fourth in the series, *Jaws: The Revenge* (1987) were all filmed at Martha's Vineyard.

• *Soul Man* (1986) was filmed at Wheaton College, which doubled as Harvard.

• Macauley Culkin's home in *The Good Son* (1992) was a large private home in Manchester-by-the-Sea on Cape Ann, known as the Pyle House. The film also featured the communities of Danvers, Beverly, Rockport, Gloucester, and Marblehead.

• Some of the battle scenes in *Glory* (1989) were filmed on Appleton Farm in Ipswich. The farm is private, but you can drive by it on Route 1-A.

• *Dad* (1989) included some beauty shots of Cape Cod, while *Amos and Andrew* (1993) had beauty shots of Martha's Vineyard.

• *Hocus Pocus* (1993) filmed some scenes at Salem 1630 (formerly Pioneer Village) in Salem's Forest River Park and in downtown Salem.

• *The Next Karate Kid* (1994) was filmed at Brookline High School, Tufts University (the site of the prom), Halibut State Park, the city of Newton, and the docks in East Boston, the site of the final fight scene.

Rhode Island

In Newport, five of the mansions on (or just off) Bellevue Avenue have hosted major productions. Rosecliff, a forty-room French château patterned after Marie Antoinette's Grand Trianon at Versailles, doubled as a hotel in Normandy in *The Great Gatsby* (1974) and as the Swiss château where Arnold Schwarzenegger tangoes with Tia Carrere in *True Lies* (1994).

For the exterior scenes of the château, director James Cameron used Ochre Court—now Salve Regina University, a private Catholic college—on Ochre Point Avenue. It was on the university grounds that Schwarzenegger crashes the diplomatic party by breaking in through an underground swimming pool. Schwarzenegger is also seen climbing the outside walls to break into a second-story room to steal information from a computer.

The Elms, modeled after the eighteenth-century Château d'Asnieres near Paris, appeared in *The Betsy* (1977), *Wind* (1992), and *Mr. North* (1988).

Marble House, built in 1892 for William K. Vanderbilt, was used in *The Great Gatsby*; and Château-sur-Meu, a Victorian mansion built around 1852, appeared in *The Bostonians* (1986) and *Mr. North*.

All of these mansions offer tours to the general public.

Tours are also given of Hammersmith Farm, on Ocean Drive, which at one time was owned by the Auchinclosses, Jacqueline Kennedy Onassis's parents. The mansion also served as the site of John and Jackie's 1953 wedding reception and as the summer White House from 1961 to 1963. In *The Great Gatsby*, Hammersmith was used as Robert Redford's Long Island mansion.

Not available for touring is the Clarendon Court mansion, on Bellevue Avenue, which was used for the filming of *High Society* (1956), which starred Bing Crosby, Frank Sinatra, and Grace Kelly in her last big-screen appearance. Clarendon Court gained notoriety more recently as the home of Claus and Sunny von Bulow. (Claus was accused of trying to kill his wife.) Permission was not granted to film at Clarendon for *Reversal of Fortune* (1990), which tells the story of Alan Dershowitz's appeal of von Bulow's attempted murder conviction, but the movie did include some aerial shots of the Bellevue Avenue mansions and Cliff Walk.

Maine

Bowdoin College
Brunswick

The soccer field of Bowdoin College in Brunswick, located 100 miles south of Rockport, served as Holyfield Academy, the military school that Nick Stahl enrolls in after being tutored by Mel Gibson in Gibson's directorial debut, *The Man Without a Face* (1993). Gibson plays a former professor who is badly disfigured in an accident, turning him into a recluse until a fatherless Stahl turns to him for help.

The movie also filmed at a private cliffside residence on Deer Isle, which served as Gibson's home, and at the Lincolnville General Store in Rockport, where Gibson shops after hours to avoid the crowds.

Other Locations in Maine

• *Peyton Place* (1957) filmed at a number of locations Camden, including at a house on Chestnut Street, which served as Lana Turner's residence; the Main Street business section, where Turner runs a shop; and at several local churches.

• The bed-and-breakfast in *Bed and Breakfast* (1990), which starred Roger Moore and Talia Shire, was the Graystone mansion in the York Cliffs section of Cape Neddick.

• *Graveyard Shift* (1990) filmed at the old Barlett Yarn Factory in Harmony.

• The Marshall Point Lighthouse near Port Clyde was featured briefly in *Forrest Gump* (1994) as the site where Tom Hanks ends one leg of his three-year-long cross-country run.

New Hampshire

Henry Fonda and Katharine Hepburn both won Academy Awards for their performances in *On Golden Pond* (1981), which holds the distinction of being New Hampshire's first major feature film, Fonda's last feature-length film, and the only one in which he costarred with his daughter, Jane. Two companies, the Original Golden Pond Tours (P.O. Box 280, Holderness, New Hampshire, 03245) and Squam Lake Tours (P.O. Box 185, Holderness, New Hampshire, 03245) offer boat rides that pass by the private house on Squam Lake featured in the movie.

Two important scenes from *The Good Son* (1993) also filmed in New Hampshire. The ice-skating sequence, in which Macauley Culkin's sister (played by his real-life sister, Quinn) falls in the ice, was filmed on Mirror Lake in the town of Jackson. And the scenes in which Culkin throws a dummy over a bridge, creating a terrible traffic accident, were filmed in the town of Newington.

Vermont

Vermont's primary movie and TV locations include:

• The Waybury Inn on Route 125 in East Middlebury, which became the Stratford Inn, run by Bob Newhart on *Newhart*. The popular comedy aired on CBS for eight years, beginning in 1982;

• J. J. Hapgood's general store in Peru, where Diane Keaton discovers that yuppies can't enough of her gourmet baby food in *Baby Boom* (1986); and

• A farmhouse in Grafton, the town square in Townshend, the town hall in Pomfret, Sid's Hideaway Cabin in Hartland, and Mill Pond, a large lake in Hartland, all used in the Chevy Chase comedy *Funny Farm* (1987).

• *Beetlejuice* (1987) was also filmed in Vermont, but the specially constructed Victorian house built on a hillside pasture overlooking the town of East Corinth—which served as Alec Baldwin and Geena Davis's house—was torn down after filming was completed.

• *The Trouble With Harry* (1954), an Alfred Hitchcock black comedy, filmed in the village of Craftsbury Common.

• *Sweet Hearts Dance* (1987), which starred Don Johnson and Susan Sarandon, filmed in Hyde Park.

• *Ethan Frome* (1992), which starred Liam Neeson, filmed around Peacham, and *The Wizard of Loneliness* (1987), which starred Lukas Haas as an embittered, orphaned twelve-year-old who moves in with his grandparents, filmed at a private home in Bristol and at the Village Green Store in New Haven, where Haas is caught shoplifting.

Waybury Inn, Newhart
*(courtesy Martin
Schuppert)*

Chapter 14

Hawaii and Alaska

Hawaii

Kauai

Much of Steven Spielberg's blockbuster *Jurassic Park* (1993) was filmed on the island of Kauai, but to see most of the sites, you will need to take one of the island's helicopter tours. Most of the tours pass by Manawaiopuna, the beautiful waterfall in Hanapepe Valley where the helipad was erected; a state forest area called the Blue Hole, near the town of Wailua, where the Jurassic Park gates once stood and where the children, waiting in a car, are terrified by a *Tyrannosaurus rex*; and Olokele Valley, where Sam Neill and the children have to climb over an electrified fence.

The helicopter tours also fly over the remote locations of several other movies. Parts of the opening sequence of *Raiders of the Lost Ark* (1981), in which Harrison Ford runs to a seaplane with natives in pursuit, and the mercenary camp in *Outbreak* (1995), were filmed on the Huleia River with the Ha'upu Range in the background.

And in the 1976 version of *King Kong*, Jessica Lange, Jeff Bridges, and the reconnaissance crew set up camp on Honopu Beach.

Most of the other attractions on Kauai are accessible by car. The Wailua Falls, the eighty-foot waterfall seen in the opening credits of *Fantasy Island*, are located outside the town of Lihue. To reach the falls from Highway 56, go west onto Highway 583 (Maalo Road) for four miles.

Also accessible by car is the Inn on the Cliffs, on 3610 Rice Street, the restaurant where Nicolas Cage tried to get back Sarah Jessica Parker in *Honeymoon in Vegas* (1992). It was outside the restaurant, on the property of what was then the Westin Kauai

Hotel, and is now the Kauai Marriott Resort and Beach Club, that Cage and James Caan, who win the right to Parker's company for a weekend, get into a fight.

Another hotel tourists flock to is the Coco Palms, on Highway 56, in Wailua. It was the setting of Elvis Presley's 1961 musical *Blue Hawaii*.

(*Note:* As this book went to press, both the Inn on the Cliffs and the Coco Palms were temporarily closed as a result of damage done by Hurricane Iniki.)

Also popular among tourists is Lumahai Beach, where Mitzi Gaynor shampoos her hair while singing "I'm Gonna Wash That Man Right Outta My Hair" in *South Pacific* (1958). Beauty shots of the beach also appeared in *North* (1994).

Several other movies have filmed on the island, including *Lord of the Flies* (1990) and *Throw Mama From the Train* (1987), which filmed on Ke'e Beach. Kathleen Turner suns herself here in the final scene of *Body Heat* (1981), while William Hurt, whom she convinces to murder her husband, languishes in jail.

North also filmed at Tunnels Beach; *Flight of the Intruder* (1989), in the Blue Hole area, near the area where the Jurassic Park gates were constructed. The area doubled as the rice paddies of Vietnam.

Oahu

Most of the movies and television shows that filmed on the island of Oahu did so on private property, but tourists can visit the Iolani Palace on South King and Richards streets, which served as Jack Lord's police headquarters in the CBS series *Hawaii Five-O*. The Victorian home, once the home of Hawaiian royalty until the monarchy's demise, served as the state's capitol building until 1969.

Also accessible is the beach in *From Here to Eternity* (1953), the site of the famous love scene between Burt Lancaster and Deborah Kerr. It was shot just to the right of the Blow Hole on Halona Cove, about eight miles south of Waikiki Beach in Honolulu.

The *Magnum, P.I.* estate—where private detective Tom Selleck served as caretaker—is nearby on Kalanianaole Highway, but the estate is hidden by foliage.

Oahu also hosted the short-lived mid-nineties television series *The Byrds of Paradise*, which filmed on the privately owned Kualoa Ranch in the Ka'a'awa Valley. Most of *Jurassic Park* filmed on the island of Kauai, but when Hurricane Iniki forced Steven Spielberg off Kauai, he finished the last day of filming on the ranch. The memorable scenes in which ostrichlike dinosaurs roam over the land were also filmed there.

Wailua Falls (Nick Galante)

Other Locations in Hawaii

• In *Black Widow* (1987), Justice Department agent Debra Winger befriends the target of her investigation, Theresa Russell, at the Mauna Lani Hotel and Bungalows on the island of Hawaii, a five-star resort hotel. The scenes in which Winger and Russell go scuba diving and Russell saves her when she loses her oxygen supply, were filmed at Lava Tree State Park. The wedding was held at the Cathedral of Our Lady of Peace, the island's first Catholic church.

• The set for *Waterworld* (1995) was built in Kawaihae Harbor on the west side of the island of Hawaii.

• *Exit to Eden* (1994) was filmed at the exclusive beachfront Manele Bay Hotel on the island of Lanai.

Alaska

Alaska's film locations include:

• Worthington Glacier, the site of the native village in *On Deadly Ground* (1993). Steven Seagal starred in the movie with Michael Caine, and it is at the glacier, located 30 miles east of Valdez, that Seagal hides from thugs of a polluting oil company.

• The seaport of Haines. In *White Fang* (1991), the 1890s mining town of Klondike City was built on a bluff overlooking the city. After the filming was completed, the set was donated to the city, moved to the Southeast Alaska State Fairgrounds, and turned into a visitor's attraction.

• Knik Glacier, which served as the ice planet Rura Penthe in *Star Trek VI* (1991). William Shatner and DeForest Kelley, accompanied by Iman, escape from a penal colony on the planet. The glacier, located in Chugach State Park about forty miles north of Anchorage, is not directly accessible but can be viewed on helicopter flights.

• Colony Glacier, also only accessible by helicopter. In *North* (1994), Elijah Wood, playing a boy looking for new parents, auditions an Eskimo couple, Graham Greene and Kathy Bates, here.

• The Alaska Railroad's southbound excursion between Gerdwood and Whittier, seen in *Runaway Train* (1985). The film starred Jon Voight and Eric Roberts as escaped prisoners who commandeer the train.

Knik Glacier (courtesy Alaska Film Office)

Acknowledgments

The list of people who helped me is quite extensive, and I hope I have remembered to include all of them here.

Essentially I contacted every film commission in existence, and either the commission directors or the location specialists on staff helped me identify the sites in the book. Virtually all of them subsequently proofread my drafts to catch any oversights or errors.

The easiest way to thank everybody is by state. For California I would like to thank Lisa Mosher, librarian, California Film Commission; Karen Norstrand, Monterey Film Commission; Joe O'Kane, San Jose Film Commission; Jeanie Rucker, film manager, city of Oakland, and Alecza Lipkin of her staff; Janet Wheeler, Kern County Board of Trade; Rich Haussmann of San Diego Film Commission; Ray Arthur, Ridgecrest Convention and Visitors Bureau; Ginger Mallette, director of tourism, Fresno County; Brian Wilkinson, director, Madera County Film Commission; Kathleen Dodge, director, El Dorado Film Commission; Donald W. Haag, film coordinator, Mariposa County film commission; Susan Peterson, Butte County film commissioner; James R. Vanko, director, Mammoth, Mono and Inyo County Film Commission; Alice Allen, permit coordinator, Santa Monica Mountains National Recreation Area; Betty Stuart, Siskiyou Film Commission; and Kathleen Gordon-Burke, film commissioner, Eureka/Humboldt County.

Thanks also to Teddy Hartry Springer, Monterey Peninsula Chamber of Commerce and Visitors and Convention Bureau; Hank Armstrong, director of Monterey Bay Aquarium; Joe Graziano, who writes the "Professor Toro" column for the *Monterey Herald*; Cammie King Conlon, marketing coordinator, Fort Bragg–Mendocino Coast Chamber of Commerce; John Sisto, curator and superintendent of Point Arena Lighthouse; Martin Blair, owner, and Ed Lockhart, manager, Kansas City Barbecue; Pamela Bellew, director, of Conference Services and Campus Filming, Occidental College; Robert Knox, special events coordinator, Dunsmuir House and Gardens, Inc.; Maggie Monroe, Santa Barbara Historical Museum; Ronnie Mellen, Santa Barbara Location Services; William Neidig, Renco Properties, for his help identifying *Terminator 2* locations;

Dan Dellinger, executive director, Crescent City Chamber of Commerce; Pat Neal, senior chief, Naval Base, San Diego; Jerry Greenbach, manager, Two Bunch Palms; Tom Rogers, curator of collections, Filoli; Mary Allely, section supervisor, Special Collections, San Diego Public Library; Doyle Minden, director, Office of University Relations, University of the Pacific; Robin McFarland, convention services manager, San Mateo County; Diana Metzler, Tulare County Planning and Development; Dave Holland, author, *On Location in Lone Pine*; Cynthia Hale, Tuolumne Visitors Bureau; Jo Ann Burns, director special events, city of Long Beach; Nancy J. Weisinger, director of public relations, Hotel del Coronado; and Ann Parker, Santa Cruz Seaside Company.

For my section on San Francisco sites I was helped by Robin Eickman, administrator, San Francisco Film and Video Arts Commission; Mark Gordon, Frisco Tours and Productions; Bob Grimes; Lasse Lidstrom, Commonwealth Club; Richard Berman of City Lights; Margaret O'Grady, Hall Realty; and Lt. Dennis Schardt, film coordinator, San Francisco Police Department.

For the Oregon film sites I would like to thank Karen Runkel, project manager, Oregon Film Office; Christopher Simpson, director, Office of Communications and Marketing, University of Oregon; Cindy Howe, Public Works Administration, city of Astoria; Jim Bocci, public relations manager, Portland Visitors Association; Diane Rinks, city recorder, Brownsville; and Joni Nelson, museum volunteer, Linn County Historic Museum (Brownsville).

For Washington I was helped by Christine Lewis, director, and Leslie Lytel, film location coordinator, Washington State Film and Video Office; Al Gilson, news bureau director, Spokane Convention and Visitors Bureau, and Carolyn Ogden, director of tourism; Jacki Skaught, former film commissioner, Tacoma; Donna James, assistant to the mayor, Seattle; Kristine Karch, assistant to the manager, Salish Lodge; and Kathy Harvey, Fine and Performing Arts, Seattle Public Library; and location manager Robert Decker.

For the western states I was helped by Lonie Stimac, director, and Maribeth Goodrich, Montana Film Commission; Bill Lindstrom, director, Wyoming Film Commission; Leigh Von Der Esch, director, and Chris Sleater, producer services, Utah Film Commission; Penny Shelley, Washington County (Utah) Travel/Convention/Film Office; Jackie Rife, Kane County (Utah) Promotion Bureau; Bette Stanton, executive director, and Tammy Snow, Moab-to-Monument Valley Film Commission; Stephanie Two Eagles, Colorado Film Commission; Greg Babcock, the assistant director of *Die Hard II*; Lana Turrou, Colorado Welcome Center; Shelley Helmerick, Boulder County Film Commission; Lynn Reed, reference librarian, Boulder Public Library; Ronald F. Pinkard, Denver Mayor's Office of Art, Culture and Film; Warren Tepper, owner, New York Deli; and Peg Crist, director, Idaho Film Commission.

For the southwestern states I was helped by Robin Holabird, deputy director, and Kate Silva, management assistant, Motion Picture Division, Commission on Economic Development, state of Nevada; Larry Rossi, Nevada Film Commission; Debbie Munch, director of public relations, Caesars Palace; Terry Lindberg, director of public relations, Flamingo Hilton; Nora Nevarez, public relations, coordinator, the Las Vegas Hilton; Gary Rembe, park supervisor, Valley of Fire State Park; William E. McCallum, Arizona Film Commission; Tom Rankin, police chief, Florence, Arizona; Matthew Bianco, communications coordinator, Arizona Department of Tourism; Luci Fontanilla Marshall, Phoenix motion picture coordinator, and Debra Knoblauch; Tom Hildebrand, Tucson Film Commission; Ann McBride, public relations, Old Tucson Studios; Greg Fister, public information officer, city of Prescott; Betsy Gottsponer, reference library, Yuma County Library District; Anna Gilbert, reference librarian, Tucson-Pima Library; Kelly Cosandaey, locations coordinator, New Mexico Film Commission; Susan Chambers-Cook, director, Mabel Dodge Luhan House; Susie Leavitt, educational intern, Randall Davey Audubon Centers; and Gerald Blea, train master, Cumbres and Toltec Scenic Railroad.

For the Plains states I would like to thank Gary Keller, director, South Dakota Film Commission; Carol Grubl, owner of the *Dances With Wolves* Summer Camp; Vicky Henley, director, Kansas Film Commission; Mary Ethel Emanuel, Nebraska Film Office; Shannon Morelli, public relations, University of Nebraska, Lincoln; Mary Nell Clark, Oklahoma Film Office; Paul Frank, location scout, Iowa Department of Economic Development; Karen Kramer, assistant director, Dyersville Area Chamber of Commerce; Jon Van Allen, university photographer, University of Iowa Foundation; Kate Arnold-Schuck, Missouri Film Commission; Micky Trost, director, and Dan Kinkaid, production/location coordinator, St. Louis Film Partnership.

For Texas I was helped by Julia Null, Texas Film Office; Lisa Campbell, production coordinator, Dallas/Fort Worth Regional Film Commission; Pat Cheshire, film permit office, Dallas Police Department; Bob Porter, director of public relations, and Sue Hilty, office manager, Sixth Floor, Dallas County Historical Foundation; Nancy Cunningham, assistant director, and Ellen Sandolowsky, Irving Film Commission; Rick Ferguson, director, and Drew Mayer-Oakes, locations coordinator, Houston Film Commission; Susie Gaines, El Paso Film Commission; Paula Mason, convention/tourism secretary,

Amarillo Convention and Visitors Council; Fran Lobpries, executive director, Archer Area Fund of Communities Foundation of Texas; Bill McCoy, director, Pasadena (Texas) Chamber of Commerce; Debra Wakeland, director, Waxahachie Convention and Visitors Bureau; Leighton Chapman, production coordinator, San Antonio; Mack Bowman, owner, Mack's Squat and Gobble; and location scouts Kate McCarley and Liz Kline.

For the upper midwestern states I was helped by Andrew Von Bank, assistant director of production, Minnesota Film Board; Stan Solheim, director, Wisconsin Film Office; Jeff Miller, University of Wisconsin-Madison News and Information; Mary Dennis, director of public relations, Greater Milwaukee Convention and Visitors Bureau; and Janet Lockwood, director, Michigan Film Office.

For my section on Chicago and Illinois I was helped by Ron Verkuilen, field scout, Illinois Film Office; Yolanda Aries and Kathy Byrne, Chicago Film Office; JoAnn K. Bongiorno, director of public relations, Drake Hotel; Carol Gifford, director of public relations, Chicago Hilton and Towers; Jerry Ostergard, public relations, Loyola University; Christopher Beauchamp, manager, Film and Entertainment Industry Sales, Omni Ambassador East Hotel; Bobby Pathan, Blackstone Hotel; Ruth Lednicer, Chicago Cultural Center; Denise Mattson, director, Media Relations, DePaul University Ken Wildes, director of university relations, and Jennifer Mathy, public relations, Northwestern University; Michelle Bjelke, Chicago Theater; Phil Bedella, coordinator of broadcasting, Chicago Cubs; and Chicago location managers Michael Malone, Betsy Bottando, and Jacolyn Baker.

For other midwestern states I was aided by Chris Pohl, Indiana Film Commission; Bruce Schumacher, director of special projects, Indianapolis Indians; Jim Leader, Huntingburg Parks Department; Dawn Martin, LaPorte (Indiana) County Public Library; Eve Lapolla, director, and Steve Cover, Ohio Film Commission; Ann Bloomberg, film liaison, Cleveland mayor's office; Beth Charlton, director of communications, Greater Cincinnati Convention and Visitors Bureau; Lois E. Smith, manager of tourist information, Greater Cincinnati Convention and Visitors Bureau; and Alan Forbes, a Cincinnati-based location manager.

For the southern states, I was assisted by Dorian M. Bennett, vice chairman, New Orleans Film Commission; Beverly Gianna, director, Public Relations, and Bonnie McErlane, New Orleans Convention and Visitors Bureau; Sal Impastato, owner, Napoleon House; Tom Finney, St. Louis Cathedral; John Pope, reporter, *New Orleans Times-Picayune*; and David Ross McCarthy, owner,

Louisiana Locations; Stacy Hamilton, director of marketing, Oak Alley Plantation; Tesa Lavioletter, executive director, Jeff Parish Film Commission; Betty G. Jones, executive director, Natchitoches Parish Tourist Commission; Betty Jones, Natchitoches, Louisiana, Chamber of Commerce; Betty Stewart, director, Tangipahoa Film Commission; Henri Fourrier, vice president, Marketing, Baton Rouge Convention and Visitors Bureau; Charles East, a former Baton Rouge reporter; William Buck, director, and Suzy Lilly and Carol VanPelt of his staff, Arkansas Motion Picture Development Office; Bill D. Ables, Chief, personnel and administration, U.S. Army garrison, Fort Chaffee; Mark Levine, Tennessee Film/Entertainment/Music Commission; Linn Sitler, executive director, and Jeanette Blakely, administrative coordinator, Memphis/Shelby County Film/Tape/Music Commission; Sally Raye, reference librarian, Public Library of Nashville and Davidson County; Ward Emling, director, and Christy Lindsey, office coordinator, Mississippi Film Office; Pamela Massey, Oxford Film Commission; Connie Taunton, Natchez Film Commission; Anne Mohon, public relations coordinator, Natchez Convention and Visitors Bureau; Ann Durham, resident manager, Rosalie (Natchez); Ms. Perry Smith, executive director, Greenwood, Mississippi, Convention and Visitors Bureau; Emmy Bullard, director, Yazoo City, Mississippi, Convention and Visitors Bureau; Michael Boyer and Courtney Parker-Murphy, Alabama Film Office; Kathy McCoy, director, Monroe County Heritage Museum, Monroeville, Alabama; Ken Hayward, vice president, Sales and Marketing, Grand Hotel; Lynn Foster, assistant director, and Albert B. Cooper, location and public relations specialist, Georgia Film and Videotape Office; Jay Brad Smith, *In the Heat of the Night* location manager; Tamara C. Richardson, director of tourism, Newton County (Georgia) Chamber of Commerce; Sara Saunders, library assistant, Atlanta History Center; and Jenny Stacy, media relations, the Savannah Area Convention and Visitors Bureau; Mark Oliphant, public relations, Morehouse College; Russ Sloane and Jim Toole, Kentucky Film Office; Laurie Viggiano, public affairs, Fort Knox; Charles King, local history librarian, Kenton County Public Library.

In Florida, Beth Nadler and Elizabeth Wentworth, Film and Television Office, Southeast Florida; Katrinka H. Van Deventer, coordinator, Orlando Film and Television Office; Bonnie King, Space Coast film commission; Virginia A. Panico, Monroe County film commissioner (Florida Keys and Key West Film Commission); Jennifer Parramore, film commissioner, St. Petersburg–Clearwater; Patricia Y. Hoyt, director for motion picture and television development, city of Tampa; Jeff Peel, director, Rick Vahan and Graham Winick, Miami-Dade Office of Film, Television and Print; Joanne Rabin, director, Production and Entertainment Sales, Biltmore Hotel, Coral Gables; Lisa Cole, director of public relations, the Fontainebleau Hilton Resort and Spa; Chuck Elderd, Palm Beach County film liaison; Patricia Haggerty, assistant, Palm Beach County Film Liaison Office; Janet Kersey, Volusia County Film Office; Susan T. Marger, communications director, Central Florida Convention and Visitors Bureau; Jenny S. Hess, Press and Publicity, Walt Disney World, Lake Buena Vista; Mike Eden, owner, Eden House Hotel; and Holly Blount, director of marketing, Vizcaya.

For the Carolinas I would like to thank Paula Wyrick and William Shaw Burney, location manager, North Carolina Film Commission; Denise Stirewalt, administrative assistant, Western North Carolina Film Committee; Joan MacNeill, vice president, Great Smoky Mountains Railway; Geoffrey Ryan, location consultant, Winston-Salem Piedmont Triad Film Commission; Lance Holland, special projects director, Fontana Village, and location scout, North Carolina Film Commission; Jane Peterson, president, Cape Fear Coast Convention and Visitors Bureau; Dick Scott, University of North Carolina, Wilmington; Beverly Tetterton, special collections librarian, New Hanover County Public Library; Melinda Stubbe, assistant director, Duke University News Service; Tony Risenbart, executive director, Thalian Hall Center for the Performing Arts; Travis P. Ledford, special projects coordinator, Biltmore Estate; Isabel Hill, director, and Daniel Rogers, project manager, South Carolina Film Office; Leo Kasprak, Rice Hope Plantation; Jeff Peth, Bay Street Inn, Beaufort; T. J. Healey, South Carolina location manager; Laura Bryant, assistant location manager, *Forrest Gump*; and Deborah B. Avery, Community Relations Office, Fort Jackson.

For the Mid-Atlantic States I was assisted by Robert Curran, Pittsburgh Film Office; Eileen Dewalt, manager of special events, Carnegie Museum; Dena H. Robins, Greater Philadelphia Film Office; and Nancy Blue, Reference Library, Cambria County Library System (Johnstown); Marcie Oberndorf-Kelso, associate director, Virginia Film Office; Sheri Winston, University Relations, University of Virginia, Charlottesville; D. Scott Little, front of house manager, Keswick Hall; Buzz Scanland, owner, Mountain Lake Resort; Mary Cruickshank, Jefferson Hotel; Glenn Flood, Pentagon Media Public Affairs; Martha M. Doss, director, Lexington Visitors Bureau; Jeff Harpold, West Virginia Film Office; Don Rigby, president, Weirton Chamber of Commerce; Keith E. Hammersla, reference librarian, Martinsburg-Berkeley County Library; Charles

Anderson, motion picture resource specialist, (District of Columbia) Mayor's Office of Motion Picture and Television Development; Rex Scouten, curator, White House; Marilyn Cohen-Brown, National Park Service; Kevin Brubaker, Washington location manager; Gloria M. Lacap, news officer, Georgetown University; Michael Styer and Jack Gerbes, Maryland Film Commission; Gil Stotler, public relations, Baltimore Convention and Visitors Bureau; Gailyn Gwin, Prince George's County Media/Film Office; Charlie Armstrong, locman, *Guarding Tess*; Linda Heyman, location manager, Baltimore, Maryland; Carol Myers, Delaware Film Office; Steven Gorelick, associate director, and David W. Schoner, Jr., production coordinator, New Jersey Motion Picture and Television Commission; Eric Hamblin and Justin Harmon, Princeton communications; Norman McNatt, director of development and public relations, Institute for Advanced Study; and Mary Jean Suopis, adult services librarian, Free Public Library of Madison (New Jersey).

For New York City I was helped by Pat Scott, commissioner, and Joyce Saffir and Pam Tomlin, New York City Mayor's Office of Film, Theater and Broadcasting; Paul Spennrath, planning officer, Police Department Movie/TV Unit; Amy Rudnick, public relations, American Museum of Natural History; Mary Jo McNally, director of public relations, Hotel Pierre; Glen Goldstein, director of marketing and public relations and Bob Policastro, banquet manager, Tavern on the Green; Kurt Gathje, manager, Office of the President, Plaza Hotel, and Dawn Williams, Dan Klores Associates; Liz Markham, public relations, Metropolitan Museum of Art; Peter Bregman, videotape librarian, CNBC; Felice Rose, general manager, Shakespeare & Co.; and location managers Charles Zalben, Peter Pastorelli, and John Hutchinson.

For New York State, I was helped by Frank Meyer, Hudson Valley Film and Video Office; Herb Mills, Sands Point Preserve; Debra Markowitz, director, Cinema/TV Promotion, Nassau County Department of Commerce and Industry; Ed Eaton, city manager, Long Beach, New York; Tom Silvestri, president, Harrison House; Monica Reischmann, Old Westbury Gardens; Cynthia Blackett, Special Collections Department, Buffalo and Erie County Public Library; Peter Blankman, director, public relations, Union College; Helen Dorsey, manager of promotions and public relations, and Nina Smiley, director of marketing, Mohonk Mountain Resort.

For New England I was helped by Rena Calcaterra, Connecticut Film Commission; Elizabeth Engelhart, marketing coordinator, Danbury Film Office; Yvette C. Stanley, executive director, Southeastern Connecticut Tourism District; John Alzapiedi, location coordinator, Massachusetts Film Office; Joe Wrinn, associate director, Harvard News Office; Marian Pierce, receptionist, Harvard Law School; Janet L. Durkion, associate director of college relations, Smith College; Julie Phillips, Trustees of Reservations, Ipswich; Rick Smith, director, Rhode Island Film Office; Kristen L. Adamo, public information officer, Salve Regina University; D. Lea Girardin, Maine Film Office; Thomas L. Gaffney, special collections librarian, Portland (Maine) Public Library; Dorothy D. Ames, archivist, Camden Public Library; Scott W. Hood, director of media relations, Bowdoin College; Ann Kennard, New Hampshire Film and TV Bureau; and Greg Gerdel, Vermont Film Office.

For Hawaii I was helped by Judy Drosd, film commissioner, and Lori Alba, Kauai Film Commission; Georgete Deemer and Colleen Y. Wasa, Hawaii Film Office. And for Alaska I would like to thank Mary Pignalberi and Kim Bieber, Alaska Film Office.

I would also like to thank Karen Sabgir and Evelyn Oschewski for editorial suggestions; my agent, Nicholas T. Smith, for guiding this project; and my editor, Kevin McDonough.

Since no book of movie and television locations can be truly complete, the author expects that he will be hearing from readers with suggestions to include in future editions.

Your ideas and suggestions are welcome. William Gordon can be contacted at P.O. Box 1463, El Toro, California, 92630.

Recommended Reading

Alleman, Richard, *The Movie Lover's Guide to New York*. New York: Perennial Library, 1988; out of print but available at libraries.

_____ . *The Movie Lover's Guide to Hollywood*. New York: Harper Colophon, 1985; out of print.

Barth, Jack. *Roadside Hollywood*. Chicago: Contemporary Books, 1991; out of print.

Gordon, William. A. *The Ultimate Hollywood Tour Book: The Incomparable Guide to Movie Stars' Homes, Movie and TV Locations, Scandals, Murders, Suicides, and All The Famous Tourist Sites*. Toluca Lake, Calif.: North Ridge Books (P.O. Box 1463, El Toro, Calif., 92630) 1992.

Holland, Dave, *On Location in Lone Pine*. Lone Pine, Calif.: Holland House (Box 1120, Lone Pine, Calif., 93545), 1990.

Ponti, James. *Hollywood East: Florida's Fabulous Flicks*. Orlando, Fla.: Tribune Publishing, 1992.

Rothel, David, *An Ambush of Ghosts: A Personal Guide to Favorite Western Film Locations*. Madison, N.C.: Empire Publishing, Inc. (Route 3, Box 83, Madison, N.C., 27025), 1990.

Smith, Leon. *Famous Hollywood Locations*. Jefferson, N.C.: McFarland & Company, 1993.

_____ . *Hollywood Goes on Location: A Guide to Famous Movie & T.V. Sites*. Los Angeles: Pomegranate Press, 1988.

_____ . *Following the Comedy Trail*. Los Angeles: Pomegranate Press, 1988.

Stanton, Bette L., *Where God Put the West: Movie Making in the Desert—A Moab-Monument Valley Movie History*. Moab, Utah: Four Corners Publications, (P.O. Box 548, 301 Crestview Dr., Moab, Utah, 84532), 1994.

Thompson, Frank. *Alamo Movies*. East Berlin, Penn.: Old Mill Books (Box 100, East Berlin, Pa., 17316), 1991.

Indexes

Film Index

Television Index

Name Index